sound within sound

sound within sound

radical composers
of the twentieth century

kate molleson

abrams press, new york

Library of Congress Control Number: 2022933889

ISBN: 978-1-4197-5356-5
eISBN: 978-1-64700-253-4

Printed and bound in the United States
10 9 8 7 6 5 4 3 2 1

Abrams books are available at special discounts when purchased in quantity for premiums and promotions as well as fundraising or educational use. Special editions can also be created to specification. For details, contact specialsales@abramsbooks.com or the address below.

ABRAMS The Art of Books
195 Broadway, New York, NY 10007
abramsbooks.com

For Nell

. . . our habitual vision of things is not necessarily right: it is only one of an infinite number, and to glimpse an unfamiliar one, even for a moment, unmakes us, but steadies us again.

Nan Shepherd, *The Living Mountain*

. . . for some time, historians of experimentalism in music have stood at a crossroads, facing a stark choice: to grow up and recognize a multicultural, multiethnic base for experimentalism in music, with a variety of perspectives, histories, traditions and methods, or to remain the chroniclers of an ethnically bound and ultimately limited tradition that appropriates freely, yet furtively, from other ethnic traditions, yet cannot recognize any histories as its own other than those based in whiteness . . . A failure to hear these new sounds constitutes not only a form of sensory deprivation, but also an addiction to exclusion-as-identity that ends up, as addictions often do, in impoverishment of the field, or even its eventual death.

George E. Lewis, *A Power Stronger than Itself*

Contents

Introduction

It was early one morning at a hotel breakfast table in Hesse that I had the pivotal conversation with George E. Lewis. That sweltering summer of 2018 we were both teaching at the Darmstadt Summer Course, a biennial happening in provincial south-west Germany that started up after the Second World War and has become an improbable new-music Mecca. Lewis – an African-American composer, trombonist and intellectual powerhouse – was a generous and jovial presence around campus that year with his resplendent chuckle and inspirational lectures on decolonising the canon. (I was meanwhile attempting to teach a bunch of fierce-minded students how to write about new music. Their conclusion: grab the subject by both shoulders, use words with wit and abandon. They were wonderful.)

On the last morning of seminars, over rye bagels and coffee, I finally summoned the courage to ask Lewis's advice about a notion I'd been mulling over for a while. 'George,' I ventured. 'I'm thinking of writing some sort of new history of twentieth-century composers. I don't mean the usual suspects. I mean composers who get left out. What do you reckon?'

Anyone who has been in Lewis's company will recognise what came next. He nodded a breezy nod. The sort of nod that says: No big deal, what are you waiting for? 'Sure,' he said, taking a bite of his bagel. 'Someone's gotta write that book. It's way overdue. You should do it.' But! I argued against my own case. Isn't the proposition too vague? Too vast? Too reductive? Too — 'Why should it be?' he shrugged. 'Choose some interesting composers who don't make it into the mainstream history books. Tell their stories. Prove that they were all doing amazing stuff. Prove that they existed. Make your readers want to hear their music. What's reductive about that? Oh, it's time.' With that, he drained his coffee and left me to it.

'Tell their stories.'

. . .

As a kid growing up in a cottage in rainy rural Scotland, I became obsessed with classical music. Who can say why, exactly, given five of my six brothers are folk musicians, but classical music is what caught my tiny ear. I fixated on the sounds emerging from the kitchen radio (ever tuned to BBC Radio 3) and from the family tape collection, which, alongside Bob Dylan and Planxty, included Mozart's late symphonies, Bach's Brandenburg Concertos and the thrillingly titled compilation *The Greatest Hits of the 17th Century*. Noticing how often I would fall asleep clutching my little Fisher-Price tape machine, Monteverdi madrigals playing on repeat, my parents bought me audio books about the lives of the 'great composers' for children. I inhaled those tales of Beethoven with his ear trumpets in Vienna, flame-haired Vivaldi on his gondola romps around Venice, Tchaikovsky heading off on steam trains to 'discover America'. These became the legends that framed the music I loved. The music I still love.

That was the 1980s. As the years passed, I pursued the radical innovation of classical music into twentieth-century repertoire – and when I reached the margins of the mainstream and discovered the ear-altering sounds made there using everything from sirens to silence, something began to irk. Why were so many innovative figures missing from my history books? It kept happening. Throughout undergraduate and postgraduate music studies in

Canada and the UK, as a newspaper music critic in my twenties, now as a presenter for BBC Radio 3 – why did the official narrative, the concert programmes, the festival line-ups, always revolve so narrowly around the same clutch of 'core' composers that I'd learned about in my kids' stories? Why were they so exclusively white and so male, so European and so American? Where were all the others? Because there were plenty of others. There are.

Things have changed somewhat in the decade since I was a student. Even since that breakfast with George Lewis in 2018, mainstream conversations around race, gender, inclusion and the arts have shifted – to an extent. In the summer of 2020, the murder of George Floyd and the subsequent expansion of the Black Lives Matter movement forced the issue into the headlines. Questions were asked, publicly and forcefully, about how we tell our histories and who gets to tell them. Statues were pulled down, alternative road names nailed up. There was a backlash. The term 'culture wars' reared its mucky head in the tabloids and in the mouths of government ministers intent on profiteering from division. Oxford University was accused of an 'attack of the woke' after it announced plans to broaden its music curriculum to include more non-Western traditions. To be clear: Oxford was not planning to drop any core repertoire from its syllabus, merely to extend the scope a little. Which it has done, as far as I know jeopardising neither the well-being of students nor the future of classical music.

Here is a myth I keep coming up against. It is an odd and spurious fear that The Great Works – the Passions of Bach, the symphonies of Beethoven and Brahms, the earth-shaking ballets of Igor Stravinsky – are somehow threatened if classical music becomes more inclusive. Nobody is mooting that we should ditch Mozart or Mahler. Nobody is suggesting that their music doesn't speak for our times and for all time. I would be the first to fight back if anyone did. So I wonder what fuels this pernicious insecurity that composers who are already in the fold will be devalued if border controls around the genre are relaxed. Societal parallels aren't too hard to spot. It is the mentality of gate-keeping, of wall-building, of door-closing behind oneself.

The irony is that the opposite is true. Stagnation will be the death of any living art form. Defensiveness is what suffocates. The longevity of the whole classical music ecosystem depends on embracing the boldest and broadest sounds as much as breathing new life into beloved old ones. The score of a Beethoven symphony is a blueprint for revolution but performed in a vacuum its message is mute. Healthy musical culture depends on who's playing, who's listening, who's genuinely impacted. The visionary director Graham Vick said that if opera has a place in the world, it must be *of* the world. He refused to watch the music he loved become 'the guarded privilege of an ever-smaller section of British society', so he took opera out of its hallowed spaces and got citizens of Birmingham singing Verdi. This was no tokenism. Disproving the false dichotomy between inclusion and excellence time and time again, Vick showed that opera can enrich every life, and in fact that the strength of the genre relies on it doing so.

Compensating for a lack of diversity in classical music of past eras is a genuine stumper. We cannot readily make up for the opportunities denied to nearly everyone except white men of previous centuries, though we must make darn sure we shout about the courageous composers who did manage to write music in spite of the odds. However: there is no excuse for ignoring the explosion of creative voices made possible by social changes around the globe after 1900. The composer Charles Seeger, husband of Ruth Crawford, admitted he had a 'not-very-high' opinion of female composers 'based mostly upon the absence of mention of them in the histories of music'. Seeger wasn't alone in his lazy assumption that if we don't generally read about someone, or hear their music much in concerts, they probably aren't good enough to be included. It's a myth of absence that pervades much of the industry. More fool us. What ear-expanding sounds we've been missing.

I write this book out of love and anger. The love: because I want to shout from the rooftops that classical music is gripping, essential, personally and politically game-changing. The anger: because I can't shout proudly about a culture that wilfully closes its doors on perceived outsiders. And it does. The Brazilian musicologist Paulo Costa Lima, who has been a great help in my research on Walter Smetak and Bahian composers of the 1960s, wrote this to me: 'Is "neglect" a mere slip of our musicological machine, or', he suggested, 'is it the very essence and substance' of how the classical music industry operates? Costa Lima pointed out that continuing to celebrate established 'centres' at the exclusion of 'peripheries' is a reaffirmation that the rest of the world 'is not capable of producing valid propositions'. In other words, he perceives Western-centric musicology as 'a colonialist enterprise renewed in the twentieth and twenty-first centuries'.

If classical music is serious about wanting change, it needs to reclaim its innate and vital sense of adventure. I mean adventurous listening as well as adventurous creating. The kind of listening that makes us vulnerable, that reawakens us, that 'unmakes us, but steadies us again', in the words of the modernist writer Nan Shepherd, who roamed the Cairngorms her whole life in search of surprise. If we want to embrace a genuine range of life experiences, we'll need to stop prescribing and start embracing a genuine range of sound. Various orchestras and institutions have scrambled in recent years to redress the demographic balance of their repertoire, plonking works by a handful of 'diverse' composers into programmes without really considering their context, or their appropriate performance practices, or whether those particular works even warrant the platform. This is the worst of box-ticking and it ends up being detrimental if the music showcased only confirms pre-existing stereotypes. The point should never be to find 'diverse' composers who write music in the model of what we already know and have deemed to be worthwhile. The answer is to look further and to open our ears wider.

Many of the musicians and musicologists around the world who helped with the preparation of this book spoke to me vehemently about the need for new narratives. From Brazil, from Mexico, from the Philippines, I heard the argument being made repeatedly: start listening to composers whose work sits outside our own spheres of reference. And when we do listen, stop exotifying the differences. Simply by doing it, the composer Muhal Richard Abrams demonstrated the plain and yet somehow controversial truth that as an African American he could write whatever music he pleased. How his music engaged with the African-American experience, or didn't, was entirely his business. As he put it, 'we know that there are different types of Black life, and therefore we know that there are different kinds of Black music. Because Black music comes forth from Black life.'

The Filipino composer José Maceda declared that 'now is the time to explore other logics and music potentials', and he acted true to his word. He also asked what classical music has to do with coconuts and rice. The question raises fundamental concerns about how a Western-born culture has spread from Europe to articulate lived experience around the world. There are many ways of answering it. Each composer in this book provides his or her own response, as varied as human voices will be. Several of them could also appear in histories of jazz, improvisation, electronic or folk music, which might explain why they get ignored from multiple angles. But overlaps are the messy, fertile stuff of real life. They cross-filter and cultivate.

Writing at the dawn of the twentieth century, the Scottish naturalist John Muir said that 'when we try to pick out anything by itself, we find it hitched to everything else in the universe'. Even for those artists who seemingly worked alone, Muir's statement rings true. Portrayals of the Soviet composer Galina Ustvolskaya, for example, have tended to suggest that she belonged entirely to her own creative universe, that she rotated on her own axis of invention, that she navigated her orbit according to no man, woman or state. But Ustvolskaya had her influences like anyone. The sinewy weave of her melodies is a feature of medieval Russian singing. In deep spirituality and rigorous polyphony she learned from her hero, Johann Sebastian Bach. With the Russian composer Modest Mussorgsky she shared a knack for monolithic rhythm and dark drama, and Igor Stravinsky, too, went in for strange rituals and obsessive repetitions. In sardonicism she surely took cues from her teacher, Dmitri Shostakovich. The French proto-minimalist Erik Satie pre-empted her capacity to hold the world still, and the music of Claude Debussy also makes us feel, physically feel, the images he conjures in sound. My point is this: recognising that Ustvolskaya was part of an artistic constellation does not diminish her originality. Maybe it makes her less easy to dismiss as 'other'.

Here is another myth I come up against a lot. It's to do with the casual, inflated and unquestioning rhetoric around 'greatness' and 'genius'. I'm guilty of it myself. These words are the hooks on which cultural histories get told and concert tickets get sold. They are words that are almost always attached to men who enjoy institutional privilege during their lifetimes and are enshrined by an industry of publishers and record labels with direct commercial interests in sustaining them. It is a lucrative myth to fuel, but a dangerous one. Genius is what puts a gulf between us (ordinary folk) and them (superhuman artists). It's what supports a permissive culture of lionising and entitlement, and denies the role of collective endeavour in favour of the romanticised lone wolf. The sooner we stop loading the onus onto the shoulders of designated star individuals, the more pluralistic, interesting and realistic the story becomes. Maybe the ethos of folk music did filter into my foundations after all.

There are ten stories in this book. Ten beautifully confounding, brave, outrageous, original and charismatic composers. I hope that each provides a gateway to exploring more music from their time and place. I hope that together they prove the marvels that exist in the margins and the overlaps. I'm not interested in making new heroes, or trying to puff up new hagiographies or invent new canons. I deliberately embraced the antagonistic and awkward characters – here's looking at you, Julián Carrillo, Walter Smetak, Galina Ustvolskaya et al. – whose cranky creativity complicates the picture nicely. You will find no single trajectory or grand chronology between these pages. That way lies exclusivity and omission, an inevitable weighing up of who's in and who's out. These composers aren't alternatives to any others, because the word 'alternative' suggests an incontrovertible core. They seek to replace nobody, but they deserve to be heard. And this is only the beginning. There are hundreds of others I could have written about. Seek them out, too, just as soon as you've finished reading.

In the twentieth century, intrepid minds across the planet harnessed the sounds of modern life. They made work out of noise, clatter, social change, new technologies, war, peace, protest, spirituality, science, their own bodies and dauntless cultural and countercultural movements. All of the composers I've written about contributed (and are still contributing, in some cases) bold creative statements against a backdrop of seismic social and geo-political change. They variously let in the dirt and absurdity, the clangour, hope, isolation and love. They tackled taboos around gender and racial self-determination, collective empowerment and deep solitude. They channelled their own faiths and deep traumas. They grappled with that age-old tug between work and mother-hood – a tug that happened to become especially pertinent to me during later stages of writing. They sounded environmental calls to arms and put us in touch with our own softest vulnerabilities.

And the resulting soundtrack? A catalogue of human endurance, depth and daring. Turn it up loud.

Julián Carrillo

(1875–1965)

Mexico's microtonal wars and the thirteenth sound revolution

1924. A war over microtonality was raging across the pages of Mexico's national newspapers. A decade of armed revolution had subsided and a period of ardent nation-building was under way. What the new Mexico would sound like was still to play for.

The immediate furore burning up the column inches of *El Universal* had to do with the specifics of the Western chromatic scale. Imagine the space between keys on a regular piano. If that space, usually a semitone, is split in half, then half again, then half again, the results narrow into quarter, eighth and sixteenth tones. An octave might be split in umpteen other ways, leading to subdivisions of thirds, fifths, sevenths of a tone – and so on. Musically, philosophically, spiritually, the pursuit of smaller intervals at the dawn of the twentieth century posed fundamental questions for composers around the globe. What were the cultural, psychological, expressive, even moral implications of warping what had been the bedrock of Western art music for the past two centuries? Crucially for some with skin in the game: who had got there first?

Rebel theorists on various continents were busy prising their way between semitones. The American Thaddeus Cahill began investigating the microtonal power of an electronic organ as early as the 1890s, splitting the octave into thirty-six parts using a proto-synthesiser which he called the Telharmonium. In Italy, Ferruccio Busoni concluded in his influential *Sketch of a New Aesthetic of Music* (1907) that standard tuning had reached a dead end. Alois Hába did similarly in (the then) Czechoslovakia, while Ivan Wyschnegradsky, a Russian émigré in Paris, wrote his first quarter-tone composition in 1918. A Soviet student named Georgy Rimsky-Korsakov extended the Technicolor reach of his famous composer grand-father, Nikolai, by founding the Quarter-Tone Circle of Leningrad. Arseny Avraamov, an impassioned chap prone to clambering up telegraph poles to conduct symphonies of fog horns, decided that the only solution was to burn all pianos and start again.

And so it went on. In the United States, Charles Ives pursued quarter tones with an early instinct that opened doors for the likes of Harry Partch, Lou Harrison, Ben Johnston, James Tenney – and, by extension, our own Éliane Radigue. In the Netherlands, the physicist Adriaan Fokker, once a junior colleague of Albert Einstein, invented a thirty-one-tone organ. In California, Mildred Couper wrote a ballet called *Xanadu* for a couple of pianos, one tuned a quarter-tone up. The Hungarian György Ligeti would repeat the trick in the 1960s in his diaphanous string work *Ramifications*. Few of the microtonal mavericks I have just mentioned were in pursuit of brute dissonance alone. For many, the aim was to break down the dichotomy of consonance and dissonance altogether – to find a more variegated gradation of 'sonances', as Arnold Schoenberg wrote about in his 1911 theory book *Harmonielehre*. Avraamov commissioned a forty-eight-tone harmonium so he could play Russian folk tunes in two parts and make the music sound 'as it might genuinely have been sung by real people'.

Back to that 1924 Mexico City fracas. In one corner was the *Grupo de los 9* (the Group of the Nine), a bunch of self-styled intel-lectuals who slung their arguments in print using increasingly uproarious rhetoric. In the other corner was the disruptive theor-etician who had sparked the debate in the first place. A violinist, composer, instrument inventor and unbiddable polemicist called Julián Carrillo. The previous year, 1923, Carrillo had published an incendiary article he titled *Teoría del Sonido 13*. His 'Theory of the Thirteenth Sound' would, he declared, uproot and seismically revolutionise the entire musical world. Carrillo did not lack ambition, or talent, or cheek. But what was his theory, exactly?

Sonido 13 was no specific note, no identifiable interval, no pindownable tone. At its simplest, Carrillo's thirteenth sound revolution foresaw a musical future built in intervals smaller than a semitone. He was certain that the twelve-tone scale – the octave divided into twelve equally tuned semitones – had reached its limit. With that he joined the ranks of avant-gardists in Vienna, St Petersburg, Prague and New York, all arguing that the inevitable direction of musical travel in the twentieth century was to break through chromaticism and embrace the notes between notes. New intervallic systems would, these microtonal vanguards believed, free the ear, the mind and the heart from our learned emotional responses to conventional harmony. Listeners would instead be able to access fresh responses that were visceral, unfiltered and futuristic.

Over the many decades of his long life, Carrillo's theorising took on a scope far greater than the logistical splitting apart of octaves. *Sonido 13* was an umbrella concept, a rhetorical provocation, a physical conjecture and a metaphysical whimsy. For some listeners it became a portal to the divine or to some far-out corner of the cosmos. One of its beauties was its conceptual breadth – or detractors might say its vagueness – which was simultaneously what enraged the *Grupo de los 9* and what allowed Carrillo's notion to mean so many things to so many interpreters, including to Carrillo himself. He wrote about his work prolifically, always in a tone of defiant and extravagant certainty, but it would take him until 1957 to settle his system in a treatise to which he gave the tantalisingly mystical title *El infinito en las escalas y los acordes* (The Infinite in Scales and Chords).

The man himself was an unlikely harbinger of such quasi-spiritual communion. Staunch and stocky, with bright-shining eyes and a thick shock of hair, Carrillo was a confounding mix of absolutist, traditionalist, visionary and shameless revisionist. He was an obsessive worker who woke daily at 5 a.m. and produced book after pamphlet extolling his latest breakthroughs. He penned and re-penned his own mythology to suit his latest polemics and simply made up facts if they might add gravitas to his required argument. Adamant that he was the very first of all the twentieth-century microtonalists, he backdated the origin story of *Sonido 13* to 1895, which he claimed (with no evidence) was the year he first subdivided the strings of a violin with a pocketknife. Maybe it was, but he neglected to mention it to anyone it until nearly thirty years later.

Never shy of an intellectual brouhaha, Carrillo had a habit of issuing blazing declarations that he would later diametrically contradict. Substantiation was secondary to rhetorical chutzpah. Here, for example, is a passage from a treatise called *Sinfonía y ópera* (1909), classic Carrillo in its rollicking use of capital letters.

> Assuming – and this is no small assumption – that symphony composers and opera composers are equally good musicians, OPERA MUSIC WILL ALWAYS BE INFERIOR TO THE SYMPHONY because it has to follow the requirements of a plot, while the symphony is ENTIRELY FREE.

(Carrillo also claimed, 'THERE IS NO symphonist who has tried to write an opera and has not succeeded', while declaring there are plenty of opera composers who have failed at symphonies. On the latter, he had a point. On the former, I can think of quite a few.)

So. Why am I telling you about Carrillo? Why devote precious space in this collection of twentieth-century pioneers to an antagonistic kook, a chronic fact-fudger? There are two main reasons.

First, despite his outlandish posturing and cranky bark, Carrillo produced a body of ear-bending, hypnotically visionary music whose daring deserves to be heard. *I Think of You* from 1928: one of his fledgling microtonal works, a Tennyson setting for voice and mixed instruments. It spins a glassy, glistening spell. The Sixth String Quartet from 1937: burly and capricious, a rugged, intrepid piece of string writing. *Horizontes* (Horizons) from 1947: scored for quarter-tone violin, eighth-tone cello, sixteenth-tone harp and a standard-tuned symphony orchestra. It is like a mirage, a bizarre concoction of romantic elegy and heightened orchestral tone poem, with virtuosic microtonal cadenzas that skew the familiar into the uncanny fantastical. These works and others are astonishing and forceful. They intoxicate. They are like nothing else.

My second reason for writing about Carrillo is that he lived an extraordinary life against prevailing political winds that always seemed to be blowing in the opposite direction. He was sidelined from official versions of Mexico's musical history because he never quite fit the mould. He refused to conform to any folk-essentialist nationalism at a time when that was really the only option going if you were an artist who wanted to get ahead. He refused to tap his own indigenous roots to make a marketably exotic version of 'Mexican composer' that would sell in Europe, in the USA and at home. Instead, he pursued his own line of strange scientific ratios with such limitless zeal that the results transcend even his own garish rhetoric to inhabit a remote, almost mystical realm. Carrillo was an awkward innovator, a problematic vanguard, a stubborn renegade. While it is always easier to quietly ignore such inconvenient misfits, his case reminds us why it is worth looking beyond the state-sanctioned stories to find the forgotten true originals.

. . .

Julián Antonio Carrillo Trujillo was born on 28 January 1875, the youngest of an indigenous Mexican family of nineteen children. His father was Nabor Carrillo, his mother was Antonia Trujillo. He grew up in a village called Ahualulco, and in an example of how passionately some people would be persuaded to jump on the *Sonido 13* cult bandwagon, his home village would briefly change its official name to Ahualulco del Sonido 13 from 1932 to 1944, after which it reverted back to plain old Ahualulco. (Nowadays both names seem to be in usage – a hint, perhaps, of the contradictory and opportunistic co-opting of Carrillo's legacy.)

As a boy, Carrillo sang and played the organ in the local church. His parents didn't have enough money for him to finish primary school, so at the age of ten when he began taking music lessons in the nearest city, twenty-four miles away in San Luis Potosí, he often boarded with his teacher to save the cost of the return journey. He studied violin, flute and kettle drums, and wrote dances for his teacher's orchestra to perform at local celebrations. Music was already a way up for young Julián. A way out, a way in.

Carrillo from Ahualulco was determined to be taken seriously. He moved to Mexico City to study at the National Conservatory where his flash violin playing won the attention of government officials, who offered him a state scholarship to study abroad. On the eve of the new century, he sailed for Europe. His destination was France, but on arrival he was told he was already too old (an elderly twenty-four!) to enrol at the famous Paris Conservatoire, so he rerouted to Leipzig. Over the next few years he studied composition and occasionally played violin with the famous orchestra of the Leipzig Gewandhaus. In his own accounts he would boast that he had been a regular member of that illustrious ensemble – in some versions he was even the orchestra's leader, which does make for a better story.

Carrillo wrote a symphony while he was in Leipzig. Later, he would claim it was the first symphony ever written by any composer from the Americas, which it wasn't, but his Symphony no. 1 was nonetheless an impressive statement from a composer still finding his voice. It opens in broad D major: an overture, a sunrise, an intake of breath. From here Carrillo strides ahead into the day, sweeping aside whole thickets of musical arcana, doffing his cap at heroes along the way. Here is Brahms in the yearning warmth of the strings and the hulking metric swagger; here is Liszt in the questing winds; here's Mendelssohn in the restless inner voices, Wagner in the bloated cadences and Richard Strauss in the tone-poetic heroism of the solo violin and horn. This was Carrillo's graduation piece, premiered in a student concert in 1902, and it's as though he wanted to pay loquacious credit to all his teachers, dead and alive.

But this was also the same Carrillo who was deeply committed to what he considered to be the inevitable march of musical evolution. The symphony ends with strings whipping themselves into an overwrought tangle. Cymbals crash, heavy brass lumbers around diminished chords, and the work reaches a thematic catharsis to arrive back at a slab of emphatic D major. Carrillo was taking stock, forming a detailed itinerary of all the ingredients of Austro-Germanic musical language. And he was already much too fiery to let anything sound merely procedural.

The Carrillo scholar Alejandro L. Madrid makes an argument whose sense will recur through this book. He writes that composers from the periphery have a certain freedom from the politics of entrenched musical factions. This point applies to the electronic music pioneer Else Marie Pade, for example, who was able to straddle the opposing schools of Pierre Schaeffer's *musique concrète* in France and Karlheinz Stockhausen's *elektronische Musik* in Germany – because as a Dane and a woman she was doubly sidelined, and so (arguably) doubly free. Composers of the periphery could, writes Madrid, 'embrace both camps' and incorporate cultural references of their own. When it comes to Carrillo's Symphony no. 1, Madrid suggests it 'is not an imitation of Brahms or Mendelssohn but rather an example of how he [Carrillo] heard, interpreted, and processed sonic Leipzig'.

I wonder what would have happened if the Paris Conservatoire had waived its age limit. Would Carrillo's sonic bricolage have been built out of French influences? Later, he did go to Belgium with the intention of studying violin with the famous virtuoso Eugène Ysaÿe (instead he landed with one of Ysaÿe's students, Albert Zimmer) but I suspect his passion for furthering a Germanic musical legacy, his belief that he was an heir to both Brahms and Wagner, was more innate than circumstantial. Carrillo was a swashbuckling rationalist. His temper was wild but his mind always searched for pattern. It was deduction, logic, a sense of ineluctable progress, that led him to *Sonido 13*.

Carrillo returned home from Europe in 1904 with a symphony, an opera (*Ossián*), a string quartet and a clutch of other chamber works under his belt. He now had some clout in the eyes of the Mexican establishment thanks to his prestigious stint overseas, but he was also tainted by it. For the rest of his life he would struggle to shake the accusation that he was a musical clone of European composers. There is an irony here, given that plenty of his contemporary Mexican composers were also heavily influenced by Europe – only, theirs tended to be French Europe while Carrillo's was German. Writing in the newspaper *El Tiempo*, his former teacher Melesio Morales mocked Carrillo's Symphony no. 1 in a review shot through with reductive nationalism. 'When composing in the German style,' Morales sniffs, 'the Mexican maestro involuntarily discovers that the pronunciation and the accent of the language itself are as unfamiliar to him as they are to his fellow Mexicans. It is music they can neither taste nor enjoy.'

This review was published in 1905, five years before the onset of revolution. The warning shot was already clear. Authentic Mexican music must break with the signifiers of past regimes. It must taste of the soil, whatever soil tastes like. Ruth Crawford would find herself faced with the same earthy prerogatives in the Depression-era United States. Not for the last time, Carrillo found himself on the wrong side of political fashion.

Still, he got to enjoy a few years as a major player in Mexican classical music. Not yet thirty, he was now professor at the National Conservatory and founder of his own Beethoven Orchestra and Quartet. As nationalist passions rose, he wrote a *Canto a la bandera* (Flag Anthem) which is still sung to this day, and a bulky patriotic opera, *Matilde*, about the forbidden love between a Mexican revolutionary and the daughter of a Spanish captain. The opera was due to be unveiled in 1910, a hundred years after the onset of Mexico's war of independence, and the premiere would have made Carrillo a cultural luminary. But it never happened. The political atmosphere in Mexico was starting to boil, the premiere was cancelled, and a whole century would pass before the opera was heard, its score unearthed from archives and stitched together for its first performance in 2010.

The Mexican Revolution broke out in 1910. Armed conflict erupted in the north of the country, inflamed by a power struggle among the elites and a dearth of basic living conditions among the agrarian poor. The long-time corrupt presidency of Porfirio Díaz was ousted and fair elections were held in 1911. Two years later, a US-backed coup deposed the new revolutionary leaders and installed the unpopular Victoriano Huerta. Naive political mover that he was, Carrillo accepted the directorship of the National

Conservatory under Huerta's short-lived regime, and a year later, when Huerta was out and a new unstable coalition was in, the composer fled the country.

For the ensuing civil war and its aftermath, Carrillo decamped to New York for what would be the first of several retreats north of the border. Depending on the decade, those periods of self-exile had various triggers. Sometimes he went to escape his own inconvenient politics; other times he was led by musical ambition, convinced that New York was home to audiences who were culturally sophisticated enough to fully appreciate the genius of his work. He did win the ear of Leopold Stokowski, a conductor with enormous commissioning power, but Carrillo's New York years never amounted to the international breakthrough he was always sure was just around the corner.

In the early 1920s, driven home by lack of funds, Carrillo returned to a very different Mexico than the one he had left. The country was newly peaceful, with a freshly drafted constitution and a chain of revolutionary generals who would remain in power for the next several decades. As well as American influence, the regime was looking to the USSR. Murals of Trotsky and Lenin started appearing on the sides of municipal buildings, and a painter called Diego Rivera was employed to emblazon great colourful frescoes in honour of the nation's revolutionary heroes. The Minister of Education announced that artists must play their part in Mexico's 'spiritual union' and 'national resurgence'.

Carrillo did at least recognise the atmosphere of avid radical rhetoric. He announced his big theory in terms he thought would chime with the times: the *Revolución del Sonido 13*. Around this musical revolution he built his own propaganda magazine (*El Sonido 13*), his own evangelistic disciples who made promotional tours of the Mexican countryside, even his own mass infrastructural plans.

He dreamed of constructing a *Sonido 13* factory in Ahualulco and a dam to provide it with energy. He foresaw a *Sonido 13* school in Mexico City. His own sonic insurgency was coming. He felt sure of it.

. . .

About *Sonido 13*, Carrillo modestly declared:

WE ARE ON THE VERGE OF WITNESSING THE MOST TRANSCENDENTAL EVENT PRODUCED IN MUSICAL TECHNIQUE NOT ONLY SINCE THE RENAISSANCE OR THE MIDDLE AGES BUT ALSO SINCE THE TIMES BEFORE JESUS CHRIST.

The *Grupo de los 9* begged to differ. They fumed at Carrillo's grandiloquence. Rather fond of capital letters themselves, they descended into personal insults. Each side denounced the other as too stupid or too obstinate to understand the basic terms of the argument. The pianist Luis A. Delgadillo, a member of the *Grupo*, declared that Carrillo was 'IMPOTENT TO CONTINUE THE POLEMIC WITHIN THE CONFINES OF STRICT SCIENTIFIC RIGOUR'. Carrillo decided that his detractors were simply not ready to recognise the magnitude of his ideas. One of his students (opting not for capitals but for the subtler exclamation mark) decried the 'Byzantine' attitude of the 'dilettanti who by questioning what they do not understand get at least to see their names in print!' Insults were flung across the pages of *El Universal* through the summer and early autumn of 1924.

Eventually, the *Grupo* called for cards on the table and demanded that Carrillo 'PROVE' his theories 'with facts and decent reasons for

the benefit of his reputation and the dignity of Mexican musicians.'
Carrillo gave a lecture on 13 September. (Of course! Thirteen was
his favourite number; he often scheduled public appointments for
the thirteenth day of the month, and he even moved into a house
whose street number was thirteen – incidentally, it was 13 Berlin
Street, which was doubly apt given his passion for Germanic culture.) The *Grupo* considered the content of Carrillo's 13 September
lecture too vague and inconclusive, so they posed a list of thirteen
questions to which Carrillo did not respond, not directly, not
straight away. The *Grupo* triumphantly held a public conference
at which they sarcastically addressed the questions themselves.
Carrillo scoffed that he had been deliberately misrepresented, and
so it went on.

What Carrillo did do in response to the *Grupo*'s challenge was
to write his first microtonal piece. *Preludio a Colón* was Carrillo's
debut microtonal manifesto in sound, an arresting, extraordinary
catalogue of possibility. Scored for soprano, flute, two violins, viola,
cello, sixteenth-tone harp and quarter-tone guitar, the piece opens
with upward surges from the lower strings. The sound is humid,
hushed, some kind of dank incantation. A spindly violin slithers
downward until the instruments meet in the middle. A harp – one
of Carrillo's specially built sixteenth-tone square constructions,
more oversized zither than pedal harp – joins up with a flute to
play what sounds like a strand of Gabriel Fauré distorted through
heat haze. Then comes the soprano singing a wordless vocalise, a
smoke curlicue wrapped around a single tone. The gentle weave of
voice and instruments is interrupted by an emphatic lament; now
the lines jump between octaves, every leap showing off the microtones in new sharp relief. The music keeps coming back to a central
pitch, a lighthouse in the fog. At the work's climax, the soprano
soars above the ensemble, her voice outlining an octave while the

instruments snake and shimmy in the microtonal mists. Carrillo couldn't help nudging around the outline of tonal chords, so there is an uncanny sense of familiar objects heard through some drowsy miasma. The close intervals feel clammy, but they also have the effect of making the octaves shine luminously bright.

Performed on 13 November (naturally) in a concert hosted by *El Universal*, *Preludio a Colón* was written as a theoretical showcase, Carrillo's last-ditch attempt to win the spat with the *Grupo de los 9* that had spiralled out of control and would never be resolved. But its impact goes far deeper than any polemical trump card. Looking back from a distance of a century, the contemporary vocalist Carmina Escobar, who has sung the piece multiple times with the Mexican new music ensemble Liminar, told me she thinks of the *Preludio* as a pop song. Escobar has learned to embody those filmy, slow-shifting microtones. 'Very melodic,' she said. 'Very natural, very seductive, just inhabiting a different scale. Once you get the hang of it, it starts to become this amazing otherworldly thing.'

One further and possibly awkward point about the *Preludio*. Its dedicatee is Cristóbal Colón. Why would Carrillo, an indigenous composer intent on carving out a place for himself in post-revolutionary Mexico, write this invocation in honour of Christopher Columbus? The answer goes to the heart of the out-of-step cultural allegiances that got Carrillo into trouble for most of his life. His own views were uncomfortably dismissive when it came to the position of contemporary indigenous Latin Americans, whose culture he considered to have been greatly improved by colonialism. Although his own ethnic roots were Indian, he claimed that his creative lineage belonged to Europe – and that was one of the many reasons why certain of his peers refused to recognise his work as sufficiently 'Mexican' at a time when 'Mexican' required an overtly nationalist, pseudo-indigenous agenda. Although Carrillo's heritage was arguably the more 'authentic', his detractors flagrantly appropriated indigenous sounds in order to promote their identity at home and abroad. Authenticity is a slippery and susceptible commodity.

Alejandro Madrid agrees that unpicking this is 'a tricky business'. Carrillo genuinely admired Columbus. He saw himself as an indigenous person who could climb the social ladder in the manner of Mexico's first indigenous president, Benito Juárez, who governed in the mid-nineteenth century. 'Juárez didn't really fight for indigenous rights at all,' Madrid explains to me:

> He was a complete integrationist. So was Carrillo. He wanted to be an icon of how an indigenous person could transcend his roots and assimilate. He felt the arrival of Columbus meant indigenous people would finally be part of a great civilised culture. He made a parallel: Columbus integrated indigenous people into the project of European modernity, and he, Carrillo, an indigenous person himself, would advance the future of modern European music.

Maybe Carrillo did initially sense, consciously or otherwise, that he had to appeal to the Western canon in order to be taken seriously on an international stage. Maybe that was a direct result of the kind of cultural imperialism that triggered me to write this book in the first place. What's striking is how his eventual shift away from such thinking represents the broader aural journey we can all take if we open our ears beyond that canon. The *Preludio*, for me, does not sing of the subjugation of land and peoples. I hear it as a liquid lament; a queasy, uneasy elegy whose European harmonic framework is infiltrated by glistening dissent. I could go as far as interpreting the *Preludio* as a threnody for lost cultures, for all victims of barbarism, even if Carrillo did not intend it as such. Maybe, sidestepping the problem, it is simply enough to hear it as a beguiling confluence of sounds.

As *Sonido 13* developed, the theory did become increasingly removed from its European lineage. Eventually Carrillo arrived at a system that rejected tones and semitones altogether – *Sonido 13* would create a world of its own, hermetically sealed, complete. In that regard, Carrillo offered a peculiar but uniquely Mexican contribution to musical history. As nationalist statements go it was admittedly an obscure one, but Carrillo felt his patriotism keenly. 'Humanity is indebted to Mexico,' he declared, 'for discovering tones 13 to 96 in the nineteenth century, and tones 97 to infinity in the twentieth.'

· · ·

There was, meanwhile, another avant-garde provocateur of Mexican new music who did not quite fit the mould. Another renegade composer-violinist who could unleash cutting parodic takedowns of the conservative status quo. His name was Silvestre Revueltas (1899–1940), and his story provides an intriguing point of triangulation to Carrillo's cultural context.

Here is Revueltas's own account of his formative years. 'I send you some facts about myself that you can arrange as you please,' he told the conductor Nicolas Slonimsky. 'You can invent whatever you wish if necessary.'

I was born somewhere in the State of Durango (Mexico). I do not think I was a child Prodigy (which is very unfortunate) but I understand that I showed some inclination for music, quite early, as the result of which I became a professional musician later on. Contributors to this were some teachers of mine from whom I fortunately did not learn too much. I guess due to a bad habit of independence.

I play the violin and I have given recitals all over the country and in the city of Mexico, but I found of no interest posing as a 'Virtuoso', so I have devoted myself to composition and conducting. (Perhaps a better pose (?).)

I like all kinds of music. I can even stand some of the classics, and some of my works, but I prefer the music of the people of ranchos and villages of my country. I get my teaching from them.

Revueltas left out a few key details. He was born on the last day of the nineteenth century into a humble family just south of the Mexico–United States border. That makes him twenty-five years younger than Carrillo, though he died twenty-five years earlier. His family was poor but had no lack of political drive or creative ambition. His brother José became a writer, his sister Rosaura became an actress and dancer, his brother Fermín and sister Consuelo both became painters. (Fermín was particularly active in an important left-wing art movement called Stridentism.) It was music that drove young Silvestre, and he travelled south to study at the National Conservatory in Mexico City then north to Austin and Chicago in the United States.

In 1924, the year of the Thirteenth Sound Polemic in *El Universal*, Revueltas was in Chicago, earning a living as a violinist and conductor of silent-film orchestras. He was also cultivating a taste for alcohol in the city's speakeasies. He married a woman named Jule and together they had a daughter, Carmen. He read the swirling French poetry of Frédéric Mistral and Paul Verlaine. In the mid-1920s, he made trips home to Mexico armed with the new music he was discovering in the United States – in 1925 he teamed up with

Carlos Chávez, a doctrinaire young pianist-composer, to play fresh works emerging from France by Erik Satie, Igor Stravinsky and Francis Poulenc. Chávez, who was rapidly becoming an architect of the new Mexican cultural movement, later convinced Revueltas to come home permanently and conduct the orchestra at the National Conservatory. Chávez recognised this was no time for the nation to lose one of its most brilliant musical talents to its cultural juggernaut of a northern neighbour.

Revueltas became politicised during his years in Chicago. Working in cinemas through the advent of new analogue sound technologies – the Vitaphone, the Movietone – he witnessed the desperation of working musicians when silent-film orchestras fell, well, silent. By 1927, 1,500 musicians in Chicago alone had lost their theatre jobs. Back home, having left Jule and Carmen in Chicago, he consolidated his ideology. The impact of the American Great Depression was spreading south and in Mexico the political agenda was lurching to the left. In the early 1930s, the ruling Partido Nacional

Revolucionario issued an ominous decree that 'foreign music whose morbid character depresses the spirit of our people must be eliminated absolutely.' Chávez jumped on the bandwagon touting 'the fruit of true Mexican tradition'.

The music Chávez wrote tended to be bright-coloured, brazen and thickset. Some of it is powerful – particularly the works dating from before he drank the nationalist elixir. After that, he started co-opting indigenous references to satisfy the party line that modern Mexico was an egalitarian state whose many cultures all coexisted in a happy *mestizo* melange. Chávez was friends with Aaron Copland in the United States. The two composers wrote to each other about their shared mission to create national musics that were unpolluted by outside influence. 'I am through with Europe, Carlos,' wrote Copland, dreaming of a wholesome American sound. 'I believe as you do, that our salvation must come from ourselves.' Chávez's Second Symphony (1936) bears the subtitle *Sinfonía india*. It pulsates to the rhythms of claves, grijutian, guiros and maracas, and quotes melodies from Yaqui, Seri and Huichol peoples. It is a sonic pamphlet for assimilation.

The contemporary Mexican composer Juan Sebastián Lach Lau explained the politics of the Chávez sound to me like this.

What he was doing with his *Sinfonía india* was appropriating an imaginary Indian culture, lapping up the *mestizo* ideology of the Mexican government and the Mexican school of painting of Diego Rivera. Whereas, in fact, what the project of assimilation did was to delete indigenous cultures, forcing them to give up their languages and practices. It was about presenting an idealised version of the indigenous past, which covers up for real oppression of the present.

And that, Lach stresses, is something that continues to this day.

The difference between Revueltas and Chávez was subtle but profound. On the surface, the rugged energy and street songs that Revueltas integrated into his music did indeed fit the fervour for a 'true' Mexican sound. He fooled the likes of Copland, who described him as 'highly spiced, like Mexican food itself' – as being 'like a modern painter who throws marvellous daubs of colour on canvas that practically take your eye out, but don't add up'. In fact, those elements that 'don't add up' are exactly the point. Revueltas revelled in unassimilated cacophony. He wrote satirical pieces juxtaposing pastiches of classic Chávez primitivism with musical derivations of that most universally recognisable Mexican insult: *Chinga tu madre* (Go fuck your mother). Within Revueltas's music, the scholar Roberto Kolb Neuhaus has identified more than twenty variations on the phrase.

By the 1930s, Revueltas was committed to representing the poor in his music. Street people, fishermen, factory workers, market sellers. The marginalised, the powerless. He refused to look to the past, increasingly interested in an un-airbrushed present that told the lives of real people verbatim. As Kolb puts it, his music is 'a bold collage that deconstructs folklorist nationalism as well as all rules of teleological modernism, proposing an avant-garde poetics of openness'. Take a piece like *Esquinas* (Street Corners), written in 1931. Jagged, thuggish, it is the music of cries, cusses, cacophony, the suffering of beggars, the barrage of hawkers. Revueltas said it depicts 'the *internal traffic* of the souls' whom he saw in doorways and gutters. This is no picturesque gloss. There is no romanticised image of any authentic, rugged spirit in his subjects. There are no pretty folk songs. The music is rough, tough and noisy. We hear the cries, the pain and the obscenities. Revueltas was coined 'the Mexican Bartók' – and yes, like the Hungarian composer Béla Bartók, he integrated vernacular elements without smoothing off the edges, without drawing any hierarchy between street and concert hall. It is what José Maceda would do in his works of amassed participation. It is perhaps what Ruth Crawford would have done, too, had she lived long enough to try.

In 1937, Revueltas travelled to Europe to fight for the Republican side in the Spanish Civil War. When he got home, he wrote his most famous piece, a ferocious work called *Sensemayá* after a poem by the Cuban writer Nicolás Guillén. The two had first met through the League of Revolutionary Writers and Artists (LEAR) and had bumped into each other again in Spain at the Second International Congress of Antifascist Writers. Guillén's poem depicts a snake and a hunter in the jungle: the oppressed and the oppressor, the enslaved and the slaver. Revueltas takes up that allegorical violence in his music. An animal hisses, writhing for its life. This is a ritual killing and we hear the heat and the brutality, the furious battle for survival. It is a ceremony of dark, taut seduction. The music has a dangerous energy in its hulking brass and deadpan percussion. There is a captivating swagger in the way the triplets jut against that unwavering march rhythm. The trumpets are shrill, the basses growl in a hard-swung dance of death. Nobody has made an orchestra sound more psychedelically variegated.

Sensemayá is the most celebrated score that Revueltas produced, and somehow it summons the tragic volatility of his own short life. He succumbed to his bleak demons and died of alcohol-induced pneumonia on 5 October 1940, the same day that his ballet *El Renacuajo Paseador* (The Tripping Tadpole) was premiered in Mexico City. He was two months shy of his forty-first birthday. The Chilean poet Pablo Neruda, heartbroken at the news, wrote that the composer had entered 'his fullest music in his sonorous silence'. It is a powerful paradox, but the memory of Revueltas should not be held in any hush. His gritty, abrasive, rebellious sound manifestos rage on.

. . .

I find it intriguing to think about Revueltas and Carrillo, this pair of concurrent outlaws, each in his own way bypassing Mexico's prescribed cultural politics of the 1930s. They both defied their nation's central narrative at their own risk and on their own terms, both resisted the dogma around what music must sound like in order to count as sufficiently 'authentic'. Of the two of them, Revueltas negotiated the game more adeptly – because, despite his knack for biting irony, his music could at least be mistaken for contributing to the national project. Carrillo, on the other hand, doggedly refused to play ball.

Carrillo was not a flexible man, though he would readily U-turn on his own diktats when it suited him. He could not be dissuaded from his microtonal mission, and continued to hone his theories, arguing that musical history is a logical progression from mono-phony (single-line music) to tonality to atonality and beyond. For him, the next step was to split semitones into incrementally tinier intervals, which he was sure the human ear was capable of recog-nising. At the outset of his *Sonido 13* revolution, Carrillo clung to equal temperament – the system developed in the early eighteenth century that divided the octave into twelve equal parts. The appeal of equal temperament for the likes of Johann Sebastian Bach was stability, flexibility, universality: because the distance between each semitone on a keyboard was now regulated, any melody could be transposed to any degree of the scale. (Think of the forty-eight preludes and fugues of Bach's *Well-Tempered Clavier*, starting on every white and black note, an inventory designed to show off a new tuning system.)

At first, Carrillo considered equal temperament to be one of humanity's greatest achievements, of which his system of subdivisions was simply a logical progression. Later, he diametrically reversed that conviction, deciding instead that equal temperament was an abomination that straitjacketed the laws of natural harmonics. Eventually, using language with disconcerting overtones of eugenics, he said he wanted to cleanse, re-purify and emotionally surpass equal temperament. His system turned out not to be about reinventing anything, but *restoring* our fundamental concept of natural consonance. He called his final book, a 600-page bumper edition published posthumously in 1976, *Universal Errors in Music and Physics.*

· · ·

Among Carrillo's most concrete contributions were instruments. He invented microtonal oboes, horns, harps, a weird string bass contraption called the octavino. He built a set of fifteen microtonal pianos, which are today housed at the Carrillo archive in San Luis Potosí. Other models of the pianos, made by the Carl Sauter piano company in Germany using Carrillo's original designs, are scattered around the world in various states of playability and decay.

In 1958, Carrillo unveiled his gaggle of close-tuned keyboards with the billing of a prize circus act:

Les Pianos Carrillo. Pianos 'metamorphosés'. Unique au monde. Rendant divers tons chacun. Des sons jamais entendu! (The Carrillo Pianos. Metamorphoser pianos. Unique in the world. They each make a different tone. Sounds never heard before!)

He had been invited to contribute to the 1958 World Fair in Brussels by Jean-Étienne Marie, a French composer who was himself keen on wonky tunings. Carrillo's *pianos metamorfoseadores* looked on the surface like any ordinary pianos: only when they were played did the difference became apparent. The space between the keys was not half a tone as usual but ranged from a third of a tone to a sixteenth of a tone – the most extreme of them had ninety-seven keys covering a grand distance of one octave. When they arrived in Brussels, the Mexican ambassador intervened to make sure this outsized exhibit was given a suitable display.

Later the same year, Carrillo travelled to Europe himself to conduct his new Concertino for third-tone piano and orchestra. Jean-Étienne Marie gathered other microtonal vanguards for the occasion. Ivan Wyschnegradsky, Alois Hába, Adriaan Fokker – there they all were, together in a room, the moment captured in a photograph that also included Carrillo's daughter Dolores and Fokker's wife Margaretha. Apparently the atmosphere was so thick it could be cut with a knife. Wyschnegradsky and Hába hated each other. When they posed for the camera, neither man would move an inch lest they had to stand any closer. It is baffling to think of the egotism that drives a man's need to be the lone wolf. Just consider the combined microtonal possibilities had the characters in that single photo recognised their shared mission and even contemplated collaboration.

After the exhibition, Carrillo's original pianos were sent to Mexico while copies were donated to institutions around Europe. One of the copies spent time at the famous Schola Cantorum in Paris, then moved to the Conservatoire de Pantin where a young clarinet student named Pascale Criton was becoming hooked on writing music and signed up for lessons with Jean-Étienne Marie. Today, Criton is herself a composer of entrancing microtonal music, and she seems delighted when I email her to say I'm curious about the works she wrote for Carrillo piano starting in the 1980s. The next day we speak on the phone. She tells me that the instrument was a game-changer for her. 'Everyone at the conservatory tried to play something familiar on that piano,' she recalls. A Chopin waltz, a Beethoven bagatelle, students amusing themselves by transforming familiar pieces into queasy microtonal mishaps. But for Criton, the allure of the Carrillo piano went deeper. She wanted to investigate the sound 'for itself', she says. 'For the closeness. For its other world of possibilities.'

The piano in Pantin was tuned in sixteenth tones: the one with ninety-seven keys covering the span of an octave. Criton points out something about the instrument that I had not thought of: Carrillo chose to pitch it to the range of the female speaking voice. 'It's a soft sound,' she says. 'It reminds me of speech, and accordingly the first pieces I wrote for it are very linked to spoken intonation. A kind of intimate, soft-spoken level.' She sings to me down the phone in a half-whisper, demonstrating the micro-inflections that it would be impossible to evoke using any standard-tuned keyboard. She describes the intervals as 'dilated', always expanding or contracting. It makes me think of Annea Lockwood and her quest for sonic intimacy. It makes me think of José Maceda and Emahoy Tsegué-Mariam Guèbru, both of them throwing clock time into flux. Of Éliane Radigue and her search for similarly 'dilated' sound within sound.

That night, Criton sends me a Dropbox folder containing private recordings of a number of pieces that she wrote for that Carrillo piano. Several of these have never been released because she still thinks of them merely as early test pieces. But I am instantly enamoured. In a piece called *La forme incontournée*, Criton stages a duet between normal piano and sixteenth-tone piano. The dialogue between the instruments is slow and courteous in the manner of two people carefully conversing across languages. There is an air of investigation, of moulding to the other's vowel sounds. Criton's *Mémoires* does exactly what its title suggests: it makes a blur of memories, some images ultra-clear, others smudged as though glimpsed through a window that keeps misting up. The strings sound as though they're being tugged upward as we listen.

The pianist Sylvaine Billier once told Criton that she became so absorbed in a performance of *Mémoires*, so completely lost in the sound, that at the end she forgot to come back on stage to accept the applause of the audience. That story strikes me as a beautiful summation of the whole Carrillo contradiction. For all his raging polemics, his music contains an immersive delicacy. He shouted plenty, but it's his quiet side that taps one's innermost thoughts.

· · ·

Alejandro Madrid tells me a fun anecdote that demonstrates Carrillo's power to skirt the supernatural and spark controversy even from beyond the grave. It happened like this.

In 1982, seventeen years after Carrillo's death, a popular Mexican morning TV show called *Hoy Mismo* invited a group of musicians to give a live performance of *Sonido 13* music for sixteenth-tone harp, quarter-tone guitar and flute. After the performance, the host, Guillermo Ochoa, announced that the network had received multiple phone calls from viewers around the country, all of them reporting a very strange phenomenon. Apparently, animals across the nation had gone berserk in response to the microtonal music coming through their television sets. Dogs in Mexico City had howled and danced. Fish in Cuernavaca had attempted suicide against the glass of their aquariums. In Puebla, canaries had battered the walls of their cages then died in ecstasy. The musicians found themselves in the unusual position of having to rapidly assure viewers that the music they played presented no lethal side effects.

What is it about *Sonido 13* that so disturbs? I'm not suggesting that the *Hoy Mismo* performance really did drive all those animals to suicidal rapture, but clearly the show's producers felt inspired to whip up a spooky storm over a bunch of microtones. It goes right back to the visceral anger of the *Grupo de los 9* six decades earlier. There is, doubtless, an air of unnerving paranormality when the familiar is skewed. It's what gives the uncanny valley, that place on the fringes of human likeness, such disturbing power. Maybe it's why many of the composers featured in this book haven't been given due recognition: people get needled, disturbed, even angered, by attempts to tread beyond the familiar. *Sonido 13* works like a gateway, a filmic warp screen, a portal to a place where senses become less presumptive and more receptive. It's that exact *unmaking* that Nan Shepherd set out across the hills to find.

Carrillo's method was nominally scientific, even morally absolute. He was, at least in principle, passionate about balance, order and rational structure. And yet his music has been embraced as whimsy, a search for the stars, even pseudo-occult spirituality. Listeners have heard heavenly zephyrs and New Age mythology, UFOs and mystic Catholicism. In the end, Carrillo came full circle with his own faith. He returned to the church liturgies he had sung in the 1880s in his home village of Ahualulco. His religious resurgence was, typically for him, an unpopular move – post-revolutionary Mexico was no place to be waving the flag of the Catholic Church. But by the 1950s and 1960s, Carrillo couldn't help but acknowledge that his pursuit of fastidious rationalism had tapped into some kind of broader spirituality. At the age of eighty-six, the now-ailing composer wrote a Latin mass in quarter tones which he dedicated to Pope John XXIII. It is an intensely concentrated piece of devotional writing, scored for unaccompanied male voices which intone the *Kyrie* in creeping, thick-meshed harmonies. Tonal triads slip-slide in and out of focus. It is as though all of musical history is entangled in this verdant plexus, unearthly and as rooted as the trees.

. . .

I hold my hands up and admit I am charmed by the zany audacity of Carrillo's vision, however obnoxious Carrillo himself could be. This is a man who boasted of creating a special piano 'which will violently advance the extension that music today spans'. He qualified: 'because instead of only eight so-called octaves, I think it's possible to increase its extension to twelve. That is, instead of reaching a C of 8,192 vibrations per second, it reaches 131,000 vibrations per second.' To be clear: what he is suggesting goes way beyond human hearing. It is a ridiculously utopian vision, basically redundant on the grounds of logical aural implausibility. Is Carrillo seriously waiting for the human ear to catch up with him? I wouldn't put it past him.

Here is another stunningly ambitious Carrillo proposal.

He envisioned 1,892 microtonal transpositions made possible within 96 divisions of the octave, plus 392 transpositions based on tones and fractions.

That equals 2,284 possible transpositions.

Multiply that by fifteen (the number of his pianos) and you have 34,000 possible transpositions.

then

Nine Beethoven symphonies × 34,000 possible transpositions equals 308,430 versions of Beethoven symphonies.

308,430 versions of Beethoven symphonies!

The same man who was criticised by his compatriots for being in thrall to European culture wanted to surpass Beethoven by making 308,430 versions of his symphonies – only nine of which would sound much like the originals at all. The nerve! The dauntless ardour!

Carrillo never trod a line of obvious nationalism, but the suggestion that his music does not speak of a true Mexican experience is as prescriptively narrow as what we'll see happening around Walter Smetak in Brazil in the 1960s, where *Tropicálistas* were hounded for polluting 'authentic' folk music with global pop culture. Who can say that the amalgam they made did not ring true to their daily lives? Why was Carlos Chávez permitted to set the sonic agenda of Mexico for so many decades?

Juan Sebastián Lach Lau tells me that even when he was a student in the 1990s, there were just two choices for a young composer in Mexico City: either sign up to the school of Mario Lavista or to the school of Julio Estrada, the two heavyweights of Mexican composition at the time. Both had been students of Chávez; Lavista was the golden boy, Estrada the rebel who retrospectively identified with Carrillo as an act of dissidence. Lach says that, happily, today's generation of Mexican composers 'doesn't follow this polarising attitude'. I ask why things have changed, and he smiles. 'Because we don't care so much about dogma any more,' he replies. 'And because the twenty-first century has taught us that there are many versions of history.'

Happily, there is already a growing interest in the music of Revueltas, though we still need to hear a wider range of it in Europe. Now it's Carrillo's turn. For all his extremes, he wrote works of singular and surprising beauty. Most of them remain way too hard to track down. Carmina Escobar considers *I Think of You* to be essential song repertoire for sopranos, but it's hardly ever sung. At the time of writing, Alejandro Madrid is pushing for Carrillo's thirteen groundbreaking string quartets to be properly published and recorded for the first time. It's infuriating that they aren't readily hearable: they are astounding works.

Carrillo's story demonstrates what we lose when a mainstream narrative dominates to the exclusion of creativity that doesn't fit within neat lines. His lines were not just wobbly. They shook the foundations.

• • •

In the United States, another composer was testing out wobbly dissonance as a modern modus operandi – and was cut short thanks to prescribed notions of nation-building and authenticity. And, in her case, womanhood.

Ruth Crawford

(1901–53)

**Wakingup, shakingup:
a new American dissonance**

'Do we ever talk to our children about who we used to be?' Peggy Seeger wags a finger in my direction. 'Nuh-uh! Course we don't. My mother never talked to us about who she'd been *before*. But you would have thought' – Seeger pauses, inhales – 'you would have thought that my father might have said to us: your mother was a wonderful classical composer.'

Oxford, early February 2020. It is a bitterly cold Sunday, the sort of winter afternoon when daylight doesn't bother much beyond lunchtime. I've cycled to the outskirts of town along the river path, past gritted-teeth college rowers and up twisting lanes of thatched-roof cottages. I'm on my way to meet Peggy Seeger. A broad garden wraps around her house, but as soon as I start looking for somewhere to lock my bike, the veteran American folk singer appears at her doorway and waves her hand at me impatiently. Bring it inside, she instructs. No ceremony here.

Seeger is eighty-four years old when we meet. She is tall, lithe, bossy, elegant and tremendous fun. Together over the next few hours we demolish multiple pots of tea and the entire box of chocolate biscuits that I bought in a posh deli in town. She installs me in her living room which is full of instruments. Autoharps, banjos, guitars, piano.

Family photographs show off three generations of broad-smiling folk musicians. There are Peggy's children Neill, Calum and Kitty. There are her legendary siblings Mike, Barbara, Penny, big half-brother Pete and the rest. There is her father, Charles, looking stern and lean in his portrait. And her mother, Ruth, sturdy as earth, eyes to the horizon, hair wrapped in braids around her head like a laurel wreath.

Wholesome, meticulous Ruth, who never swore, who crocheted on the porch and read Perry Mason detective novels. Ruth who sang around the house while she sewed and while she cleaned, while she checked her children's clothes for moths and their hair for lice. Seeger remembers how her mother would 'make caves under the piano' and how she would 'magic herself' into the world of her children's imaginations. How she would sit them at the keyboard and invent fantastical musical fairy tales with 'leaps and arpeggios for the rabbits, squeaks for the mice, thunder for the wicked step-mothers and lions'. But the image Seeger can paint from memories alone is incomplete. 'I knew her as a folk-music mom and a piano teacher.' She shakes her head. 'I didn't know the rest. I had no idea.'

Ruth Crawford (the 'Seeger' came later; I shall stick with her maiden name) was a sensationally skilled composer who fell in love with her teacher, got married, had children and near enough stopped writing music altogether. She got swept up in a double tidal wave of what she called 'composing babies' and the nascent American folk movement that emerged out of the Great Depression, during which she became a folk-song transcriber and a writer of books. 'I folded my wings and breathed good friendly dust,' is how Crawford herself put it, by which she meant she folded her audacious compositional wings. And she meant 'dust' in the most positive way, because dust was what real people planted their feet in. Not the highfalutin – what, marble? ether? – of the avant-garde.

It wasn't that Crawford ever stopped working. She worked arguably too hard all her life, including during her two decades of compositional near-silence after she got married. She published multiple books, taught piano, raised four children and ran a busy household right up to her death from cancer at the age of fifty-two.

By that point, she was a star of the folk-education movement, respected across the nation for her songbooks that graced parlour pianos from Phoenix to Philadelphia. She was one of the Seegers, and the Seegers taught America to sing its own songs.

What about before she folded those wings? More pressingly: why did she fold them?

Peggy Seeger points out that if her mother ever called something 'sweet', she did not intend it as a compliment. Ruth Crawford was a pioneer of hard-hitting, distinctly un-sweet American modernism. In her twenties she composed caustic little piano pieces, blindsidingly intense songs, a series of exploratory duets that pivot instruments around each other like pairs of sparring martial artists. Hers was unapologetic music that blazed a trail for a new national paradigm – or might have done, had she kept going with it. Adventuring alone in Berlin in the early 1930s, she came up with a choral sound that thrums with strange mysticism, note clusters and invented languages. And there is her masterpiece, the utterly original *String Quartet 1931*, the date in its title still a reminder of just how ahead of its time her music was. One critic admiringly admitted that Ruth Crawford could 'sling dissonances as mean as any of them'. Them: the men.

That small but formidably original body of work – that's the *before* that Charles Seeger never told his children about. 'Oh, my father?' Peggy Seeger's tone is blunt now, the kind of bluntness only family members can get away with when talking about each other. 'My father composed, too, but he wasn't nearly as good as she was. I think there was something operating there.' I note the lifetime of observation and experience contained within the phrase. *Something operating.*

. . .

Peggy Seeger's hair is cropped short. Mine is too, as it happens. 'When?' she points at my head, demanding the backstory, so I find myself abruptly explaining how I chopped it out of restlessness and resolve at the painful end of a relationship. We take a lengthy tangent on the politics of hair styles. Ruth Crawford cut hers short in the early 1920s when she moved from Florida to Chicago. Crawford's life was a constellation: acts of bold conviction linked by stretches of work and acquiescence. Moving to Chicago was one of those acts of conviction, and cutting her hair short was another.

Crawford was born in 1901 in the mill town of East Liverpool, Ohio, and raised in various Methodist congregations across Indiana, Missouri and Florida. Her father was Clark Crawford, a minister who died of tuberculosis when Ruth was twelve, at which point the family was unceremoniously kicked out of the parsonage and Ruth and her brother were raised by her mother, a resourceful woman named Clara who was not a bad pianist herself. Before Clara met Clark, she had turned down a couple of marriage proposals and set out to make her fortune as an independent woman. Once wed, she sat in a low-cut dress for a portrait that Clark didn't see until the painting was done, at which point he demanded that the artist colour in the neckline for the sake of decorum. After Clark died, Clara started doing all kinds of things. She set up a boarding house despite knowing nothing about the hospitality business. She took up painting. Eventually, she followed her daughter to Chicago. Peggy Seeger believes in inherited family traits, and she says that tenacity is passed down the line of Crawford women. 'I myself have been willing to take risks, or willing to be stupid,' she says. 'I think my mother was too, and so was my mother's mother. And they were both the kind of mothers that their daughters wanted to have around.'

As a girl, Ruth Crawford was whimsical, assiduous, with a jagged home-cut fringe, heavy-set brow and a wide, friendly face that remained that way till the end. And she was determined. When she was seven she decided she would be a poet; by sixteen she had written 200 poems and upgraded her ambitions to 'authoress'. As a pianist she was exceptional, earning a reputation as one of the top players and teachers in Jacksonville. When she was nineteen, her mother agreed she could go to the American Conservatory of Music in Chicago – on the condition she would return to Florida after a year and set up a teaching studio. Clara hoped that Ruth would become a 'real lady musician, with nice manners and poise and self-confidence and pretty clothes'.

It's hard to work out how many of those aspirations Ruth Crawford met or didn't. Sartorially, she went way off-piste. Peggy Seeger recalls a night in 1952 when her mother was awarded a top prize from the National Association for American Composers and Conductors. Before the ceremony, she took Crawford shopping for a new red blouse and sewed her an accompanying black taffeta skirt, but she didn't think to check on the footwear. 'I see her plainly now,' Seeger writes in her memoir, *First Time Ever*. 'Dear, dear stranger-mother, in her definitely *un*fashionable everyday unpolished men's lace-ups, no jewellery at all, just her lovely colouring of black hair, very red cheeks and lively face – moving across the stage like a self-conscious child to accept her prize.' As for the poise and self-confidence that Clara Crawford wished for her daughter: those qualities did emerge in Ruth, if gradually.

Ruth Crawford arrived in Chicago in 1921 and checked into the YWCA on South Michigan Avenue, a seven-storey red-brick hostel that had housed working women since the late 1800s. She was twenty years old, unworldly, diligent, driven. The city would blow open the mind of this Methodist minister's daughter. Almost every week she attended concerts given by the Chicago Symphony Orchestra, which at the time was conducted by the moustachioed German violinist Frederick Stock, who had played in Cologne under Brahms, Tchaikovsky and Richard Strauss. Chicago in the 1920s was a major touring destination for Russian musicians seeking an audience in the new world while the old one was in upheaval. Pianists Arthur Rubinstein and Leopold Godowsky, composers Rachmaninov and Prokofiev – they all came through town during Crawford's very first year there. Chicago was where, in 1921, Prokofiev premiered *The Love for Three Oranges*, his opera about melancholy and mirth and a prince who is unable to laugh. Reviewers wanted to know who Prokofiev was poking fun at: them? The audience? Art itself? 'All I had been trying to do', the composer later shrugged, 'was to write an amusing opera.' Chicago is also where, nine years after Crawford showed up at the YWCA, a certain Muhal Richard Abrams was born a few streets away on the South Side.

Crawford threw herself into her studies. She practised piano so hard that her left arm 'went on strike' with a condition called occupational neuritis, which didn't stop her winning an end-of-year prize for her razor-sharp performance of Chopin's *Polonaise-Fantaisie* op. 61. Meanwhile, she witnessed herself prising open. 'I feel myself broadening,' she wrote in her diary. 'My ear – the inner ear whose good judgement and training is of infinite value to composers – is hearing better than it did last year.' Twelve months in Chicago turned into another year, then another, and eventually Clara Crawford resigned herself to her daughter's tenacity, sold up the Florida home and headed for Illinois, where Ruth declared that she wanted to be a composer. Moreover – that she wanted to write music 'which will be *different*'. Her earliest surviving work dates from 1922. She called it *Little Waltz*. It's a tiny, spicy triple-time number with a lopsided grin and a boogie-woogie spring in its step.

. . .

Spring, 1927. Ruth Crawford watched an envelope buffeting about in the relentless winds that sweep across Lake Michigan. She wrote in her diary about this dancing envelope, how it 'cut such capers when the wind found its cup, first rushing across the sidewalk, then sidling enticingly, slowly, as tho doing a bit of quiet flirting, then suddenly turning most unladylike somersets into a grass plot, where it lay discontented till it could creep stealthily back to the sidewalk for more acrobatics'. The shimmy of that little bit of paper was so full of music – 'such a perfect scherzo of rhythmic variety and subtlety' – that Ruth Crawford laughed out loud.

In the five years since she had written that tentatively daring *Little Waltz*, Crawford had gone through some major personal transformations. Her creative parameters had stretched until the lines between sound, spirituality and conventional music started dissolving altogether. Her ears were now saturated with the multi-sensorial colour spectrum of the Russian mystic composer Alexander Scriabin, and she was writing her own hot-breathed piano pieces in response: intensely numinous preludes, unflinchingly mathematical canons, the flamboyantly titled *Kaleidoscopic Changes on an Original Theme*. 'What do you think of the name!!!' she scribbled on a programme booklet, those three exclamation marks revealing how far she had managed to surprise herself. Her spry *Adventures of Tom Thumb* for piano and narrator is a Rust-Belt answer to Prokofiev's musical picture book *Peter and the Wolf*. Her *Music for Small Orchestra* is sultry summer music with languid flutes, toying ostinatos and clammy string clusters. A violin circles an atonal refrain in eerie harmonics like someone humming a fragment of a forgotten dream. The second movement is marked 'in roguish humour', motoring along with a wit so dry it could combust.

By now, the young Ruth Crawford was turning heads. Thanks to the arresting charisma of these early pieces, she was being hailed as part of an artistic movement of sorts – a small group of composers that included Charles Ives, her friend Henry Cowell, and Carl Ruggles, who once sat at his piano banging out the same chord for more than an hour because he wanted to make sure it sounded as good the multiple thousandth time as it did the first. All these composers were seeking to clinch a new and distinctly American brand of modernism. They were labelled 'ultra-moderns' and their mascot was dissonance. Dissonance was the way they would break from the historical trappings of the old world and set out an expressive language fit for the new. They worked apart, these ultra-moderns, and in some cases (Ives) they held fairly unreconstructed attitudes about the plausibility of a woman being a member of the vanguard. But they all shared an inkling that tonal freedom and social freedom must have something in common.

Ruth Crawford's most striking piece from her Chicago years is the Sonata for Violin and Piano (1926), which flings into action with every muscle flexing. The opening chords are a kind of atonal detonation. Out of the wreckage the piano tolls and the violin line unfurls like limbs not quite ready to be obedient. The third movement is low, carnal, celestial, marked '*mistico*' and '*intenso*'. The middle movement is 'buoyant', the instruments orbiting each other like counterbalanced points on a Calder mobile – a poised, shifting equilibrium that would become a signature of Crawford's sound. This sonata has immense conviction. It is a composer limbering up with intent, evidently thrilled by the sound and symbolism of dissonance but also playful enough to have fun with the sensuality of it all.

In life as in music, Ruth Crawford had begun to unbutton what she called her 'coat of steel'. She had fallen into Chicago's bohemian circuit, attending incense-rich soirées that were a universe away from her Florida life of a decade earlier. Now she explored

Eastern mystics and read Walt Whitman, underlining long passages in *Leaves of Grass*. She became friendly with the Chicago poet
and 'people's troubadour' Carl Sandburg and wrote piano parts
for his 1927 anthology *The American Songbag*. Significant spiritual
doors were being opened by her piano teacher, Djane Lavoie-Herz,
a fabulously worldly woman who wore exotic caftans and had spent
time with Alexander Scriabin himself in Brussels. Herz introduced
Crawford to Theosophy – a philosophical movement founded by
the Russian esotericist Helena Blavatsky, who claimed to possess
powers including telepathy and clairvoyance and wrote volumin-
ous treatises based on encounters, real or invented, with various
Tibetan Mahatmas. For many Western artists and intellectuals of
the early twentieth century, Theosophy was a gateway to all kinds of
alternative thought. It was for Crawford, and would be for Walter
Smetak two decades later.

Herz's apartment was a focal point for beatnik Chicago in the
1920s, and Crawford was a regular guest. Before long she herself
was writing intense poems with names like *Shades of Dead Planets*:

For you are the sun,
But I am the creator of the Sun.

'Looking back on it now' – Peggy Seeger holds an impish finger
aloft – 'looking back on it, I'll bet they were lovers.' Seeger has
been mulling over a photograph from 1925 in which her mother
stands next to Djane Lavoie-Herz on the shores of Lake Michigan.
Crawford wears a boxy shirt and her trademark brogues. Herz looks
archly stylish in black. Both have notably cropped hair. A couple of
years later, not long before she married, Crawford would experience another female friendship passionate enough that she and the
woman in question felt the need to discuss what they referred to as

the 'lesbian subject'. Peggy Seeger's supposition is part daughter's hunch – mischievous speculation about her mother's premarital love affairs. It is another part empathy, because she herself has loved men and women and appreciates the wonders and complications of both. 'Oh, I wish I could speak to my mother about it all,' Seeger sighs. That same wish becomes a recurring refrain in our conversation.

For her part, Seeger wound up living here, where we are talking in this hedgerowed corner of Old England, because of a story that began in 1956. She was twenty years old. She walked into a room filled with smoke and men, perched herself on a high stool and started to play the banjo. One of the men was the folk singer Ewan MacColl. He was twenty years older than Seeger and married, and would remain so while she gave birth to their eldest son, Neill. Seeger shares with me an uncomfortable episode from that first pregnancy. Ewan's mother Betsy came to stay and sat in their home knitting a baby blanket. When Seeger thanked her, Betsy replied that she was knitting it for Ewan's wife, Jean, whom Seeger discovered, via that blanket, was also pregnant at the time. Three decades, three children and one of the most fabled romances in folk music later, Seeger fell in love with her best friend, Irene, and began to reassess how some marriages can numb a woman's sense of agency and desire. She was now equipped with terms like 'gaslighting' and 'feminism'.

'That's another thing my father did.' Seeger says this with a steely expression. 'My mother cut off relations with the female friends and people she had known in her twenties. I recognise it very well, because it's what I did. It's a pattern. It's what they do. I'm not excusing it. I'm just passing it over to you as information.' She assesses me from across the coffee table. 'You've not been married, have you?' No. 'Children?' No. Well, not at that point, anyway.

'OK. I've been married, I've had children. Let me share a common saying you hear among married women. *I do this to keep the peace.*'

Later, Seeger quizzes me about my own family. 'Six brothers? Oh, woman!' She slaps the arm of her chair and chuckles. 'I can relate!' she cackles. 'We also have a preponderance of boys. Four brothers, and they've had a lot of sons among them. And', she leans back, crunching into a biscuit, 'let me tell you about my father.'

. . .

Summer, 1929. Ruth Crawford wrote to a friend: 'I am beginning to think life is what I want.'

She never did go back to Florida to set up that piano studio she had promised her mother. Instead, she left Chicago and headed east to New York City to study with a teacher who came highly recommended by her friend and fellow composer Henry Cowell. The teacher's name was Charles Louis Seeger. He was a fine thinker and an unremarkable composer. He came from a New England family that owned a rambling house in Patterson, New York, and he strode with a sense of entitlement to match. He had a Harvard education and three sons (Charles, John and little Peter) from his first marriage to a violinist called Constance. What he did not have was the esteemed composition career he felt he deserved. Nobody seemed particularly interested in the earnestly procedural music he was writing. It was as a teacher, a theorist and a song collector in the burgeoning field of ethnomusicology that Charles Seeger would leave his mark.

'Tall, aristocratic, ultra-refined, a bit cold' was Crawford's first impression of the future father of her children. 'Five feet of ice and ten feet of books' was another astute description. Seeger spoke with slow gravitas in the drawn-out drawl of moneyed New England. He considered the music of the firebrand French composer Edgard Varèse to be 'lousy' and he decided George Gershwin was a fake. He had a low opinion of female composers, mostly because he didn't read about them much in history books. The prospect of teaching a woman did not enthuse him and he wrote to Crawford before they met to tell her as much.

Seeger was not an entirely happy man. His parents disapproved of his career choice ('gentlemen are not musicians') and his marriage was in bad shape. He wasn't getting much attention or money for his compositions. 'My father wanted to be a conductor then he found out he was going deaf,' Peggy Seeger interjects, trying to rationalise what she interprets as a deep-set need to prove himself. 'That was a real blow to him. The music that my mother was making was so advanced. He understood what she was doing, I'm absolutely sure of it. Understood, but that doesn't mean he was able to accept it.'

Some attitudes die hard. There was the time that Charles Seeger wouldn't let Crawford join a gathering of musicologists – it was for

men only, he insisted, but if she really wanted in on the discussion
she could sit on the other side of the closed door and eavesdrop.
When she conveyed to him her less-than-impressed feelings about
being excluded, he told her: 'Your integrity compelled my admiration.' Presumably it's the 1920s equivalent of 'You look sexy
when you're angry.' Years later, he would inform his kids that
women could not write symphonies – this despite examples to the
contrary by (in the United States alone) Amy Beach, Marion Bauer
and Florence Price. But Peggy Seeger remembers her father saying it clearly. 'He would look down his long nose at me as he said
it, almost like a confession.' She waves a hand dismissively. She
has spent decades coming to terms with all this. 'Personally,' she
shrugs, 'I think a symphony is a rather bloated form, don't you?
Very male. Maybe he was right.'

Crawford arrived in New York in the autumn of 1929, ignoring
Charles Seeger's letter, or possibly fired up to prove him wrong.
She lodged on the edge of Central Park in the same apartment
where Henry Cowell was a regular visitor and Béla Bartók had
been a guest a couple of years earlier. Her composition lessons
were a mutual triumph. Seeger's intellect gripped her – gave her
'airplane views', as she rhapsodised. A new concision, a new thrifti-
ness, began to emerge in her sinewy *Diaphonic Suites*, a series of
tiny works whose fleet astringency would resurface in the music of
György Kurtág and Elliott Carter many decades later. Crawford's
third suite is scored for two clarinets. The instruments snake and
jostle around each other with magnetic drama. No movement lasts
for more than ninety seconds, but their proud strut makes these
miniatures feel monumental.

Seeger took full credit for Crawford's new mettle, claiming she
had been an 'imitator' until 'she had studied with Charles Seeger
and she had form'. Actually, she had been investigating how to

make sleek dissonance mean something pertinent for half a decade and counting. What changed was that she now had the assurance to scrape away every bit of excess and reveal the gleaming essentials.

And yes, Crawford and Seeger fell for each other, even if it took them both a while to admit it. Their passion ignited as they co-authored a treatise on dissonant counterpoint. The nitty-gritty of atonal polyphony – hardly sounds the stuff of hot romance, but for them the treatise represented an ideological thrust that set both minds alight. Surely they could have read the signs. Instead of focusing on writing her own music in the summer of 1930, Crawford decided to devote her energy to helping Seeger write his book, which was essentially a summary of the ideas they had discussed together during their lessons. With his three sons in tow (and relations now downright frosty with his wife Constance), the pair of polyphonic paramours retreated to the rambling Seeger homestead in Patterson. They set up office in a barn and got to work compiling their magnum opus. On hot summer evenings, Seeger would play guitar while the family sang camp songs under the wide East Coast skies. Young Pete was eleven years old, and already learning to join in with the harmonies.

By the end of that sepia summer, Ruth Crawford was all but subsumed into Seeger family life. She worked with them, she sang with them, but she was not quite ready to give up her independence altogether. That year, 1930, she became the first woman to be awarded a Guggenheim fellowship as a composer, and she would not pass up that chance, not even for love. She decided to spend the fellowship stipend on a year in Berlin to immerse herself in post-war Germanic modernism. Seeger borrowed an old Ford Runabout and drove her north to Quebec from where Crawford would board the RMS *Empress of Scotland* bound for Europe. They stopped on a bridge in Vermont and at last articulated the feelings that had been hanging in the air all summer. Later, they would quote the birdsong they heard on that bridge as musical code in their love letters. That night, they rented a room near the Canadian border, on the bucolic little archipelago of sandy islands known as North and South Hero that cut through the heart of Lake Champlain.

. . .

Autumn, 1930. Berlin was on the cusp of its darkest political decade. Nazism was on the rise. Kurt Weill and Bertolt Brecht had coined the sound of Germany's Weimar-age high life, grinning on the next cliff edge, soundtracking pleasure on the brink of collapse, but by the time Ruth Crawford reached the city even that blithe partnership had collapsed.

Crawford noticed that the trains in Germany ran in 5/8. She was offered introductions to the paterfamilias of atonalism, Arnold Schoenberg, but she held fast, determined not to leap into studying with anyone. Maybe she refused to meet Schoenberg out of loyalty to her American teacher – maybe she was convinced that she already had access to a mind finer than that of any European. Maybe that was a mistake, limiting her options to appease the pride of Charles Seeger. I am reminded of Peggy's words: *I do this to keep the peace*.

Regardless, it was alone in Berlin that Crawford made her two masterpieces. First she composed the *Three Chants for Women's Chorus*, an extraordinary breakthrough in choral writing. Crawford's sound is rapturously, blazingly inventive. Drawing on the Theosophical penchant for Eastern religions she had encountered via Djane Lavoie-Herz back in Chicago, she initially wondered about setting a piece of Hindu scripture. When she couldn't track down a decent translation of the Sanskrit, she decided to make up her own language instead. Pure sound, she figured, could trigger the mystical effect she was after. She also borrowed a vocal technique from a Chinese opera star called Mei Lanfang, whom she had heard performing earlier in the year. 'Approach a note by a slide from below, and sustain the note,' she had noted in her diary. 'Or by a slide from above and sustain the note. Or leave the note in either of these ways . . .'

The outer movements of the *Three Chants* are dedicated 'To an Unkind God' and 'To a Kind God'. The voices of the middle movement, the hypnotic 'To an Angel', glide about like slow skaters on an astral ice rink. The final note of the piece is a dense hum that hangs in a supernatural mist – the sort of eerie galactic throb that Ligeti would summon thirty years later, or which Kaija Saariaho, Finnish composer of bewitching illusions, would pursue in her twenty-first-century whispered confessionals.

Berlin was not a particularly happy or healthy home for Ruth Crawford. She didn't feel welcomed by the city's music circles. She was spurned, she perceived, by a double snobbery towards her as a woman and as an American. 'Germans simply can't stand the hurt of having to admit that there is anything someone else can understand better than they,' she wrote home to Seeger, feeling dejected. Maybe their four-day love affair had scuppered her chances of enjoying Berlin before she had even boarded the RMS *Empress of Scotland*. She spent a lot of her time alone, reporting back to Seeger in letters filled with frustration and soul-searching.

And yet out of that struggle she composed her finest work of all: the *String Quartet 1931*. Its distilled sound play and uncompromising, sharp-chiselled mathematics make it a harbinger of the avant-garde music that emerged nearly two decades later out of the wreckage of the Second World War. The writing is fastidiously constructed using modernist procedures including tone rows, staggered dynamics and rhythmic cells – procedures that in other hands might sound clinical, but not in hers. As well as its astringency, Crawford's Quartet is ruinously expressive. The *Andante* alone is devastating: a four-minute threnody, strings grasping and galvanising as though trying to escape the dark clouds that were building around Europe. No work of music articulates the pre-war moment with more unflinching premonition and power.

In the spring of 1931, with the tiny bit of money she had left from the Guggenheim fellowship, Crawford bought herself some train tickets and at last went visiting. In Vienna she turned up on the doorstep of the composer Alban Berg, whom she found a disappointment ('more Schoenberg worshipper than I would have thought' was her cool assessment). In Budapest she called in on Béla Bartók, who was anything but a disappointment. Bartók was one of the first composer-ethnomusicologists to travel extensively armed with new recording technology and a genuine respect for folk culture. His thousands of field recordings influenced his own music integrally but never in a cheap or approximate way: he adopted the rogue rhythms of vernacular songs, the untameable angles of dances, and his writing grew increasingly taut, jagged and original as a result. A 'dear quiet shy little person' is how Crawford described him after they spent an afternoon together. He showed her a collection of traditional flutes, which he had collected in North Africa and Hungary. The two composers shared a mutual delight in talking about the sort of open intervals and overtones that such instruments might magic up. From that day she held him in highest esteem, and she cried when he died in 1945.

Bartók and Crawford were kindred spirits in more ways than they perhaps recognised at the time. Within a few years, she would be taking up his mantle, spending the next two decades transcribing folk songs with an attentiveness to the integrity of the material that was rare among classical composers. It is tantalising to wonder what might have happened had she met Bartók sooner, or had she kept in touch with him better, or had she kept composing for longer. Would she have become America's Bartók? Would she, too, have found a way of synthesising folk music and modernism, rather than effectively cleaving the two and renouncing the latter? I put the notion to Peggy Seeger, who nods emphatically but says she cannot allow herself to dwell on the what-ifs. That way lies agony, she shakes her head.

As Crawford and Seeger continued writing to each other, him in New York, her in Berlin, they returned again and again to a question that had been preoccupying them both. Was it possible for a woman to have children and keep composing? In a typically pithy summation, Crawford called it her 'career vs love and children battle'. And she was torn apart by it, a split that women the world over will recognise. At times, she felt sure that anything was possible, that she could win in both camps. At other times she was despondent. She was not ready to choose.

In the summer of 1931, as her Guggenheim fellowship ran out and her stay in Europe came to an end, Crawford's mood was crestfallen. Seeger crossed the ocean to meet her in Paris and they spent the night walking through the city streets. She asked him, tears streaming down her cheeks, 'What's going to happen to me?' He put an arm around her shoulder and replied, presumably with the intention of reassuring her, that they would get married and have 'some lovely children'. Which is what they did.

. . .

Winter, 1935. New York was in the thick of the Great Depression. Six years after the stock markets crashed on Wall Street, two years after Franklin D. Roosevelt declared that the only thing to fear was fear itself, four years after Ruth Crawford returned from Berlin, life back home in the United States had not been easy. Seeger had assured her 'there is no obstacle to the loving that enough loving (feeling) cannot overcome', but they had no money and no work, he (Seeger) was still married to someone else and his parents were refusing to welcome her (Crawford) into their house. Once the divorce papers finally came through, the former teacher-and-student couple seized their moment, drove west and eloped to Nevada. Their first child, Michael, was born ten months later. Crawford burned the score of her Sonata for Violin and Piano, the work that in 1926 had been one of her bravest statements. Maybe it was just too raw a reminder of a creative future that no longer seemed possible.

Roosevelt's New Deal was sweeping the nation with make-work projects and amassed patriotism. By the mid-1930s, the political left was becoming preoccupied with celebrating and edifying proletariat culture, which threw left-leaning avant-garde artists into existential crisis. Could prepared pianos ever be the instrument of the American worker? Could dissonant counterpoint express the social urgencies of the Dust Bowl? Later generations would find ways to reconcile those false polarities, but for Charles Seeger – whose career as a modernist composer was anyway in the doldrums – the route forward looked clear at last. He told the folk-singing union activist Aunt Molly Jackson: 'You're on the right track and we're on the wrong track.'

In his mind, the 'right track' was folk music. Not the anodyne versions that had previously made it onto commercial records, but the real thing – the rugged voices and banjo picking, the fiddle tunes and work songs that were being sung and played across America under the radar of most academics and record producers. Seeger took up a post with Roosevelt's New Deal workforce, joining a battalion of artists now employed to 'keep up morale'. He was tasked with sourcing authentic rural folk songs and bringing them back to the cities, thus instilling urban workers with honest, all-American music and a healthy dose of national identity on the side. By the summer of 1936, Seeger was rigging up his newfangled Presto Disc recording device at farms from Alabama to Arkansas. His son Pete, now a spindly seventeen-year-old, tagged along to a traditional music festival in Asheville, North Carolina, where he heard his very first five-string banjo under the rolling peaks of the Great Smoky Mountains.

The Seegers befriended another father-and-son team. John Lomax had begun recording Texan cowboy songs into an Edison cylinder in the early years of the 1900s. When his wife died and he lost his bank job to the Great Depression, Lomax packed young Alan into the back of a car along with a Presto Disc and set off to record the authentic sounds of America. The Lomaxes would go on to make more than 10,000 recordings, from zydeco waltzes to vaquero love songs on the Rio Grande. They devoted special attention to collecting Anglo-American and African-American ballads. One of the first singers they recorded was an inmate at a Louisiana prison: a black man by the name of Huddie William Ledbetter, better known as Lead Belly. He was interned for murder and sang stoic, earth-cracked versions of 'Midnight Special' and 'Goodnight, Irene'.

. . .

By now it is fully dark in Oxford, and Peggy Seeger sashays across her living room to switch on a couple of lamps while ordering me into the kitchen to refill the kettle. 'I think she loved my father,' she says plainly, when I walk back into the room carrying the teapot. 'She respected him, and because her own father had died when she was twelve, Charles became a father figure for her. In the same way that Ewan was a father figure to me. By the way,' she cracks her mischievous smile, 'Ewan wouldn't recognise who I am now. I'm so different. I think he was worried when I became interested in feminism. It takes a strong man to be with a feminist woman.'

Long after Crawford died, Charles Seeger would describe his late wife as an 'ardent feminist' because she believed (he said) in the basics of gender equality. Did she really? 'You'd be in trouble if you tried to argue with her,' Charles Seeger reflected, which suggests that he had tried to argue and that she had pushed back. But when an elderly Virgil Thomson visited the Seeger household, he noted that 'he worked her too hard and she cooked too much'. As Crawford herself wrote to her brother in 1945, 'All during the housecleaning I was thinking of the books I might be working on.' If she did believe in the basics of gender equality, she never found a way of laying them down in her own home.

Peggy Seeger has a deft tactic for dealing with her own prefeminist years. She looks back with bemused detachment at scenarios she would never accept now. 'I wasn't a feminist then,' is her succinct appraisal – it's the same self-forgiving reflection I encounter in Annea Lockwood, and in my own mother. Two decades after Ewan MacColl died, Seeger edited *The Essential Ewan MacColl Songbook* and addressed the problem head on in her introduction. 'As a budding eco-feminist,' she writes,

> I find the subject matter of many of the songs in this book very hard to deal with. A developed eco-feminist would probably not have undertaken this book at all. Ewan was a Marxist, a

militant, gut-political product of the tail-end of the industrial revolution. In most of his songs, men are digging, slashing, cutting, building, re-shaping, raping, controlling, humanising the earth and being praised for doing so for the good of mankind. Humanity and the class struggle were Ewan's main preoccupations but his songs deal with MEN: men's work, men's lives, men's activities and many veiled (and not so veiled) references to the power of the penis. Even where it is obvious that both sexes are being referred to, Ewan (like myself in my early songs and like most people in our patriarchal society) employs the masculine pronouns.

Ruth Crawford never got her chance for such retrospection. And she certainly never ever described herself as a 'woman' composer. 'I suspect she was a closet feminist,' Seeger surmises. What would Crawford have thought of the term? That refrain comes around once again. 'Oh, I wish she was here to ask.'

• • •

'We were a close family,' Peggy Seeger remembers. 'Held together by music and by our parents' love for each other. We drifted together naturally on Friday nights and sang in the room where Dio and Charlie's desks stood back to back.' Dio was the name toddler Mike had given his mother, mimicking the way his father stretched out the word 'dear' in his New England twang. There was no radio or television in the Seeger house, but there was music all the time. In 1948, young Peggy went AWOL in a Washington department store and was picked up by a tall and practical black woman who stayed with the child until she was reunited with her mother. That woman's name was Elizabeth Cotten, and she had been a star singer at her church in North Carolina until she hit puberty and got taken out of school and married off. Ruth Crawford was so impressed by Cotten's composure in the department store that she offered her work in the household, where the family guitar was always hanging on the kitchen wall. 'I came in after school one day and found Libba playing it left-handed,' Seeger recalls, using the family's affectionate name for Cotten. (The Seegers were big on nicknames.) 'Index finger swinging away doing the job of the thumb, her thumb relegated to fingerdom. We heard "Freight Train" for the first time.' Later, when Peggy was at college, Cotten would bake enormous chocolate cakes and post them north to her in Vermont.

Crawford joined the folk movement. How could she not? Her own music went against the prevailing winds within her own house, where Seeger declared it 'almost immoral' to 'closet oneself in one's comfortable room and compose music for its own delight'. At first, Crawford wondered if there might be some kind of amalgam – some way to serve the populist cause with music that didn't apologise for its complexity. In 1932, she wrote two overtly political songs to the angry proletarian poetry of a young Chinese dissident called H. T. Tsiang. The first song is 'Sacco, Vanzetti', honouring a pair of anarchists who were executed for crimes they almost certainly didn't commit. The piano pounds oppressively while the voice intones with steely gaze. The second song is 'Chinaman, Laundryman', and here Crawford's brilliance with repetition takes on a menacing grind: the exploited worker so downtrodden by the mechanisms of capitalism that even his song complies. In the background, the piano provides the incessant tumbling of laundromat washing machines. The soprano who was booked to premiere the songs in 1933 refused to sing them because they were too controversial. Anyway, angular settings of proletarian texts were not the future for Crawford. 'My father put a cap on her composing when he called it "music for musicians",' Peggy Seeger tells me. The pursuit of a new American dissonance would have to wait.

Crawford gamely rebranded herself 'Krawford the Kommunist' and threw herself into the cause. When John and Alan Lomax returned from their field recording trips, they would hand over carloads of heavy shellac records and it was Crawford's job to make meticulous transcriptions. In many cases it was the first time these songs had been written down. She would listen to a line sometimes eighty times over, noting every detail, labouring over some tricksy time signature or the critical difference between a B and a B-flat (the truth was often somewhere in the middle). Meanwhile the whole Seeger clan sang. 'We sang all the time,' Peggy says. 'We sang the songs my mother was transcribing. That's how we learned. She kept lifting the needle, playing back the same line over and over. After a while we were dying for her to get to the next line.'

The Lomaxes gave Crawford a down payment of one dollar per transcription. She loved the utility of what she heard in these songs: the sense that they were sung for purpose, for necessity. She was moved by their everydayness – they were songs, she wrote,

> sung as though they might continue off into space. This singing
> and playing is a close accompaniment to living: to working, to
> playing games, to dancing all night, to doing nothing, to doing
> anything a long time, to jogging down a night road behind the
> unhurried clop-clop of the old mare's hoofs, or riding along in
> a car or truck with miles rolling away underneath.

Sometimes she wrote piano accompaniments to go with the melodies. She created books for schools: *American Folk Songs for Children*, *Animal Folk Songs*, *American Folk Songs for Christmas*. Her books earned her repute in educational and musical circles. Woody

Guthrie wrote a letter to the Seegers and the Lomaxes in 1948: 'All of you make such a good team that I'd say America's waking-up, shakingup, looking up folksongs and ballads.' Other times, Crawford simply transcribed, with a fearsome ear for accuracy. She always sought out the real thing. She said she wanted the *breath of the singer* to feel as close as possible. 'She was a perfectionist,' Peggy Seeger points out.

> I think she had a bit of contempt for some of the people who were putting out folk music for children, making it *dumpty-dumpty*. She wrote beautiful accompaniments. They sound simple but they are bloody hard to play. You can play them or you can sing them, but try doing both! A lot of her folk accompaniments were contrapuntal. She didn't just put chords all over the place. She would create countermelodies. Often she wouldn't give us a resolution. She'd make a song that was in the Ionian mode sound as though it was in the Dorian. She would do things you wouldn't expect and then she would only half resolve them.

Her mother was, Seeger concludes, still composing after all.

. . .

In the late 1940s, Ruth Crawford began composing full works again. Late at night, after the family had gone to bed, after the house had been put right, she worked on a second quartet, whose sketches are torturously lost, and she wrote a bright and brief orchestral piece called *Rissolty, Rossolty* that sparks and fizzes with folk-fibrous energy (though doesn't reach anything like the audacity of her earlier works). In 1948, in a letter to the composer Edgard Varèse, she

explained some of the elements that she felt characterised her musical style. Clear melodies, she listed, as well as independent rhythmic
parts, musical cohesion, and above all – dissonance. She admitted
she still stood by these compositional convictions. 'I believe when
I write more music these elements will still be there.' Although
nearly two decades had passed since her searing *String Quartet
1931*, Crawford remained a modernist to the core in the way she
embraced dissonance and rejected convention, commercialism, the
excesses of romanticism. Remember: she hated polish, hated sweet-
ness. 'Ugliness is also a very beautiful thing,' she declared. 'That is,
things that many other people might consider ugly.'

In 1952, Crawford entered and won a competition with her new
Suite for Wind Quintet, which regains at least some of her original
poise and attack. The bassoon beetles away with an atonal boogie-
woogie bass line while the other instruments flit and shimmy,
testing their equilibrium. Nobody does counterbalancing better
than Ruth Crawford. Now that three of her children were nearly
grown up and the uncompromising politics around the Great
Depression-era proletarian cause had started to soften, her signature style was creeping back. 'I believe I'm going to work again,' she
wrote to her friends Carl and Charlotte Ruggles. 'More! If I live to
be 99 as my grandfather did, that gives me 48 more years.' What
galling optimism hangs in those determined words. A year later,
Ruth Crawford died of cancer.

Her old Chicago friend Carl Sandburg once observed that he
himself would probably die 'propped up in bed trying to write a
poem about America'. In a sense, that's exactly what happened to
Crawford. According to Pete Seeger, she didn't go gently at all.
She worked furiously on her next book until the very end. Who
knows what she might have done with those forty-seven lost years.
Musically, she was on the brink of something new. She was in a

unique position, with one foot in America's modernist vanguard and the other in America's great folk dynasty.

'I don't think she wanted to be famous,' Peggy Seeger sighs, standing, stretching, clearing away the mugs. She is tired. We have talked at length. In the distance, the bells of Oxford are ringing for Evensong. It's time I removed my bicycle from her hallway. 'My mother just felt the need to create,' she says over her shoulder as she heads towards the kitchen. 'She had such respect for folk music. I don't think she would have been a Benjamin Britten or a Ralph Vaughan Williams – in the sense that she would have never been *nostalgic* about folk music. And think. Just think of the double expertise she had. My mother died when she had under her belt a terrific knowledge of classical music and a terrific knowledge of folk music. The real thing. Do I think she would have found a way to put them together? Of course I do. I think she would have been absolutely extraordinary.'

Ruth Crawford was extraordinary already. Her formidable early works stand for themselves: the two pieces she wrote during her single year in Berlin are reason enough to shout about her. But the impact of *Three Chants* and *String Quartet 1931* is doubly potent because of the silence that followed. Hers is the story of women everywhere who feel they must choose. She lived on the brink of a feminist freedom she could not quite grasp. If her presence in this book represents the 'lost' female composer, it is the 'lost' potential of unsupported working mothers the world over.

For Walter Smetak, it was the choice to quit classical music's central European heartland and head for the tropics that consigned him to the periphery of musical history – and sparked his anarchic creativity.

Walter Smetak

(1913–84)

**From Brazil to caossonance: introducing
Tak-Tak, godfather of *Tropicália***

The noise of a city has no single seed. No lone authorship. Charismatic mavericks can shape a time, imprint headline identity on a place, but it's the collisions and intersections, the overlaps and undercurrents, that cumulatively and haphazardly make a sound, a scene, a creative stamp. Walter Smetak had an instrument workshop in the basement of a university building in Salvador da Bahia, north-eastern Brazil. In the 1960s and 1970s, that workshop was a regular meeting place for musicians of wild and questioning minds.

Salvador was, still is, one of the most intensively multicultural cities in Brazil, which makes it one of the most multicultural cities in the world. During a buoyant decade and a half in the 1950s and early 1960s, a brief hiatus between military regimes in the changing capital cities (Rio de Janeiro then Brasilia), Bahia germinated a joyous cultural movement. Artists from this poor sugar state challenged doctrine about what it meant to look Brazilian, to sound Brazilian, to be Brazilian. Smetak, a Swiss immigrant, tuned into Salvador's exuberant spirit of invention, and he added his own outlandish sounds to the mix.

One of his former colleagues told me that Smetak smelled of wood varnish and pipe smoke. That he had a temper nobody wanted to cross, this taciturn, craggily handsome buckaroo of Bahia who growled at students and walked with dozens of keys jangling from his belt so you could hear him coming all through the music department. Smetak cut an unmistakable image with his white hair, white beard and wayfarer shades, tearing around Salvador on a motorbike, which he nicknamed the 'Whore of Babylon'. He looked like a gonzo luthier. He called himself a 'de-composer'. He claimed that he contained so much spirit it was almost physical. He declared he was going to create 'a new genre of music: a poor music, a music of the beggars, a Craft Music. Music that is not commercialised.' He fused the social conscience of Revueltas with the dogged cheek and outlandish ambition of Carrillo.

Smetak composed, but I've included him in this book because of his musical sculptures. *Plásticas sonoras*, he called them (sound plastics). They channelled ley lines. They were tuned to the moon. They embodied the feverish resonances of his adopted city. Tapping the multitudinous energy of the place, his instruments could often be played by several people at once. What Smetak called 'deep Brazil' was, for him, 'the land of possible impossibilities'. He might have been describing himself. The man of possible impossibilities. He was a cellist, initially, and a cello teacher, but Brazil radicalised him into becoming an inventor of instruments, a composer of aural sculptures, an improviser, a magician of microtonal intermedia noise-making. 'I am the pre-balance,' he stated, 'the asymmetry, the reaction.'

His creative mind was sprawling, poetic, unpredictable, sometimes downright unachievable. He painted and sculpted, wrote spiritual–theoretical treatises, books and plays. He practised a special branch of Theosophist spirituality called Eubiose, which prophesied that the next Buddha would be reincarnated in Brazil in the year 2005. Leaving aside all the zany messianic stuff, Smetak's writings reveal a free thinker who was always on the hunt for more profound and interconnected ways of understanding music and the universe. His texts, which include a series of roving aphorisms, linger somewhere between science, science fiction, self-help and horoscope, with subjects flitting from radioactivity and mortality to reincarnation, fertility (eggs crop up a lot) and his own beard as

metaphor for the jungle. Thoughts frequently skirt the apocalyptic.
Sometimes he simply poses whimsical little riddles like:

O céu se chove, um barco furado?
(Is the sky raining a punctured boat?)

Or

A borboleta dá beijos sem beijar . . .
(The butterfly kisses without kissing . . .)

Or

Esta escada irregular que desce à minha casa é aleatória.
É uma escala. Também tu podes subir nela.
(This irregular staircase that goes down to my house is random.
It is a scale. You too can climb on it.)

As a composer, Smetak did write down some of his music, and
in the 1970s he made two albums of arcane and wonky beauty. But
it was his hand-built collection of cosmic, carnal instruments that
proved to be his life's work.

Like Annea Lockwood, Smetak thought about bodies, be they
musical or human bodies, as resonating chambers. But whereas
Lockwood turns her attention inward, for Smetak these chambers
were attuned to planetary vibrations. There is an earthy, Dionysian
abandon to many of his creations. Take his collective flute. It is
made of bamboo and it is very long (five metres). It has twenty-two
holes, and can be played by twenty-two people at the same time.
Here he is describing one hot afternoon when this oversized holed
tube was transported from workshop to concert hall:

It was summer. People were wearing many colours and were in high spirits. They formed a kind of procession and tried to play the flute. It was hilarious; some people were shorter and some people were taller, and of course the taller people had it easier. The shortest people could not get their mouths up to the holes so they were struggling a lot; they were walking on their tiptoes in order to be able to blow at all. And the taller people were laughing so hard they weren't able to play either.

When the assembled flautists finally stopped laughing and made it into the concert hall, they adjusted their seating so that they all reached around the same height and they started to play. The pitches came out according to the dimensions of each bamboo segment, some of which were wider than others. The giant pipe warbled in close microtones, twenty-two voices contributing to one motley wheeze.

Smetak's instruments aren't fancy. They are made of ordinary things like bamboo, wire, plastic, rubber gloves and vegetables. They are not usually tuned to any particular scale. Some are painted to look like planets or stars or human faces. Some operate like a one-man band, while others, like that overstretched flute, require multiple people to play them at once. Others still, like the elegant *Metástese* (Metastasis), are all poise and lunar balance and make no sound at all. Smetak's ultimate aim was nothing if not lofty. Through his instruments, he wanted to achieve a meta-sensory state that would transcend all boundaries between light and sound, between sight and hearing. And maybe, he believed, just maybe, this heightened state would allow a human being 'to glimpse existence'.

· · ·

Smetak felt he belonged everywhere and also somewhere very specific. He was Brazilian by chance and by choice – he called himself 'a very Brazilian Brazilian, with my feet in the water up to my knees' – and his instruments owe their porous nonconformity to Salvador in its golden age. But this story begins five thousand miles north-east of Salvador, in the colder, sterner hills of northern Switzerland.

Anton Walter Smetak was born in Zurich on 12 February 1913. The music world was in upheaval. It was the year Louis Armstrong was arrested for firing his stepfather's gun at a New Year's celebration and was sent to the New Orleans Colored Waifs' Home where he first picked up a cornet. In Paris, it was the year Lili Boulanger became the first woman to win the Prix de Rome composition prize and Stravinsky unleashed his pulverising ballet *Le Sacre du printemps* on a gobsmacked audience at the Théâtre des Champs-Élysées. In Vienna, it was the year Arnold Schoenberg conducted what became known as the *Skandalkonzert* (the scandal concert), also nicknamed the *Watschenkonzert* (slap concert) after its organiser walloped a rioting audience member in the face. In Rio de Janeiro, Heitor Villa-Lobos – who would come to dominate Brazilian classical music for the next four decades – began publishing his works.

Smetak's childhood was peaceful, according to his eldest daughter, Barbara, who sends me lively emails in Portuguese about her father. She tells me that young Walter had a good relationship with his parents and with his sister Leone, and that the family home was full of music. His mother Frederica was a Swiss-Austrian singer who had met his father Anton, a Czech zither player, when both were studying music in Vienna. Barbara tells me a story that hints at her father's early inspiration: when Anton taught his zither lessons at home, little Walter would sit with his ear against a table and listen to the music resonating through the wood. Anton hoped his son would follow in his footsteps as a zither virtuoso, but Walter's love of Bach led him first to the piano, then, after a hand injury, to the cello, which he went on to study in Salzburg and Vienna. Smetak was always fascinated in how instruments were made. Ear against wood, he fixated on the physical properties that produce resonance. Whichever city he was in, he would track down the local luthiers and linger for long hours around their workshops.

On graduating from the conservatory in Vienna, Smetak was offered a job playing cello in an orchestra in Porto Alegre, Brazil. He packed up his instrument and headed across the Atlantic to join the Orquestra Internacional Farroupilha at the mouth of the Patos Lagoon. The year was 1937; he was twenty-four years old, and had plenty of reasons to turn his back on Europe. When the Porto Alegre orchestra dissolved less than two years later, he did not get back on the boat and go home. It was better, he said, to immerse himself in the *desordem e a liberalidade dos trópicos* (the disorder and freedom of the tropics) than to surrender himself to the 'European miseries instigated by Adolf Hitler'.

But Brazil was in the grip of a new authoritarianism of its own. The government was flirting with fascism. In November 1937, President Getúlio Vargas claimed that the only way to suppress the threat of communist uprising (real or invented) was to shut down his own legislature and rule by martial law. Relations with the United States wore a fixed grin under the so-called 'Good Neighbor Policy', promoting the likes of the singer Carmen Miranda as poster girl for what amounted to a US soft-power grab across Latin America. Miranda herself is a fascinating construct: Portuguese by birth, samba superstar by trade, she adopted tropical headgear and the flag of multicultural Bahia to make herself credible as a performer of Afro-Brazilian music. Her career skyrocketed under the strident nationalism of the Vargas regime. Meanwhile the classical music establishment was dominated by the prolific composer Heitor Villa-Lobos. Like his counterpart Carlos Chávez in Mexico, Villa-Lobos landed on a sonorous integration of folk music from all corners of the country, which suited the dictatorship's one-nation integrationist agenda to a tee.

Smetak recorded with Carmen Miranda. Her swoopy string section was just one of the odd jobs that kept him busy during his first two decades as a gigging cellist in Brazil. He freelanced in casinos and radio orchestras, in dance bands in São Paulo and Rio de Janeiro. He played chamber music with the Trio Schubert and taught cello in Porto Alegre. In 1941, he married a pianist named Maja Fausel who was twenty years older than him and a fellow Swiss immigrant. He wrote unremarkable little pieces for solo cello, for piano or small ensembles, and deployed the skills he had gleaned from the luthiers of central Europe to build and repair string instruments. Already intrigued by acoustics, he designed but failed to patent a form of close-contact microphone for pianos which he called the Meta-Sound.

Then came a spiritual awakening. In 1948, a colleague in the Brazilian Symphony Orchestra introduced Smetak to the Sociedade Brasileira de Eubiose. 'It is difficult to define why my father was so interested,' Barbara Smetak writes to me in an email. 'It was a process of conversion, a calling he felt for a way of seeing the world, life, the universe.' Eubiose is a Brazilian branch of Theosophy, the same philosophical movement that had sparked the synapses of Ruth Crawford in Chicago two decades earlier. Its esoteric teachings would underpin the rest of Smetak's life and work. Eubiose colour-codes the planets, the days of the week, the metals and the body parts. It seeks systems to connect the sacred and profane, the divine, the human and the intergalactic, and teaches that there are three suns, that indigenous Americans are the original population of Atlantis who survived the flooding 80,000 years ago, and that Brazil will be the cradle of a new civilisation. Eubiose is keen on planetary icons and obelisks. Smetak was particularly captivated by the central idea that light and sound might evolve from the same ethereal starting point.

His understanding of music and of himself was transforming. He began practising yoga. He studied directly with the founder of Eubiose, Henrique José de Souza, the man who had reconfigured Blavatsky for the Brazilian context. In the mid-1950s, De Souza pointed north to Bahia, where he intuited that there were particular earth energies in need of investigation.

Smetak arrived in Salvador in 1957. It was two decades since he left Europe, four years since the suicide of President Getúlio Vargas. In Tokyo, it was the year Tōru Takemitsu unveiled his Requiem, a severe, muted-string threnody. In Cologne, Karlheinz Stockhausen tested a gargantuan sonic-panning effect via his triple-orchestra score *Gruppen*. In Buenos Aires, Astor Piazzolla was incensing the establishment with his internationalist take on tango. In St Petersburg, Galina Ustvolskaya turned her eyes to the heavens, summoning bells in her Fourth Piano Sonata. In Chicago, Richard Abrams laid down the jagged piano lines of his first jazz record. In Liverpool, John Lennon and Paul McCartney met for the first time at a garden fete at the church where Eleanor Rigby was buried along with her name. In Rio de Janeiro, the new president Juscelino Kubitschek, promising an era of progress and optimism for Brazil, commissioned the architect Oscar Niemeyer to build a brand-new capital city to be finished by the dawn of the next decade.

. . .

The Bahian poet Antônio Brasileiro wrote:

A verdade é uma só: são muitas
(The truth is only one: there are many)

Salvador da Bahia was founded by the Portuguese in 1549 on a peninsula that juts out between the broad Baía de Todos os Santos (All Saints' Bay) and the Atlantic Ocean. The city is a great jumble. A centuries-old place of convergence. Nearly 1.5 million human beings were unloaded from ships here before slavery was at last abolished in Brazil in 1888. 'We are', says Paulo Costa Lima, composer and former culture secretary of Salvador, 'the diaspora of many Africas.' In 1928, the modernist poet Oswald de Andrade used his *Manifesto Antropófago* to argue that ingesting multiple cultures (his word was 'cannibalising') was one of the reasons for Brazil's great vibrancy. Costa Lima shrugs at the terminology. 'This cultural anthropophagy had been happening here in Bahia for centuries without any theory. The state of Bahia', the former culture secretary adds with some pride, 'was postmodern before it was modern.'

The anthropologist Antonio Risério writes in *Avant-garde na Bahia* that Salvador is 'a society given to contacts, exchanges, interpenetrations, transfusions and contagion' – and that contagion he refers to plays out in sound. Sound is everywhere in this city of multitudes. There are more than a thousand *Candomblé* houses: places of worship for a religion that is itself an amalgam of West African gods and Catholic saints. For the *Candomblé* faithful, spirits are summoned through singing, dancing and drumming. It's a clever religion that ensures every Mass kicks off like a mini carnival. When it comes to actual carnival (which Salvadorians will tell you is the best in Brazil), the city streets are thronged with *afoxé* bands dancing to Nigerian *ijezá* rhythms. João Gilberto, Bahian-born luminary of bossa nova, charged his guitar riffs with an extra frenetic drive borrowed from Afro-Brazilian *batucada* players. Any notion of 'purebred' or 'authentic' here assumes fusion as a starting point.

In the late 1950s and early 1960s, a confluence of free thinkers, immigrants and local radicals arrived at the Federal University of Bahia (UFBA). Bahia went big on the arts, asserting itself as a centre of cultural gravity that celebrated the dynamism of its own population instead of taking cues from Rio de Janeiro or São Paulo, let alone Paris or Vienna. The university established schools of Music (1954), Theatre (1955) and Dance (1955) – and invited a figure of the avant-garde to head up each faculty. Its series of *Seminários livres de música* (experimental music seminars) blossomed into the most vibrant music department in Brazil.

One of the key players in the Bahian classical music renaissance was the composer Ernst Widmer, a Swiss immigrant who taught seminars at UFBA using what Paulo Costa Lima describes as a bold 'horizontal method'. Students and teachers generated ideas together, supposedly without any hierarchy. Another influential figure here was the composer Hans-Joachim Koellreutter: born in Freiburg, he refused to join the Nazi party, proposed to a Jewish woman (a crime for which his own parents denounced him to the Gestapo) and turned his back on Europe in the late 1930s. Koellreutter played principal flute in the Brazilian Symphony Orchestra and set up a contemporary music series called Música Viva. His 1946 manifesto was a brazenly political agenda with points including:

(1) Music represents the reflection of social reality

(7) Abandon the concept of 'beauty', aiming to transform music into an art-action

(8) Refute the false nationalism that, through folklore, stimulated 'egocentric and individualistic tendencies that separate men'

(10) Value the importance of popular music from an artistic and social point of view.

When Koellreutter arrived at the university in Salvador, he set about creating an orchestra. In search of string players, he hired an eccentric cellist whom he had heard playing in São Paulo three years earlier.

• • •

Walter Smetak was initially recruited by Koellreutter as a teacher and cellist for the UFBA Symphony Orchestra, but his life's work would take place in the basement of the music department where he had been designated a workshop and the responsibility for mending staff and student instruments. Before long, that's where he started inventing new instruments, too.

In 1961, the year John Cage published a collection of lectures and writings under the title *Silence*, Walter Smetak travelled to the Vanguard Music Week at the Theatro Municipal in Rio de Janeiro. He heard performances by international new-music luminaries including the composer Luciano Berio and the pianist-composer David Tudor. He himself appeared as soloist in a work by Paul Hindemith (*Kammermusik no. 3* for cello and ten solo instruments). Back home in Salvador, still buzzing from the festival, he attended a performance of works by Koellreutter and experienced what he later described in his book *Simbologia dos instrumentos* (Symbology of the Instruments) as a 'revelation'.

The works he heard were written using techniques of *musique concrète* – a game-changing post-war method that used new tape technology to make music out of chopped-up and manipulated recordings of real ('concrete') sounds. The techniques of *musique concrète* were kickstarted in Cairo in 1944 when a young agricultural engineer called Halim El-Dabh recorded women singing at a religious ceremony. The term was coined in Paris in the late 1940s when Pierre Schaeffer turned the screech and clang of trains running along railway tracks into a symphony of noise. By the early 1960s, when Smetak experienced his epiphany in Salvador, there were *musique concrète* practitioners around the globe, thrilled by the permission to emancipate musical ingredients, to take any raw noise and craft it into polyphony, to slip between cultivated contexts and the everyday.

What Koellreuter's *musique concrète* seemed to ignite in Smetak's imagination was some ephemeral sense of alchemic possibility. Many composers were concurrently enthralled by the taxonomies of sound that new technologies opened up in the aftermath of the Second World War, but few would make the interconnections that Smetak did between engineering, acoustical physics, abstract spiritual philosophies and the human body. Through his instruments, he would spend the rest of his life in pursuit of that grand alchemy.

'If we divide the word in half,' Smetak explained, 'two Latin roots appear. *Instruere*, from instruct, and *mens*, the mind.' So he thought of an instrument as a tool to instruct the mind. He borrowed every available book on organology from the university library, placed a coconut shell inside a calabash and attached a broom handle and a single guitar string. It was the first of his *plásticas sonoras*, and he called it *Mundo* (World).

Smetak built more than 150 *plásticas sonoras* over the next two decades. They were wind, string and percussion instruments with fantastical names like *Máquina do Silêncio* (Machine of Silence) and

Anjo Soprador (Blowing Angle); *Mulher do Vento* (Woman of the Wind), *Espaço e Nuvens* (Space and Clouds), *Namorados Abstratos* (Abstract Lovers), *Andrógino* (Androgyny) and *Imprevisto* (Unexpected). He made a whole family of *Borés* which look like unravelled bulbous bugles, or maybe toilet plungers. The *Piston Cretino* (Foolish Trumpet) is a plastic tube with a trumpet mouthpiece at one end and a kitchen funnel at the other. In performance, Smetak would hold the funnel against his belly and wobble it like a wah-wah mute. What you see is what you get with the *plásticas sonoras*. Sight and sound go together in these uniquely Bahian readymades. There are no extraneous gimmicks. In appearance they are oddball, benign, somehow animal, a little alien, like wonky cubist temples of sound. It was important to Smetak that he sourced local and cheap materials. Old strings, bits of broken guitars, hoses, rubber gloves, chunks of Styrofoam, a lot of calabashes. The composer and Smetak scholar Marco Scarassatti thinks of the instruments as 'compositions' because of the multi-textural dimensions they contain. There is counterpoint in the mechanisms, polyphony between the elements.

Some of Smetak's *plásticas sonoras* rotate like a hog roast. Some are bright-painted spinning suns with strings that ping as they swivel. Pitch is not necessarily important – often Smetak did not even specify – and neither is virtuosity. In most cases, anyone who can blow or pluck or hold a bow can play these instruments.

Here are some of my favourites:

Amén is an eye, a calabash as its retina.

Colloquio involves two heads painted gold and a string between them. The heads face each other as if in conversation, and when they move, the string makes a wobbly sound.

Constelação is a painting of the night sky with strings connecting the stars. The strings can be plucked like a cosmic zither.

M-2005 is an intriguingly anthropomorphic creature. A human figure is set on a little plinth, with a face painted on a gourd and a little hat fixed to the top of the head. Strings run from the man's body to where his feet should be. The figure is holding a plastic globe and an orbiting moon. Smetak imagined the character 'floating on a block of ice, drifting from the North Pole southward toward the equator to land on shore. A penguin with an innocent nature accompanies this being, whose name begins with the letter *m* . . .' That would be 'M' for Avatara Maitreya, the future divinity who, according to Eubiose prophecy, was due to appear in this world in 2005. Incidentally, Smetak believed that he, too, would be reincarnated that same year.

Pindorama looks like – what – a palm tree? A planetary system? A mop? An octopus? It is more than two metres high, with seven calabash gourds and multiple cowbells suspended from a frame, whose six points Smetak thought of as navigational points on a mystic sextant: North, South, East, West, Nadir and Zenith. Hanging from the gourds are dozens of clear plastic tubes with flute mouthpieces fixed to their ends. 'The instrument is sensitive,' Smetak cautioned. 'If you offend it, the bells begin to ring.' Up to sixty musicians can play the *Pindorama* at the same time. The musician Tuzé de Abreu, who performed with Smetak, described the effect when everybody plays the instrument together, each tooting away on their own bendy flute. He said the harmonics sound like sun shining on water.

Maybe the most extraordinary of them all is the *Vina*, something between a snake, a sonic shrine, a blobby cello and a one-man band.

There is a fingerboard strung with three strings. There is a spike and a bow. There are three calabashes representing the Hindu deities Shiva, Vishnu and, chunkiest of them all, Brahma. There is a tube containing a sympathetic string to represent the serpent Kundalini. A clock spring is attached to the biggest calabash. There are bells, an electric tremolo effect, a mouthpiece attached to a plastic tube and a triangular zither resting inside one of the cala- bashes which reminded Smetak of a pregnant woman about to give birth. The musician sits with her back to the audience, possibly (and Smetak encouraged this) wearing a white cloak and a mask. The player absorbs the sound through the calabashes. When she strikes, strums, blows or bows, she channels a deep, tantric energy.

• • •

Love must be a soft thing, Smetak wrote in one of his many aphorisms. Love must arrive without causing a disturbance. 'If it is the other way around, it is just a passion, full of trouble.'

Smetak met his second wife, Julieta, not long after arriving in Bahia. He was on tour with the UFBA Symphony Orchestra in the city of Aracaju. Barbara Smetak relays the meeting with dig- nified economy. 'Smetak was enchanted with the young Julieta,' she writes, 'and invited her to live with him in Bahia. The young woman accepted the invitation, moved to Salvador and brought up five children.' The family lived in the Federação neighbourhood of the city where, says Barbara, 'we had a simple house, without luxury. We played, listened to a lot of music, studied and were happy.'

Contrary to his beatnik artistic image, Barbara describes her father as 'a conservative man' who refused to admit that his chil- dren might 'know about matters or participate in conversations regarding dating or sex before we were the right age. Everything at the right time. He was a very serious man.' Smetak held Eubiose seminars at that house in Federação. Gilberto Gil, godfather to Smetak's youngest son, called him 'a mix of mad scientist and Santa Claus'. Barbara remembers the two of them clambering onto the roof, scanning the night sky for UFOs.

When it came to institutional matters, Smetak was often a lousy team player – frankly, he sounds like a nightmare of a colleague. Maybe, like Julián Carrillo, he felt a certain licence to cause friction, or in fact that pre-emptively courting outcry might allow him more room to test. He claimed that achieving his desired creative alchemy required him to be in a particular state of mind, sinking into some trance-like communion with the divine, and that his most fertile state of mind was unstable, volatile, chaotic. In staff meetings he would sit in a corner smoking a pipe and refusing to speak much. His colleagues tended to leave him alone. Ernst Widmer described him as 'critical, grumpy, sometimes elusive, sometimes glorious, humble, radiant, severe and irreverent'. Scarassatti writes about Smetak's 'transparency' – he was someone who said what he wanted when he wanted. This corresponds with a story about a journalist arriving at Smetak's house for an interview and finding the composer outside mending his motorbike. When Smetak demanded to know whether the journalist could help him fix the bike and the journalist admitted he could not, Smetak declared the interview over before it had begun.

Paulo Costa Lima tells me about an incident involving Smetak and a cello spike.

I was 18, and the orchestra had a recording session. We were waiting for the session to begin, and Smetak arrived with this wonderful cello that he almost never used. He began to play in one corner of the room. The sound was amazing. Wonderful. I went up to him and said, 'Professor, what a beautiful sound.'

He grunted. I moved away, but a moment later we heard him muttering bad words at me. Then he stood up and ran at me with his cello. An old lady who ran the orchestra chastised him. He stormed off and wouldn't play in the session. The next day I was sitting in front of the school and he walked past. He couldn't bring himself to apologise, but he muttered some sort of conversational remarks in my directions. Much later I found out that he lashed out because he thought I was making fun of him. He hadn't played for a while and he was self-conscious about sounding bad. But you see? Woe to anyone who provoked him in any way.

Many years later, Costa Lima bought that same cello from Smetak, taking out a loan of $5,000 in order to help pay for it. Smetak changed his mind at the last minute. 'I told him about my loan and he grudgingly sold it to me, but two days later he called and said, "Bring the cello back! I can't sleep without it!"' By now Costa Lima knew him well enough not to take the mood swings to heart, so he simply avoided the instrument inventor for a few months until one day the two men bumped into each other in the music department. 'Paulo!' Smetak bellowed from the other end of a long corridor. 'You don't need to hide any more! I've overcome it!' This was the man, Costa Lima smiles with great affection. *This was the man.*

Despite his seeming antipathy to organised group activity, Smetak did closely involve himself with a remarkable artistic anti-movement founded in Salvador in 1966. The motto of the *Grupo de Compositores da Bahia* (the Group of Composers of Bahia) was a defiant one-liner –

IN PRINCIPLE WE ARE AGAINST
ALL AND EVERY PRINCIPLE!

– and it was this spirited *Grupo* that spurred Smetak to pursue his experiments in instrument building. Formed by Ernst Widmer and a generation of composers whose minds he and Koellreutter had expanded over the previous decade through Salvador's experimental music seminars, 'its source of energy', says Costa Lima,

> was to *dare*. The group asserted that it was possible to create avant-garde music in Bahia. That it was possible to make work that was high enough quality that the rest of Brazil realised there was something happening here. That in itself was still a subversive idea in 1966. At the beginning of the '60s, nobody would have suggested that the decade might end with Bahia recognised as a genuine laboratory for experimental sound.

• • •

In 1964, 'The Girl from Ipanema' was sweeping the world. Astrud Gilberto sang of Brazil as a paradise for the tall, tanned and lovely while the country's democracy was overthrown by a military junta. The song's muggy lilt of sex and *saudade* (longing) was an easy opiate but also a soft-shuffling cultural coup. Augusto de Campos, the nation's leading concrete poet, applauded bossa nova for beating the First World at its own game. This uniquely Brazilian hybrid of samba-plus-cool-jazz proved with delicious nonchalance that an underdeveloped country could produce exquisitely developed art. Bossa nova was the soundtrack of Brazil's modern renaissance, and it was selling across the globe.

Around the time that 'Ipanema' hit the charts, the artist Hélio Oiticica lost interest in painting flat things and started making work that people could wear and hold and move in. He called his objects *Parangolés* after a *favela* slang word that can variously mean nonsense, sudden confusion or a sticky situation. Oiticica's objects likewise meant whatever the users made of them. The new military dictatorship was cracking down on personal freedoms after Brazil's brief and burgeoning interlude of democracy, and Oiticica emblazoned capes with political statements that flashed or didn't, depending on how the wearer decided to dance – a stroke of libertinism that handed agency back to individuals and acknowledged the futility of fixing real life into a flat-surfaced, sun-soaked gloss.

In 1967, Oiticica built a shack in a gallery in Rio de Janeiro and surrounded it with tropical birds and plants. He plonked a television set in the middle of his installation, goading his viewers into admitting how readily they would buy into the numbing thrall of mass media in order to dodge the muck and confusion of the streets. The widespread arrival of television in the past decade had, he inferred, acted as a sedative on the collective Brazilian consciousness. He forced a disruption with this *favela*-meets-avant-garde, low-life-meets-high-art, natural-world-meets-consumerism, and he coined a word for it. He called it *Tropicália*.

Musicians in Salvador seized on Oiticica's technicolored truth telling. As the 1960s drew to a close and the grip of the military regime tightened, they made sounds that celebrated the multifarious dances and dangers of daily life in South America's mega cities. Stuff breaks in *Tropicália*. Bombs go off. Musical styles crash, clatter and explode. Surreal wordplay encodes forbidden political commentary. Sweet-sounding vocals and swooning strings erupt into parodic marching bands, and out of the wreckage grows a music of venomous and irreverent energy. The singer Tom Zé called the *Tropicália* movement a 'tornado' that uprooted the 'fertilisers, nutrients and compost' of the country's subsoil.

If one album stands as a manifesto for this feracious countercultural cyclone it is *Tropicália: ou Panis et Circencis* (1968), Brazil's answer to *Sgt. Pepper's Lonely Hearts Club Band*. The record is a riot. Its line-up brings together *Tropicália* luminaries Caetano Veloso, Gilberto Gil, Gal Costa, Tom Zé and a troupe of dissident rockers called Os Mutantes. The opening track begins with a faux church chorale and proceeds with a tuneful impudence that is so flagrant and seductive it would clearly never be allowed to last. And indeed that chorale did turn out to be a pre-emptive funeral dirge for a movement that had only just burst into life. *Tropicália* was so rambunctiously anarchic, so rebelliously and jarringly joyous, that it enraged commentators on all sides of the political spectrum.

Left-wingers who wished to build their new Brazil in the image of some invented folk nationalism attacked the *Tropicálistas* for being too frivolous, too in bed with global pop culture, too cavalier with 'authentic' Brazilian sounds. 'I have nothing to do with this purity,' declared Gilberto Gil, refusing an award in 1972. He was damned, he said, if anyone was going to make him 'a "good negro samba singer", as they want all blacks to be who really know their place'. Anyway, as Revueltas in Mexico had sensed four decades earlier, what was 'authenticity' if not the multi-strata experience he lived every day? On the other side of the political spectrum, the authorities would not tolerate such exuberantly volatile creativity. They clamped down and arrested many of the *Tropicálistas*. Gil and Veloso both spent time in solitary confinement where their glamorous hair was shaved to the scalp. At the end of the 1960s, they were sent across the ocean to England, where it was hoped their pizzazz would wash out in the drizzle. It did not.

In 1972, Veloso, not long back in Brazil after political imprisonment and exile, released a sensationally off-kilter pop album called *Araçá Azul*. His mood was audacious. His range of influences was voracious. *Araçá Azul* includes a song called 'Épico' (Epic) which swings from action-movie pastiche (timpani, squealing trumpets) to sultry flute and traffic jams. Over a chorus of car horns and exhaust fumes, Veloso incants a protest against pollution. Then in the second verse he rhymes the word 'musak' – for this is a commentary on mass consumer culture, too – with one repeated name. It goes like this:

Smetak, Smetak, e Musak e Smetak
E Musak e Smetak, e Musak e razão

Yes, it's Walter Smetak, gruff underground innovator and unlikely occult godfather of *Tropicália*. These anarchic pop artists seized his all-embracing creative mantra and aligned with his uncurbed sonic bricolage. They made a raucous roots music for a culture whose roots are unruly, just as Smetak, too, made instruments that did justice to the explosively vibrant pluralism of his adopted home. Given the industrious noises that emerged from his subterranean laboratory, Veloso and Gil gave Smetak an affectionate nickname: they called him Tak-Tak. Gil even wrote Tak-Tak into the lyrics of his song 'Língua do Pê', which he sung in staccato offbeats with the hypnotic-voiced Gal Costa in 1970:

Smetak tak tak tak (tak tak tak tak tak)

Such were the sonic collisions of Salvador.

• • •

One morning in the early 1970s, Smetak hung up a freshly varnished guitar to dry on a washing line. The wind blew through the strings like an Aeolian harp and Smetak was so thrilled by the resonance that he fetched a microphone and recorded the interior of the instrument for twenty minutes. He felt the sound had as profound an impact as hearing the word 'om' in meditation. He became aware of frequencies that seemed alive in the smallest of intervals – an awakening that Éliane Radigue experienced around the same time through her synthesiser experiments – and at that moment he decided that microtones were the future. Sound within sound. He wrote a poem called *Microtonização* (Microtonisation) which begins with the instructive line 'microtonise yourself, never to be exalted again with the Pythagorean harmonies' and proceeds with the rhythmic insistence of a New Age preacher intoning a sort of call to arms for self-actualisation. When Smetak was introduced to the work of Julián Carrillo, he felt galvanised by the Mexican composer's thirteenth sound theories which envisioned a fresh future beyond the diatonic scale. 'We can squeeze almost nothing more out of our old musical system,' Smetak wrote enthusiastically. 'Over the next century, we're going to need other scales.'

In 1977, Smetak released his first self-titled album, produced by Gilberto Gil and Caetano Veloso. Smetak plays his own instrument, the *Vina*, in his composition *Mantram* (Mantra). Even though he had worked for nine months to finesse the beast, the *Vina* still sounds raw and rickety, a newborn animal finding its feet. The tone gradually strengthens over the course of the recording. Then comes an astonishing contrapuntal passage, Smetak telescoping time as he borrows a line from J. S. Bach. It is a fleeting disjunct, this calabash baroque, and the piece soon spirals back to tentative natural overtones.

For his second and last album, *Interregno*, Smetak put together a group of musicians under the name *Conjutu de Microtons* (Group of Microtones). This Smetakian orchestra plays on various of his *plasticás sonoras*, a Yamaha organ and six microtonally tuned guitars. Each guitar is strung with six identical strings, all tuned within the narrow

range of a semitone. The range of each instrument corresponds to
the notes of a regular guitar (E, A, D, G, B, E) – in other words, Smetak takes standard guitar tuning, spaces it out across six instruments
and divides each note by six. The result is an astral smirr, a pointil-
listic smudge, a crowded and inky night sky like a microtonal Milky
Way, all of it emerging as though from one meta instrument.

The loose weave of *Interregno* is the product of collective improvisation – for Smetak, 'a free form of composition'. The difference
between composition and improvisation, he wrote in his essay *Arte
Transcendental da Improvisação* (The Transcendental Art of Improvisation), is only 'that there is no author. There are many authors
whose minds have to work simultaneously.' Improvisation, the art
of the city.

Here is another of Smetak's instructions on improvisation:

Aqueles que sabem cantar, cantem. Aqueles outros que não
cantam se preocupem com funções rítmicas. Ou toquem
instrumentos escolhidos por eles. Os que não servem para uma
coisa nem outra, dancem.
(Those who know how to sing, sing. Those who don't sing,
take care of the rhythmic. Or play instruments of their choice.
Those who are not fit for one thing or the other, dance.)

• • •

In the early 1980s, Smetak was invited to Berlin for a residency. He
wanted to take some of his instruments with him but they weren't
built to travel, so when he got to Germany he constructed seven
cube-like single-string sound-generators and adorned them with
planetary symbology. At the end of his stay in Germany he wrote a
letter filled with weariness and renewed purpose. This was not the

Smetak of the spiritual bravado or the cello-spike attacks. This was a man who was not yet ill but somehow sensed he was nearing the end.

I have to go back home. I have to work. Here in Berlin I have nothing left to do. But now I'm not interested in building more instruments. I have no room left; where should I put them? Besides, the instruments I already have are constantly breaking from the heat – or the woodworm eats them, or the strings rust due to moisture. I'll never be finished with all the repair work anyway – as soon as the last one is repaired, the first one is broken again. In addition, the instruments now have to be stored in a barrack, far away from the school. I'll find out soon how they endured these two months; let's hope for the best. But nature is so powerful we can never overcome it, not a chance.

I'm planning on moving to Minos next year. If I'm not able to store the instruments somewhere, maybe I'd like to take them with me and set up a school there. But I don't know. It's about three thousand kilometres to Minos – with a truck! The instruments will suffer. The calabashes can't tolerate any jolts. And I don't have any more strength to start over.

If nothing comes up, I thought I would stack the instruments into a big pile, pour gasoline over them and light them. A Chinese sage once said to his student, 'If you can play your instrument well, if you really master all the playing techniques, you can throw the instrument away.'

Smetak died on 30 May 1984 of pulmonary emphysema, having smoked that pipe to his destruction. He was seventy-one years old. He drove himself to the hospital on his motorbike, believing that after death he would travel as far as the centre of the earth before reincarnating in Brazil just over two decades later.

'He liked to shock,' said the composer Ernst Widmer. He liked to 'catapult the listener from inertia to new reflections'. Subsequent generations at the University of Bahia have noted how his presence is still palpable in the institution, how, even decades after his death, he is still reverently referred to with nicknames like 'the old wizard' and 'alchemist of sound'. The composer and musicologist Marco Scarassatti rather wonderfully refers to Smetak's work as *multimídia desplugada* (unplugged multimedia), a term that makes me realise how much his pursuit of interdisciplinary acoustic bricolage reappears in the work of subsequent generations of sound sculptors, from Joaquín Orellana to Ellen Fullman to Sarah Kenchington, and indeed to Annea Lockwood. In some ways, Smetak was right about the reincarnation.

Not unlike Hélio Oiticica and his *Parangolés*, Smetak wanted his *plásticas sonoras* to summon a new harmony between shape, space, spirit and humanity. He dreamed of travelling beyond notions of consonance and dissonance, beyond sight and hearing and past and present to arrive at a state he called *caossonance*, where light becomes sound and a grand union of the senses is achieved. Scarassatti writes about 'a predominance of rewiring' in Smetak's approach, whose rhetoric and logic 'are not constituted through the development of Western music and thought'. Instead, Smetak deconstructs, dismantles and reconstructs the context of everyday Brazilian materials. Nan Shepherd's unmaking and steadying.

Of the 176 instruments he built, around forty remain today, and of those some are broken, disintegrating or have simply gone missing. There are other agonising absences: what would I not give to hear the theatre music he wrote for a 1970 production of *Macbeth*, for which he recorded instruments underwater. But maybe that unheard sound is the point. Maybe Smetak's greatest invention was the one he never made. The *Estudio Ovo* (Egg Studio) is where his concepts of space, place and bodies, microphones, microtones and spiritual ley lines all came together. Smetak dreamed of making a twenty-two-metre oval pavilion out of fibreglass, inside which he would install hundreds of microtonally tuned resonating strings. The bottom of the structure, the widest part of the egg, would be buried in the ground, and the floor would move on a hydraulic platform with propellers swishing about the water beneath and hydrophones capturing the sound of the currents. Tubes would pipe in sounds from the outside world and propeller fans would be positioned around the space to play with the overtones. *Ovo* was to be a temple and a research centre, a recording studio and full-body immersive instrument from which sound would not escape. To enter would be like stepping inside an organ, or a womb, to be completely enveloped by the thrum.

He sketched his *Estudio Ovo* in detail, specifying everything from proportions and materials to what kind of ground it should be built on (a spiral surrounded by a square atop a green grassy hill). There was more: Smetak wanted to create a new university curriculum designed as a solar system. Students would grow their own food and take classes in subjects ranging from mathematics, nuclear physics and alternative agriculture to ceramics, instrument-making, litera-ture, Eubiose, cinema and sculpture. The teaching would happen inside various planetary structures, of which the *Ovo* studio would be a centre for acoustic and electronic research.

The University of Brasilia did actually pursue the idea of get-ting *Ovo* constructed. After all, the entire city of Brasilia had been designed and built from scratch in four years; what was one extra egg-shaped studio? But neither *Ovo* nor its holistic curriculum would come to be. Maybe Smetak was just not enough of a political operator. Maybe out of diffidence, he wrote that, in any case, it was not necessary 'to build every idea you have in your head or to really hear all the sounds'. It was not necessary, he claimed, to construct everything just to prove it exists.

In the unheard spaces of *Ovo*, which Smetak called his *instrumento total*, the impossibilities remain possible. 'It's all over,' he wrote. 'The rest is siiiiilence.' It is his ultimate soundless sculpture, a member of that most esoteric family of *plásticas sonoras* that propose noise without ever actually making it. These mute instruments are Smetak's greatest anarchic act of all but they're also his most generous, inviting us to ponder the potential of transcending form altogether and deciding for ourselves. Audience becomes composer – a transfer of agency which Annea Lockwood grants through her most intimate calls to attentiveness.

Meanwhile, at the opposite end of the scale, a composer in the Philippines was testing out a similar transfer of agency via extremes of mass participation. While Smetak distilled the collective spirit of a city, José Maceda harnessed the physical involvement of an entire global metropolis.

José Maceda

(1917–2004)

**Filipino drone time:
orchestrating city and century**

In the 1960s, the Filipino composer José Maceda dreamed of a futuristic multi-spatial spectacular involving thousands of cars playing recordings of indigenous Asian instruments. The cars would blast out these recordings through loudspeakers while cruising the multi-level freeways of, for example, Los Angeles. Maceda wanted drivers and passengers to take on the role of performers in a 'maze of sounds, where musical function becomes a recreation'. In his vision, man becomes 'part of the machine, but he is not its slave, for he can turn it off anytime'. He went as far as applying for funding to stage this ballet for automobiles. He even submitted a proposal to the Ford Motor Company to fit out their cars with loudspeakers and interconnected radios but was, alas, turned down.

Next, Maceda dreamed of an even bigger work, a work scored for twenty radio stations and literally millions of performers. Each of those twenty radio stations would play a separate part of the score. Broadcast simultaneously, the amassed sounds would envelop an entire global city. For the duration of the performance there would be nothing but song and rhythm filling the streets. The aftermath would be a new kind of collective harmony. The experience would be as sociologically transformative as it was musically audacious.

This time Maceda was not turned down. The dream in question was *Ugnayan*, and on 1 January 1974, between 6 and 7 p.m., every one of the thirty-seven radio stations in the Filipino capital Manila was involved in the simultaneous broadcast of Maceda's magnum opus. Lasting nearly an hour, covering a geographic range of one hundred kilometres, this was an avant-garde musical happening of unprecedented magnitude. Anyone within radio signal of Manila, population 4.7 million at the time, could tune in – and indeed was strongly compelled by the authorities to do so.

There's more. The sounds being broadcast by those thirty-seven radio stations came from twenty pre-recorded tape parts (some stations doubled up), and each recording involved five musicians playing traditional Filipino instruments. So there were one hundred individual parts in all. The audience did not simply switch on and listen; they actively created the work by doing so. Meeting points were designated in parks, community centres and multiple other public spaces around the metropolitan area, citizens instructed to bring along their portable transistor radios and then roam freely. The piece was effectively being performed by its listeners – it was their movements, their unchoreographed meandering that determined the final mix. As crowds gathered, lingered and dispersed, the output of their individual radios overlapped to form vast clouds of sound. And because nobody would hear exactly the same combination of stations, depending on which other radios were within earshot, the music was uniquely balanced for every person's position within the throng. Nobody would experience it in quite the same way. And *that* meant that despite its unfathomable enormousness, *Ugnayan* was a bespoke experience for every one of the millions of listeners who heard it that day.

There is an awesome dauntlessness about this ritual of metropole-encompassing scale. The concept is just so bold, so neat, so exhilaratingly complete! No other radio programme was available during the allotted performance time, so if you were within signal of Metro Manila on that New Year's Day, for that hour between 6 and 7 p.m., and if you switched on a radio, you had to be part of the piece whether you wanted to be or not. Maceda's avant-garde music was hijacking the airwaves of an entire global megalopolis.

It should be noted that there was a not-insignificant authoritarian backdrop to the staging of *Ugnayan*. In practical terms, Maceda could not have done it without the kleptocratic Marcos regime on his side. The work was personally supported by the First Lady of the Philippines, Imelda Marcos, as one of her grand nation-building cultural projects. Radio stations were essentially ordered to take part, and citizens had little choice in their state-imposed provision of mass entertainment. As an independent nation, the Philippines was not yet three decades young, and its last colonisers (the United States) still wielded major cultural influence. The regime seized on the premiere of *Ugnayan* as a highly symbolic moment, with its celebration of pre-Western traditional Filipino instruments and its amassed coming together of citizens to make music in the model of collective human labour.

And so the mild-mannered, diligent Maceda found himself inadvertently, or naively, the instigator of not only a groundbreaking sonic experiment but also a bloated patriotic spectacle of gargantuan scale. Later, he regretted how his work had (he felt) been co-opted, though he did acknowledge there was no other way of making the piece actually happen. And he did share some of the regime's broadest ideals – particularly around the value and potential of collective endeavour. But he was not interested in being part of any modern ethnic nationalism.

This gentle, deep-thinking ethnomusicologist was mainly driven by a passion for indigenous musics that pre-date European influence and don't comply with the contemporary borders etched across Asia. In the Philippines alone there are 7,641 islands. Ethnically, linguistically, geographically, politically, musically, the archipelago is varied, intermingled and very complicated. Maceda spent half a century investigating the traditions of those islands and elsewhere, making music that is rooted in specific cultures but that transcends specific nationalism. I find it intriguing to note that while Julián Carrillo felt his ticket to internationalism was to distance himself from any traditional culture, Maceda believed precisely the opposite. For him, the act of preserving multiple indigenous practices was an act of resistance against cultural hegemony. When he was in his seventies, he explained that he didn't want to be identified as anything. 'As coming from anywhere,' he said. 'Not Nigeria or Madagascar or Kalinga, or the Moon.'

Maceda loved to blur lines across borders, between audience and performers, to make everyone feel part of a traditional communal gathering. At the heart of it all is the idea of the *malleable drone*. The shifting constant. Maceda wanted to create sounds of such fluid and multitudinous layering that the effect for listeners (who, remember, were often also participants) was like joining a murmuration of starlings, or a loose, immersive drumming ceremony. He was transfixed by the intricate rhythmic weave of natural formations; he loved the way multipart rhythms could flux and cross-hatch. He wanted time to ripple as it does in the rainforest, millions of musical parts coming together like the buzzing of insects or the shaking of leaves. And, by using new technologies, he wanted to preserve the pre-colonial traditions that he was hearing in the remotest parts of Asia by translocating them into the modern metropolis. He wanted village to become city – space collapsed, hut and ancient temple beamed into the parking lots of 1970s municipal edifices in downtown Manila. He wanted past to become present. Out of the old, out of the organic, he wanted to make a new music fit for all Asia.

. . .

There are no written records of specifically Filipino music from the time before Ferdinand Magellan arrived in 1521. The Portuguese explorer landed on the island of Cebu having found his coveted passage east through South America, if somewhat underestimating the girth of the globe. Fragmented accounts of Filipino culture then start appearing via travelling monks and merchants. There are reports from the mid-1500s of songs of passage and ritual: children's rhymes, heroic ballads, songs for birth and death, songs for work to the rhythms of fishing, harvesting and planting. There are reports of instruments made of bronze or bamboo. When the Spanish colonised the archipelago in 1565, they implanted their church music and concert culture, which Filipino musicians evolved in their own way. New local styles grew out of old – distinct takes on marching bands and *rondalla* ensembles. And there are the heart-sore love ballads, the *kundiman*, sung in Tagalog, the official national language of the Philippines.

Three hundred and thirty-three years of Spanish rule ended less than two decades before José Maceda was born. Many Filipinos sided against their imperialists in the Spanish-American War of 1898 because the Americans seemed to promise liberation. Things did not exactly pan out that way. After two months of nervy independence, US forces took charge of the archipelago on the eve of the new century and Filipino resistance raged on against one coloniser to the next. In 1916, the American president Woodrow Wilson promised there would be independence, but it took until 1935 even for a date to be set. During the Second World War, the Japanese occupied the Philippines for three blood-soaked, food-deprived years, at the end of which many Filipinos welcomed the Americans back once again as liberators. The USA at last granted independence to the Philippines in 1946, after nearly half a century of promise. It was the same year that José Maceda, not quite thirty, moved to the United States. And it was in the United States that Maceda would tune his ear back towards home and start to really hear his own culture.

. . .

José Montserrat Maceda was born on 31 January 1917. His family came from the town of Pila, south-east of Manila on the shores of the shamrock-shaped Laguna Lake. His maternal grandfather, Pablo Montserrat, was an organist and band master. His mother, Concepción Montserrat y Salamanca, was a pianist. His father, Castro Maceda y Norona, was a judge. José was the oldest of four brothers: Adelfo became a lawyer, Emilio a businessman, Hernando a Jesuit priest. That little José would be a musician seemed destined from the start. By seven, he was entertaining his family at the piano, trotting out tunes from Ponchielli's opera *La Gioconda*.

To give him the best chance at a musical education, young Maceda was sent to Manila where he was cared for by an aunt named Aguida. He returned to Pila only for holidays – fiestas such as the Maytime pageants *Flores de Mayo*, or *Pabasa* (when epic poems are chanted in unison for Holy Week), or *Simbang Gabi* (a series of night masses leading up to Christmas). José absorbed these ritualised, intensely mystery-laden ceremonies of Filipino Catholicism, but no actual traditional music featured in his upbringing. The realities of life in a rural village were about as far removed from this boy's experience as they would have been for any middle-class city kid growing up in Madrid, Tokyo or New York.

He was clearly gifted as a pianist. He excelled in his studies at Manila's Academy of Music, and after his graduation it was decided that he should go to Vienna to study with Emil von Sauer, who had been a pupil of the nineteenth-century Hungarian virtuoso Franz

Liszt. Funds were gathered from the *Asociacion Musical de Filipinas* – but when a touring French pianist called Youra Guller came to Manila and heard Maceda's touch at the keyboard, she picked up on something fine-grained and searching. She felt he was geared toward subtle gradation and fluctuation. Try Paris, she suggested. And that's why twenty-year-old Maceda found himself in the French capital in 1937, enrolling at the École Normale de Musique.

Maceda's Paris years were formative and tough. He studied with the resplendently named Madame Bascourret de Gueraldi and with the eminent pianist Alfred Cortot, who was a grand-pupil of Chopin. He practised diligently, devoting himself to upholding Cortot's pedigree, but he was also inquisitive enough to talk his way into classes with the fearsome pedagogue Nadia Boulanger.

(While we're on the subject of pedigree: Boulanger was respon-
sible for educating an eminent swathe of twentieth-century
musical minds, among them Aaron Copland, Ruth Anderson,
Elliott Carter, Grażyna Bacewicz, Quincy Jones, Astor Piazzolla,
Beatriz Ferreyra, Burt Bacharach, Per Nørgård, Thea Musgrave
– the complete list is staggering.) When he wasn't at the piano
or eavesdropping on Boulanger's classes, Maceda would wander
the streets, drinking in the Parisian language and culture until it
was part of him and he of it, or so he hoped. Five decades later, he
could still remember how fellow students made him feel the outsider. There was one particular question he was frequently asked
by dorm-mates in his boarding house: 'José, why are you studying
the piano?' Only later did it dawn on him that what the question
really meant was: *José, why are you studying an instrument that is not
part of your culture?*

Four years at the École honed a flawless pianistic technique, and
on graduating, Maceda was awarded a *Diplôme de Virtuosité* with
distinction. In 1941, a year into Germany's occupation of France,
he set out for home, travelling across wartime Europe, through
the Panama Canal then onwards through the USA where he was
dangerously misidentified as Japanese as he crossed the continent.
When he eventually arrived back in the Philippines, he gave a homecoming recital at the Metropolitan Theatre in Manila. He played
Chopin, Debussy, Ravel, Albéniz, Liszt, Busoni – and Beethoven's
Appassionata Sonata, which became a fixture of his repertoire for
the next decade. On the surface it was perhaps a surprising choice
for Maceda, devotee of French pianism. But the *Appassionata* also
makes sense. Beethoven began working on the sonata in 1804, a
time later labelled as part of his 'middle period' when his music
raged with ungovernable thunder. He was becoming deaf and his
response was to reach inward and express the torment. He also had

a new piano to test to its limits, an Érard with a (then) extended range of five and a half octaves. If he was going to articulate the emotional extremes that he felt, Beethoven needed the full extent of the instrument, its full sonic shock and wonder. He needed to place his listeners at the eye of the storm. Of course Maceda loved it: that immersion, that abandon to the whim of forces more organic and enveloping than reason alone.

· · ·

The United States granted sovereignty to the Philippines on 4 July 1946. Designating the date of its own independence day was a final twist of, what, subjugation? Eleventh-hour bridling? Filipinos would later cut that particular chain and shift their national cele-brations to 12 June, marking the end of Spanish rule in 1898.

Maceda's personal American sojourn was just beginning. When the Second World War was over, he moved to California, intent on picking up his instrumental studies with a pianist called E. Robert Schmitz, whose lineage led straight back to Claude Debussy. Virgil Thomson thought of Schmitz as a musician's musician, the sort of pianist whom other pianists tended to admire; Maceda would later remember how elegantly his teacher could shape a phrase in a Mozart sonata, which was never about the first beat of the bar but about the line that unfurled thereafter. Although his future did not involve him performing much Mozart, Maceda did retain that way of drifting across barlines, of floating through downbeats and spin-ning webs of sound outwith the bounds of regulated time.

It was around this time that his attention began to shift from the keyboard. 'There were more and more pianists' is how he later put it – and during his first few years in America he started to feel that jostling for space on the carousel of touring recitalists might not be the best use of him. Moreover, he found himself increasingly drawn to the work of composers who were testing out alternatives. He was interested in Pierre Schaeffer's experiments in repurposing everyday noises into *musique concrète* (he would later spend some time at Schaeffer's studio in Paris). He was beguiled by the Greek architect-composer Iannis Xenakis and his ventures into sonic acoustics. Above all, he was drawn to the rebellious French composer Edgard Varèse, who had disrupted the orchestra, flung open the doors of the concert hall and let in the noises of the world. Meanwhile, Maceda found himself preoccupied by a fundamental concern. Schmitz, Mozart, Schaeffer, Varèse, orchestras, concert halls – 'What', Maceda pondered, 'has all this got to do with coconuts and rice?'

What he meant was not that Asian artistic horizons should be limited to what grows in Asian soil. He meant: how can classical music, its ideologies seeded in Europe, articulate the lived experience of human beings around the world? For Maceda, the answer would come from figuring out how the tools of modern classical music might be used to honour and repurpose the traditions of his own culture. He took up anthropology. He enrolled in newly launched ethnomusicology courses in Chicago, New York and Los Angeles, for the first time scrutinising his own roots as a source of musical richness. When he went home to a faculty post at the University of the Philippines, he poured his energies into researching the music that came *before*. Music that had survived three centuries of Spanish colonisation and fifty years (and counting) of American cultural swagger. Sounds were fast disappearing, local traditions dying out across the archipelago. Flanked by teams of researchers, Maceda set out to record as much as he physically could.

In the 1950s, he field-tripped voraciously. 'Portability meant a 10-kilo Uher [a reel-to-reel recording device] and a 10-kilo Remington typewriter,' notes the Maceda scholar and curator

Dayang Yraola. 'He literally crossed mountains and rivers while burdened by gigantic tape recorders to gather ethnic music traditions.' Maceda travelled across the country, across all South-East Asia and beyond, recording flutes, mouth harps, manifold bamboo instruments, dancers, gongs, songs. He crossed Thailand, Malaysia, Burma, India, Indonesia, Japan and China. Ghana, Uganda, Nigeria. Fuelled by a research grant from the Rockefeller Center, he spent a year (1968) studying the music of *Candomblé* ceremonies in Brazil's Bahia province – he was a visiting professor in Salvador where Walter Smetak was busy concocting instruments that could summon the energy of the streets and the stars. The two crossed paths on a daily basis, and when Maceda returned to the Philippines he left behind a significant influence on a generation of composers in Salvador, and a set of gongs that remain at the university to this day.

Maceda would later pinpoint a moment of epiphany in 1952 when, listening to a particularly soulful *kinaban* (mouth harp) player on the Filipino island of Mindoro, he palpably experienced his own centre of musical gravity shifting – as he described it, from West to East. He gave his last official public piano recital in February 1957. The programme included much of the music that had shaped his early musical self: Mozart and Prokofiev alongside his French pianistic heartland of Chopin, Debussy, Ravel. After that, he sat at the piano only for his own pleasure. According to Dr LaVerne C. de la Peña, Dean of the College of Music at the University of the Philippines and Director of the UP Center for Ethnomusicology, 'You'd go past his house, and you would often hear that someone was playing jazz.'

There was also another member of the Maceda household who played the piano. Back in San Francisco in the late 1940s, Maceda had met and fallen in love with a talented and adventurous

French-Canadian pianist called Madelyn Clifford. They married in 1954. Their wedding photograph shows Clifford with a bridal bouquet, hair swept off her forehead by a simple band. Maceda wears a white suit and white tie, signature round glasses, hands clasped neatly on his lap. His mother sits birdlike to his left in a shiny gown. His three brothers stand behind him, all in white. His father proudly flanks Clifford on her right. Clifford gave up her own burgeoning career as a concert pianist to support Maceda's work. They married a year after Ruth Crawford died, but the world had moved on little from the 'career vs love and children battle' that Crawford had faced two decades earlier. The Macedas spent their honeymoon in the southern Maguindanao province of the Philippines, collecting field recordings and musical instruments for José's research.

Instead of playing concerts, Clifford raised four daughters (Marion, Madeleine, Kate and Eileen) and became piano teacher to the faculty children who grew up on campus at the University of the Philippines. And for all the social openness and egalitarianism of his musical structures, Maceda never let go of his domestic conventions. 'He was in a way . . . let's say he was not the father who was closely involved with the kids,' de la Peña tells me, stressing this was typical of Filipino fathers of that generation. 'He was focused on his work. Instead of hanging out with his kids in the living room, straight after dinner he would go to his study.' Dayang Yraola remembers that Maceda 'found no reason why kids had to be noisy'. She herself was one of those kids: her mother worked with Maceda for decades, so she grew up spending time around the composer's household. The professor was 'always clueless about which knick-knacks made the best gifts for which grandchild', Yraola laughs, pondering aloud how a man of 'such creative brilliance' could be so puzzled by something so simple.

In the end, Clifford's mind eroded into Alzheimer's. During her final years she would sit at the piano every day and try to play a piece from memory. If she forgot a passage, Maceda would gently speak the notes until she got back on track.

· · ·

Maceda's first publication as an ethnomusicologist was the laboriously titled *Music of the Bukids of Mindoro; Hanunoo Music of the Philippines; Music – where East and West Meet*. The Filipino musicologist Ramón Pagayon Santos notes that the points of reference in Maceda's early academic writings were largely Western (Gregorian chant, parlando style, tonal centres, tonic and dominant triadic harmony) but that those references soon shifted.

By the 1960s, Maceda had parity on the brain. He started recruiting folk musicians into the music department at the University of the Philippines, actively seeking out players who might work day jobs as janitors or security men but whose grasp of traditional techniques was second to none. In 1961, he travelled to the East–West Music Encounter in Tokyo, where he watched uncomfortably as the conference organisers showcased music by Luciano Berio, Bruno Maderna, Luigi Nono – major heavyweights of European new music – without also platforming any compelling Asian counterparts. He felt increasingly clear about where his own loyalties lay. He recognised that he had been 'moulded' by the Philippines and Asiatic culture and 'influenced' by Europe and America – and that he was no longer interested in trying to emulate the latter.

Was it coincidental that Maceda wrote his first composition proper from afar? Distance seemed to spur him on and send him searching inwards. *Ugma-Ugma* was performed in Los Angeles as part of a UCLA Monday night concert series in 1963. The name means 'Structures'. The line-up includes *shō* (Japanese mouth organ), *kubing* (Filipino mouth harp), *gambang* (xylophone) and *gendèr* (Indonesian metallophone), plus various gongs, rattles, bells, buzzers, clappers and scrapers, as well as the horn of a water buffalo and mixed chorus. In the score, the instruments are grouped according to the general sounds they make: Maceda wanted high falsetto noises to create 'an intense situation' against a background of 'sharp and slow' decay, with extremes of 'almost inaudible twangs and heavily cluttered noises' working in opposition. Listeners in Los Angeles were largely nonplussed by the results, a reaction that Maceda later shrugged off. 'Let's face it,' he told the composer Chris Brown in 1992, when Brown showed up at his house in Manila and switched on a recording device to capture a long afternoon of conversation. 'LA was conservative,' Maceda stated. 'One critic dismissed the piece in a couple of words. He just didn't get it.'

But the shock factor of his music would need to be overcome at home, too. Most urban Filipinos knew next to nothing about their own traditional music. Maceda's plan was to start a two-way exchange. On the one hand, he wanted to introduce city folk to the spirit of village ritual, and on the other hand he wanted to grant villagers a place in modern Filipino identity. Above all, he was in pursuit of a contemporary musical ethos and broader philosophical context that didn't take all its cues from a Western world view. 'Where new musical horizons are being sought,' he wrote, 'it is this incursion into the past that may lead to a discovery of other thoughts and perceptions. In other words, to another humanism that cannot be extracted alone from technique and technology.'

In 1968, Maceda wrote a mass called *Pagsamba* (Worship). A hundred voices chant high and chant low. A hundred instruments provide a backdrop, a mesh of whistle flutes, clappers, buzzers, scrapers and sticks. Sixteen low gongs shroud the sound in mellow resonance. The text is a Tagalog translation of the Catholic liturgy, but Maceda often stretches the vowels until they become abstract sound. Sombre and elated, the voices incant, sigh, murmur and ululate. They roll in like tidal surges. Maceda specified that any performance of *Pagsamba* must happen in a round space – it was written for the UP Chapel, a broad, circular structure – so in a sense he folded the architecture into the score. He instructed that performers should be interspersed among the audience. Everyone should face towards the centre of the circle. As with *Ugnayan*, there are no bystanders here, not even the building.

Maceda had been raised a Catholic and remained so all his life. *Pagsamba* is deeply sacred music, but it also taps a non--denominational spirituality that is about prayer, trance, almost animism in regards to respecting the powerful forces of nature. Ethnic tensions were afoot in the Philippines while he was writing. The year 1968 saw the Jabidah Massacre, when Muslim Moro soldiers were murdered by members of the Filipino armed forces, kickstarting the Muslim Independence Movement and the subsequent Moro National Liberation Front. Imelda Marcos would later travel to Tripoli to beseech the Libyan leader Muammar Gaddafi to stop funding the MNLF via Malaysia. The countries signed a shaky peace agreement that established autonomy in secessionist southern regions of the Philippines. All the while, Maceda continued his pan-Asian field trips, resolutely ignoring contemporary ethnic, religious, linguistic and political boundaries that he felt had little relevance to the ancient cross-border musical traditions he was recording. He found that the *kulitang* gong players in Muslim Mindanao were especially skilled, so he recorded them assiduously. 'We don't really have such a thing as "Muslim" music,' de la Peña tells me. 'It's just music that happens to be played by people who are Muslim. The music was there before.'

. . .

Maceda thought a lot about time. He once noted, on a flight from New Zealand to the Philippines, that the particular recording of a Chopin Berceuse being played through the tannoy 'was so stiff that I wanted to jump out of the plane!' He knew what he didn't want musical time to be: stiff, like that Chopin on the plane. And he had an inkling of what a more flexible approach to time might open up.

In a 1975 paper for the Third Asian Composers' League Conference and Festival in Manila, he laid out his proposal for a reimagined sense of Asian musical time. This would not be measured by the clock, he explained, nor by barlines or time signatures, but through natural events such as the migration of birds and the flowering of plants. Accordingly, his own music plays tricks on regulated time. It moves at a pace that refuses to be either steady or erratic – somehow it is both and more, an eddying equilibrium, a fluidity that gives the impression of being totally loose and organic. I say 'impression', because in fact his seemingly elemental flux is meticulously constructed.

Maceda thought a lot about drones. By 'drone' he did not mean a monotonous repeated note or single long sound. His drones are more coruscating than static, made of hundreds or thousands of enmeshed individual parts, and the overall effect is a shifting continuum. Imagine a shoal of fish. That's the iridescent constant he was getting at.

Maceda thought a lot about opposites, and how they seemed to him to be a Western obsession. In an essay called *A Concept of Time in a Music of Southeast Asia*, he references Jacques Derrida on the subject:

Good vs. evil, being vs. nothingness, presence vs. absence, truth vs. error, identity vs. difference, mind vs. matter, man vs. woman, soul vs. body, life vs. death, nature vs. culture, and equal entities. The second term in each pair is considered a negative, corrupt, undesirable version of the first. In other words, the two terms are not simply opposed in their meanings, but are arranged in hierarchical order which gives the first term *priority*.

Add to that list: tonic versus dominant, the linchpin relationship around which tonal harmony pivots. (Take the key of C major: C is tonic, G is dominant.) Maceda believed that Western tonal music is dominated by an obsession with closure – and that although such an obsession might give comfort and seem to solve problems simply, he considered it a 'narrow view' that 'may lose its contact with other perspectives, especially a concept of the larger space, infinity, a metaphysical construct of the universe'. He lamented that 'there is less room for qualities like patience, sorrow, doubt and humility, and other spiritual attributes which are spurned by the righteousness of logic and precision'. Maceda, like Nan Shepherd, sought to be *unmade*.

He knew full well about the many movements that were concurrently trying to break down the post-Aristotelian dualism that had been at the heart of Western classical music for centuries. Movements including atonalism, total serialism, *musique concrète*, aleatoricism, modal jazz, free improv, minimalism and more. But his particular way of prising open the tonic/dominant supremacy was to build an alternative based on Asian foundations. He favoured the egalitarianism of the five-note pentatonic scale (imagine playing only the black notes on a piano), which he felt gave every note equal importance. He was also increasingly interested in mass participation as a way of dodging hierarchy in performance. He began writing works in which every voice and limb contributed to the whole.

In 1971, Maceda made a piece for a hundred cassette tapes. A hundred performers with a hundred portable tape players infiltrated the lobby of the Cultural Center of the Philippines. He called the piece *Cassettes 100*, and the tapes played recordings of indigenous instruments and natural sounds, together making a happy heap of field material and *musique concrète*. 'The recordings are my dictionary,' he explained. 'They are a receptacle of ideas from which I can pull at any time.' As the participants moved their bodies in slow choreographed gestures, brandishing tape players in their outstretched arms, the sounds swirled accordingly. *Cassettes 100* was the first time Maceda brought the village to the heart of the city, and the first time he braved a large-scale performance happening. Three years later, he would repeat the act in *Ugnayan*, this time involving millions.

· · ·

Ugnayan begins with forty *kolitongs* (zithers), all playing tiny melodies, all tuned slightly apart. Beaters patter off strings like rain on a tin roof, insects flitting against lightbulbs. There is no measurable pulse, no regular beat. Then in come the hectic *balingbings* (rasping bamboo buzzers) and the low, docile *bungbungs* (bamboo flutes that sound like slow-moving herbivores). The rain gets heavier then eases off; *bangibangs* (yoked-shaped wooden bars that are struck with beaters) join the party, all at their own pace. The *bungbungs* layer up; the *kolitongs* whip themselves into a frenzy then fix on single pitches. A new voice arrives: the *ongiyong* whistles, short, sharp, shrill. An exquisite dance ensues, circling between buzzers, gongs and Chinese

HIGH PITCHED ZITHERS
ONE ZITHER EACH LINE
TWO STRINGS EACH LINE
TWO STICKS
♩= MM 60
TWO STRINGS

cymbals. And then – thirty-seven minutes into this amassed percussive ritual – human voices! Emerging from all directions, intoning a single syllable: *YAA!* All on the same pitch at first, then they move ever so slightly apart, and there is a narcotic sensation of being *in the thick* of this incantation, that the music is swirlingly multidimensional. The vocalists murmur then open their mouths, dazed, ecstatic, elastic. Cymbals crash, gongs gong, *kolitongs* flicker then fade into breath. The *ongiyong* whistle flutes have the last word, and then it's all over, cloudburst cleared as suddenly as it began.

. . .

The early decades of independence had been a bumpy ride for the Philippines. On the back of rising crime and regional unrest, a botched assassination attempt on a key government figure (possibly staged by the government) and the potential of a communist uprising backed by China, President Ferdinand Marcos declared martial law on 21 September 1972. He slashed press freedoms, opposition politics and the powers of congress. Protesters were exiled or just plain murdered; poverty soared and human rights were trashed while Marcos and his wife stole billions in public money to collect gold kilobars and, infamously, a lot of shoes.

As well as designer footwear, Imelda Marcos had a taste for lavish cultural and infrastructure projects. She went in for exorbitant, staunchly brutalist architecture like the snaking San Juanico Bridge (a birthday present from Ferdinand in 1973) and the breathtakingly austere pyramid bunker of the National Arts Center. These projects and others earned her dubious notoriety for having an 'edifice complex', but it was not just buildings she indulged in. The vast scale of Maceda's *Ugnayan* was possible only thanks to the First Lady's personal support.

'They used me,' said Maceda. 'They changed the word. *Ugnayan*. It means "working together".' Initially, Maceda had a different name in mind. He originally wanted to call it *Atmospheres* – for him, the thrill of the ginormousness mainly had to do with the amassed multi-textured sounds made possible by the sheer number of participants. But he had to acknowledge that 'there was a political side to it. I agreed to it just so I could do the project. One letter from Mrs Marcos to all the radio stations and, well, I got what I wanted. At least in theory.' Promotional blurbs that appeared in newspapers and pamphlets in the lead-up to the premiere explicitly aligned Maceda's work with the regime's agenda. Here is one such advert:

As a creative ideology for unity and community . . . *Ugnayan* can operate in large or small groups . . . brought together or linked together for positive ends. It would be difficult for this nation to develop its full potentials, to experience its longed-for democratic revolution . . . in the generation of a new reform-oriented and a compassionate development-oriented society, unless its people are one in body and in spirit.

The Marcos regime aimed to foster an image of collective harmony, and to cast Manila's cultural elite as a central civilising force in its prosperous new society. 'For the regime, it was convenient to have someone like Maceda around,' says de la Peña. 'Someone who was respected internationally and who kind of paralleled their agenda.' De la Peña was still a child in 1974 but he remembers the hype and the literal noise around the event. 'Martial law – it was a bit like lockdown now,' he tells me during the coronavirus pandemic, 'but even worse. New Year's Eve in Manila is usually very loud. For the first time in 1972–3 it had been silent because of martial law. Then came 1973–4, only the second time we had

New Year's under martial law. And they staged this piece. It was packaged for us as the new way of merry-making. Like: who needs fireworks when you've got *Ugnayan!*'

How should we understand the symbolism of *Ugnayan* now? As a musical experience, it was surely designed to incite collective attentiveness, collaboration and zen. The year of the premiere, 1974, Maceda spelled out what he saw as the positive ideological overtones, writing that 'the idea that only large groups of people can put together sounds spread out over a big area is paralleled by the co-operation necessary for large numbers of people to achieve a certain purpose'. In his history of Filipino noise music, the musician Cedrik Fermont hints that, for him, Maceda's political collusion taints the spirit of *Ugnayan*. For him, despite Maceda's claims to transcend nationalism, the composer's 'emphasis on the identity and the history of the Filipino people felt well under the appreciation of the President's views of national values'.

Dayang Yraola is more equivocal, explaining that these are still sticky subjects among Filipino academics and musicians. 'The Marcos regime, as you know, is a whole murky story on its own,' she explains to me, and proceeds to give a precis of what happens when a political history is oversimplified and a national artist is lionised beyond scrutiny. 'People have been avoiding this for a long time,' she emails. 'At present, when many are against all of the Marcos legacy (regardless of its actual effect on the nation), how would you reconcile the association of rare talent such as Maceda, who is now considered pride of the nation? Enemy of the Nation + Talent = Pride of the Nation.' She concludes: 'This is not actually a viable equation.'

. . .

The scale of *Ugnayan* could not and never would be matched, but Maceda kept chasing those shifting clouds of sound. In 1975, a year after the premiere of *Ugnayan*, he unveiled another drone-based ritual piece for unlimited numbers of participants. Emphatically open-spirited, the score for *Udlot-Udlot* (Hesitations) specifies its forces: *for 6, 60, 600 or more performers*. The first performance involved 800 high-school students congregating in a parking lot at the University of the Philippines. As the sun set over Manila Bay, the students chanted and played instruments they had made by hand. The musicologist Arsenio Nicolas remembers the atmosphere at the premiere as reminiscent of 'rituals in villages where people converged in the central square, in megalithic arenas, in rice fields, in sacred water springs and trees, in village temples or crossroads, in mountain sanctuaries, in ancestral graves and monuments, where powerful spirits reside and preside over the affairs of humans'.

Nicolas also describes a 1976 performance of *Udlot-Udlot* which took place in his own hometown of Calauag, Quezon, about 300 kilometres south-east of Manila on the island of Luzon. 'The town plaza was closed to vehicular traffic to create an atmosphere of serenity, zenitude and contemplation,' Nicolas notes. 'At an appointed time in the afternoon, some 30 sections of all four years of the high school were dispersed to all the farthest boundaries of the town proper and, from there, walked towards the town plaza playing the basic rhythm with their instruments.' I find this a tremendously heartening image, the traffic halted to make way for the 'zenitude' of rhythmically enmeshed students. Later that same day, the organisers of the performance went for tea at Nicolas's house, where his mother sang *kundiman* love songs and Maceda accompanied her on the piano.

Maybe because of its mutability, maybe because it does not require any special technical devices or city-wide infrastructure,

Udlot-Udlot is the piece of Maceda's that gets restaged most often. It can work with virtually any number of performers in virtually any space. There have been renditions in Bonn, in Buddhist temples in Tokyo, in Jakarta, Kuala Lumpur, in Hong Kong, in Berlin. In 2000, the composer Chris Brown invited Maceda to Mills College, California's hotbed of adventurous composition, and together they staged an enactment of *Udlot-Udlot* in San Francisco's Yerba Buena Gardens. A Filipino film crew was in attendance for the event, so we have footage of that golden mid-October day. The American participants wore short sleeves while Maceda was dressed in a white woollen jumper as he led the ceremony from the front. 'Look at me!' he instructed the crowd. 'Because there is a certain manner of walking!' He thrust his arms out in front of him. 'It is a *ritual*. You're showing off!' He brandished a couple of wooden beaters. 'These are a pair of good, nice sticks. Show that!'

For Chris Brown, the most memorable moment of that day came at the end of the performance. On one side of Yerba Buena Gardens is a Catholic church. 'A mass was just ending,' Brown recalls.

That neighbourhood had always been heavily populated by Filipinos. Coming out of the church, they were walking across the park and they encountered this performance of traditional Filipino music and an old Filipino guy with a shock of white hair conducting it, waving his arms about. It was beautiful. He greeted them, they talked. In that way he connected with the Filipino American community.

At the end of the performance, Maceda took a microphone. 'Thank you, everyone,' he beamed. 'You see how easy it is to make music? Very serious meaning with very simple music. You don't have to study piano for a hundred years, nor violin, nor singing. You just play. Isn't it fun?'

. . .

In hindsight, Imelda Marcos might have wondered whether ordering people onto the streets and fomenting creative excitement through the medium of radio was a potentially risky strategy. Just over a decade after the premiere of *Ugnayan*, mass media turned against her, citizens of Manila were galvanised into collective action by the outspoken broadcasts of Radio Veritas. Protesters took to the streets wearing yellow in a revolution that overthrew two decades of the Marcos regime in just four days.

Radio Veritas had been broadcasting revolutionary information to anti-Marcos factions across the nation. At dawn on Sunday 23 February 1986, government troops tore down the station's central transmitter, at which point Veritas operators switched to a smaller transmitter and carried on broadcasting as far as they could reach. Hundreds of thousands of demonstrators called time on two decades of corruption and human rights violations. Ferdinand and Imelda Marcos fled to Hawaii, leaving their Malacañang Palace to be stormed by protesters who wandered the vast hallways of sunken bathtubs and cavernous closets. Bewilderingly, Imelda Marcos would eventually come back to Manila to make a museum of her footwear, uttering that most immortally tone-deaf of lines: 'They went into my closets looking for skeletons, but thank God, all they found were shoes, beautiful shoes.'

Things changed for Maceda after the Marcos era of bumper culture funds. The incoming president Corazon Aquino was clear that she wanted to break from perceived vanity projects and reset the political agenda in favour of economic stability. No more Coconut

Palaces, no more film theatres, no more amassed avant-garde radio happenings. Maceda's post-Marcos works downsized significantly, and when I ask Dayang Yraola how much that had to do with the change in regime rather than aesthetic choice, she responds with typical diplomacy. 'This is a probability,' she replies. 'It is a claim I have used too on some occasions, like when we restaged *Ugnayan* in 2010' – that was part of a three-day *Ugnayan 2010* festival, which saw the piece enacted in modest proportions around a plaza in the University of the Philippines. 'I mentioned that we cannot restage it the way it was staged in the 1970s because we do not have Imelda now who will tell the National Telecommunication Commission that they will play only Maceda's music for one hour.'

After the regime change, for the first time in his life, Maceda started writing for Western instruments. But he didn't go in for any East-meets-West fusion of pianos plus pentatonicism. His aim was more profound than that. He wanted to wipe all slates clean. When he writes for violins, flutes and pianos, the instruments don't really *behave* as they conventionally should. The musicologist Ramón Pagayon Santos uses charged language to stress the point – he suggests that Maceda wanted to 'liberate' the instruments from their cultural trappings, that he was 'practically invading the exclusive domain of Western musical thought and supplanting his own transformed and metamorphosed sensibilities on the very tools and mediums of Western musical expression'. I think of Julián Carrillo and his 308,430 versions of Beethoven symphonies. Is Santos deliberately co-opting the vocabulary of colonisation when he writes that Maceda performed an 'attack' on the integrity of these instruments, 'subjecting them to perform under an alien aesthetic order'? Did Maceda see it that way?

Certainly, he enacted a very elegant coup in his later works. Take a piece he wrote in 1987: a twenty-minute beauty called *Strata*.

The scoring is for five flutes, five guitars and five cellos with ten *balingbing* buzzers and five tam-tams – if you want to play the numbers game, the elements of East and West are perfectly balanced at the starting whistle. And what happens next is an all-round draw. Neither side wins or dominates. The *balingbings* provide an overture. Flutes tendril upward, green shoots reaching for light. Cellos follow suit in an unruly pack, then guitars. Vegetation grows fast in this rainforest. The piece saunters. It jostles. It is a fiesta of polyrhythms, a clattering dance of the earth propelled by subterranean eruptions from the gongs. The momentum is hypnotic. A guitar riff cuts through; a gurgle of flutes surfaces. 'In a tropical jungle there is a heck of a lot of sound,' says Chris Brown, who recorded the piece for the Tzadik label in the 1990s. 'Sound is all around you. There is so much rhythm. And that rhythm certainly doesn't all come together on a downbeat.'

Three years later, Maceda wrote a bewitching half-hour orchestral work called *Dissemination*, scored for twenty-five Western instruments plus *olimongs* (shrill whistle flutes) and gongs. The opening is so high it's almost inaudible, as though Maceda is reminding us there are more things in heaven and earth than are dreamt of in conventional accounts of musical feasibility. The music swarms, laps and circles. It builds and rebuilds, dense and multiform, drone constantly on the move, oboes keening in the midst. Maceda invokes living organisms out of sound. The music breathes. It billows.

One of his pieces that has surprised and captivated me most of all is a rhapsodic, dare I say *impressionist*, work that at last brought Maceda back to the instrument where he began. It took a lot of convincing for him to even consider writing for piano. The Japanese pianist Aki Takahashi asked him for a piece; Maceda refused her request, arguing he could not summon his motley drones using one instrument alone. Eventually he agreed – but only if he could use multiple instruments. *Music for Five Pianos* (1993) is a homecoming of sorts. It opens with octaves, as though Maceda is preparing bare earth as a stage. The octaves begin to fill in, pitch by capricious pitch like birds landing on the keys and dancing out patterns that tug, strobe and coalesce into unexpectedly lush colours. Maceda turns his piano ensemble into a gamelan orchestra. A gagaku court band. A whirlpool that sweeps through uncharted vistas to arrive, bedazzled, at some suddenly redolent place.

The Japanese composer-pianist Yuji Takahashi was a great friend of Maceda, a fellow explorer of playful musical alternatives. In his sleeve notes to a recording of José Maceda's *Music for Five Pianos*, Takahashi writes:

> Time without beginning without end, scintillating colour points, immense space open to manifold events arising and passing, a peaceful atmosphere wherein many different kinds of trees, flowers, bamboo, birds, animals and people are allowed to live together.
>
> Maceda's music is a proposal and exemplar for a profound change in our feeling and thinking toward the society and culture in this troubled world. It gives a vision for each of us to investigate.

· · ·

The grandeur of Maceda's massive performance pieces is seductive, but it's the humanity of his works that makes them really gleam. The man was a polyglot, a lateral thinker. Dayang Yraola writes that Maceda's creative practice 'was actually that of a drifter, which only means that his philosophies and work cross over the imaginary line that divides the artistic disciplines'. At the close of the twentieth century, by now an elderly man, Maceda still reached for horizons yet to be ventured. 'Now', he mused, 'is the time to explore other logics and musical potentials.'

When he died in 2004, Maceda was honoured with the highest prizes an artist in the Philippines can achieve. A funeral procession accompanied his body between the concert hall and the Catholic chapel, two of the places that had been fixtures all his life at the University of the Philippines. The entourage was accompanied not by the usual marching band, but by gongs.

As a composer, Maceda was not prolific. By the end of his life, his total work list numbered only twenty-three. (Twenty-four, if you include a piece called *Accordion and Mandolin with Special Orchestra*, which at the time of writing is yet to be performed in full.) His vision took time to percolate. He didn't write his first composition until he was nearly fifty, by which point he had already notched up two other careers as pianist and as ethnomusicologist. When he did turn to creating music, what he proposed was nothing less than a radical new philosophy based on the collective rhythms of ancient village rituals. His music re-examines sound, temporality, space, individual agency. He dreamed of a music that forms and floats like mist. A music that could free time. A music that could loosely unify thousands, millions of individual parts and transplant the oldest sounds into the newest devices. A music that could repurpose hyper-local practices into an international sound for the future. Tradition, as the critic Theodor W. Adorno once grudgingly admitted, is yet present time.

And if there is a nationalism in Maceda's music, it is an inquisitive and abstract nationalism akin to that of Julián Carrillo, or Ruth Crawford, or even Walter Smetak and his rambunctious comrades in *Tropicália*. It is a nationalism that ventures new sorts of identity, new realms of thought, new radical and rooted sounds that speak of life where he lived it. In the next chapter we meet a composer who also articulated the bluntest truths of her reality. But while Maceda made music under the widest skies, Galina Ustvolskaya drove deeper and deeper inward.

Galina Ustvolskaya

(1919–2006)

Sound poet of St Petersburg:
sonic realism, holy terror

June, 2019. A century after the birth of Galina Ustvolskaya. The buildings of St Petersburg are all yellows and fierce golds. The city that Dostoevsky called foul and slimy and Pushkin imagined forever lurking in the mists is gleaming under the midsummer sun. Gulls screech over the Neva river and drunk teenagers swarm the streets celebrating high-school graduation. I have tracked down the address where my grandfather grew up – an apartment in an imposing central block on Sadovaya Street – and I stand staring at the stones for long minutes. I suppose I'm trying to figure out what I feel.

My grandfather, Andrei Viktorovich Ivitsky, escaped from post-revolutionary St Petersburg in 1919, the same year that Ustvolskaya was born here. At the age of twelve, Andrei was held hostage by the authorities in an attempt to prevent his father, a railway engineer, from deserting to the UK. Andrei bribed a guard who took his money but phoned ahead to the border anyway; when he discovered the train was being searched for him, Andrei swiftly disembarked, crawled under the carriages and crossed into Finland. He made it to England and wound up being sent to an uncaring school for boys in south London.

I knew him only when he was an elderly man and long since embittered. By then he had settled in the Netherlands and occasionally visited our family in Scotland. He was not too fond of children. I remember my parents suggesting I play him whatever I was learning on the piano, to which he responded by slamming the lid on my fingers.

Maybe there is a reason why I'm so intrigued by Ustvolskaya's music. Music of astounding strength and determination, as well as wilful and often inexorable cruelty.

I take the metro five stops south from Sadovaya Street and emerge in a neighbourhood lined with birch trees. A park next to the metro station has a little pond, a chapel, a pavement stall selling flowers. I buy a bunch of harebells (I'm told Ustvolskaya had a fondness for wildflowers) and walk for ten minutes through neat apartment blocks and communal gardens full of bright plastic climbing frames. A street cleaner notices me searching for apartment numbers and guides me into an inner courtyard. This is where the composer once lived.

· · ·

In 1973, Ustvolskaya wrote a piece of obliteratingly brutal music scored for eight double basses, piano and a large wooden box, which is to be struck by a percussionist and which in some performances has been built to resemble a coffin. The work is a setting of the *Dies irae* – the Latin hymn for the Day of Wrath. Over the course of ten merciless movements, the bass players dig into their strings and the pianist attacks the keyboard with the incisive hack of a butcher. As for the box: Ustvolskaya gave detailed instructions about how it should be constructed. It should not be resonant. Its voice should be hollow. It should sound dead behind the eyes.

In 1988, two years after the explosion at Chernobyl nuclear power station, Ustvolskaya composed her sixth and final piano sonata. This time the score contains nothing but tone clusters – piles of notes crammed together and unleashed all at once. By now, she had found new ways of embodying terror in her music. She instructed her performer to sound the instrument with palms and elbows. The pianist Maria Cizmic later wrote about what it feels like to play this sonata. 'Fingers smart as they strike against the keys' hard edges,' Cizmic relates. 'The side of the hand flushes with colour. The amount of repetition required to learn this work causes experiences of pain to amass and exist in the private hours of practising.'

That physical pain is no accident, and neither is the trauma that builds up through a performance and lingers long after. There is a steely discipline at work here. Whether exorcism or catharsis, litany or lacerating meditation, this music is an exacting ritual of sorts. And in the middle of all the violence there is a moment of fleeting, galling tenderness. A clutch of pianissimo chords whose impact is more shocking than all the noise.

Ustvolskaya gave up on time signatures in 1949. Like Maceda and his malleable drones, her music refuses to be bound, unless she set the rules herself – and when she did, she applied them with ineluctable rigour. Here was a woman who could and did write an entire intransigent movement out of nothing but crotchets (the Second Piano Sonata). Critics over the years have given her pithy nicknames including 'the lady with the hammer' and 'the high priestess of sado-minimalism'. Like most nicknames, they gloss the nuance, but it's true that almost nothing she wrote makes for comfortable listening. And why should it?

I recently discovered that one of the living composers I admire most is also an Ustvolskaya devotee. Rebecca Saunders, a British composer long based in Berlin, herself writes music of fearsome intellect and exacting demands. She takes no prisoners in the way she talks about her work or in the rigour she requires from performers and listeners. (Her music can also be tender, tactile, gleefully playful.) Saunders told me she loves Ustvolskaya for her 'uncompromising directness and honesty'. Ustvolskaya's music is,

says Saunders, 'an example of ultimate musical courage. It is completely unfiltered. Skeletal, precise. Nothing is superfluous. She
goes straight to the heart.'

Saunders first discovered Ustvolskaya through her Duet for
violin and piano, composed in 1964. She remembers hearing it as
one of the true moments of mind-expanding inspiration in her life.
'This music does something that very few composers have dared
to do,' she explains. 'There is a deep emotionality that Ustvolskaya
does not hide. There is no shame. And there is profound fragility.' Fragility? It's not a word I expected to hear in relation to all
that directness and daring. 'Ah, yes!' Saunders corrects me, nod-
ding emphatically. 'That's the nub of the existential stuff. It's what
Beckett is all about, too. Fragility is the brutality of what they open
up and allowed us to confront.'

· · ·

A tiny elevator creaks to the sixth floor of the apartment block in
St Petersburg where I am greeted by an elderly gentleman wearing
large glasses and a T-shirt tucked into velvet floral trousers. This
is Konstantin Bagrenin, Ustvolskaya's widower. There is a shyness
about him, or maybe a wariness. He accepts the bunch of harebells
that I bought outside the metro and gestures around the apartment. Even with only a few shared words, he manages to convey
quite a lot about his late wife.

Galina Ustvolskaya was born in what was then Petrograd on
17 June 1919, a year and a half after the Bolshevik Revolution. Her
father was a lawyer and her mother was a teacher. She had a twin
sister, Tatyana, who became a mathematician. One early photograph shows the sisters aged around five, both unsmiling, both
wearing frilly white dresses and identical ribbons in their severely

cut hair. One holds a cuddly toy shaped like a rabbit. The other clutches a doll that is distinctly macabre.

Galina did not get along with her mother. Her father was a little deaf, so everyone shouted around the home. Her safe space was under the piano. She was a lonely child who often skived school to wander around galleries and museums. Pervasive solitude channelled into art – it's a theme that makes me think of Else Marie Pade inventing sonic fairy tales from her sickbed in Aarhus around the same time. Ustvolskaya's favourite composers were Mahler, Stravinsky, Mussorgsky and above all J. S. Bach. When asked what she wanted to be when she grew up, she said she wanted to be an orchestra.

The city variously called Petrograd, Leningrad and St Petersburg was her home for her whole life, save a brief wartime stint in the

Uzbek capital, Tashkent. She was nine years old in 1928 when Joseph Stalin implemented his first Five-Year Plan, severing dialogue with the West and strangulating Soviet cultural life. The Russian Association of Proletarian Musicians ruled that concert music was not as useful as collective singing, and thus began the persecution of anyone deemed to be a 'progressive' composer. Ustvolskaya enrolled at the (then) Rimsky-Korsakov Music Conservatory in 1937, a year after Stalin walked out of Shostakovich's opera *Lady Macbeth of the Mtsensk District* and the state newspaper, *Pravda*, published a hatchet job on the piece titled 'Muddle Instead of Music'. This was the height of the Great Terror, not an ideal time to be making headway as a radical thinker in Leningrad. Ustvolskaya was not the only one having to weigh up the balance between asserting a creative voice and staying alive.

She joined the class of Shostakovich at what was by then the Leningrad State Conservatoire (the institution's name changed repeatedly) in 1939. He was her senior by thirteen years and Ustvolskaya won his esteem. Shostakovich later declared he was 'convinced' that her music 'will achieve world fame, and be valued by all who hold truth to be the essential element of music'. He admired his brilliant student highly enough to send her his unpublished scores, keen to hear her advice. 'It is not you who are influenced by me,' he told her, 'but rather it is I who am influenced by you.' In perhaps the highest compliment of all, he quoted her music in his. A theme from her early Trio for clarinet, violin and piano (1949) turns up in his Fifth String Quartet (1952). It turns up again in the song 'Night' from his *Suite on Verses of Michelangelo Buonarroti* (1974), a work Shostakovich wrote just a year before he died. Over the decades, his own creative voice had shapeshifted multiple times, but his respect for Ustvolskaya's musical plainspeak held fast until the end.

Ustvolskaya's Clarinet Trio is in three movements. There are no tempo indications, but there are expressive instructions – *Espressivo*, *Dolce* and *Energico*. Compared with most of her scores, there is disarming emotional subtlety in this piece. The middle movement is a whispered lament, so introverted that it ends up swallowing itself completely. What's gripping about the gnarled counterpoint of the outer movements is how absolutely stark the writing is, how intently chiselled, how remote. The landscape is unforgiving but the instrumental lines venture on, like tough little roads snaking through blasted rock.

Ustvolskaya gave the impression that she was uncompromising. That she was dogged in the model of Julián Carrillo, never adjusting her style to suit the cultural hegemony of the times. That, instead, she opted to isolate herself and leave her genuine music unperformed rather than taint her integrity by writing state-sanctioned 'Soviet' works, as Shostakovich and Prokofiev both did. It helped that she wiped out nearly every one of those early 'Soviet' works from her official catalogue. But they did exist, with rousing titles to match such as *Hail, Youth!* (1950), *Dawn over the Homeland* (1952), *The Hero's Exploit* (1957) and *Lights in the Steppe* (1958). As it turns out, Ustvolskaya could compose patriotism with finesse, and – for some of the works, at least – was praised by critics of the day for making music of such exemplary ideals.

My personal favourite of these state-approved works is her 1956 score to *The Girl and the Crocodile*, a cautionary film in which a rope-skipping Soviet girl called Katya is put in charge of a collection of caged rabbits, reptiles and an unfortunate thrush, then accidentally manages to set them all free. Cue various japes and running about the city, after which the animals are re-caged and important life lessons are learned. Ustvolskaya's film score is perky and tuneful, full of clever patterns. The crocodile gets an ominous little staccato on the bassoon against a choir of roaming oboes.

A couple of years later, in 1959, Ustvolskaya wrote her Grand Duet for cello and piano. Now there are no cute life lessons at play. The piano drives at the extremities of the keyboard. The cello rages alongside, hoofing at the ground, all snarling jaws and sinew stretched to the limit. In the end, the beast loses strength, or just gives up: the Grand Duet fades to leave the cello alone playing a gallingly tender elegy. Again, it's that fragility which feels the most brutal. But a sense of elegiac closure would be too trite. The piano gets the final word, stabbing out any hint of consolation with three bitter thrusts.

. . .

Konstantin Bagrenin shows me a soft-focus portrait from the 1950s. The photograph was taken around the time Ustvolskaya was writing her First Symphony, which is a score crowded with menacing vignettes. Doomed merry-go-rounds, nervy Saturday nights, tales of child poverty and the oppression of American workers. A couple of boys' voices intone to the backdrop of thrawn strings and eerie chimes. The music fits together in chunks, serrated pieces of some ominous jigsaw. Rhythms are lopsided, intervals are stark. The symphony consists of two instrumental movements bookending eight songs, the last of which is called 'Sun', but any optimism is soon snuffed out. Bagrenin writes out the date of the photograph for me and mimes until I understand. In the picture, Ustvolskaya is reaching for the sun. He points at the blinds in the study, indicating how, in later life, she would keep them lowered because she could not bear composing in the light.

It came as a surprise to many who knew her when, in 1966, Ustvolskaya proposed to Konstantin. She was forty-seven and

Kostya, her student, was twenty-four. They would live together for the next forty years. The only photograph of the couple on display in the apartment was printed and framed on a trip to Amsterdam, one of the few occasions she ever left St Petersburg. Ustvolskaya is wearing her trademark huge square glasses and Bagrenin sports a black beret. They are both grinning.

The apartment consists of four rooms: study, kitchen, bedroom and bathroom. The place is spotless. The bedroom has green floral wallpaper. The kitchen has mustard yellow cabinets, tomatoes ripening on the windowsill and magnets on the fridge. The study has an upright piano, a couple of bookcases and a glass cabinet full of gifts from Ustvolskaya's students. She is usually portrayed as a recluse, but this cabinet contains proof in the shape of dozens of miniature wood and china figurines that her students adored her.

A Van Gogh print hangs on the wall and a sculpture of Jesus is placed on the shelf above one of the bookcases. In the hallway, a black-and-white photograph shows a wooden church in the remote Karelia region north of St Petersburg. The nature of Ustvolskaya's relationship to organised religion still puzzles me. She more or less refused to discuss the matter publicly, so exactly what her faith entailed remains a matter between her and her God. Certainly it seems that no higher being she believed in was about to provide any easy comfort, and her spiritual music is no luminous, holy minimalism in the vein of her Estonian counterpart Arvo Pärt.

Some of her later works are explicitly sacred. Her three *Compositions* (1971–5) all carry religious subtitles: *Dona nobis pacem*, *Dies irae* and *Benedictus qui venit*. Four of her symphonies include texts that implore God directly. Ustvolskaya made statements about how she composed 'in a state of grace', about how God was the only one who could, strictly speaking, commission her. She was not a regular churchgoer, and her world view did not seem to involve much

Christian absolution. She took pains to distinguish religion from spirituality, which she considered far more fundamental: 'Spirituality', she said, 'is what remains of a person if you disregard the rest.' Hers was a grand, uncontainable vision of the almighty.

Was the sacred in her music also a form of resistance? She despised the atheist state, which for most of her life had oppressed the Church and promoted the Soviet project as a new religion in its place. Was the very act of composing forbidden complex music some sort of defiant worship? Her Second Symphony (1979) plays out in brute slabs. Scored for the typically weird line-up of six flutes, six oboes and six trumpets plus single trombone, tuba, piano, bass drum, tenor drum and voice, the music pounds along like a pile driver in slow motion. Ustvolskaya said it cost her a lot of effort to bring the symphony into this world. The text, delivered by a narrator, was written by an eleventh-century Benedictine monk called Hermannus Contractus, who was born with a physical disability and could barely speak. Pain is already ingrained in these words. From the throat of an individual who is almost literally silenced, the text beseeches God in guttural repetitions: *Gospodi*. The words beg for truth, mercy, eternity. In Russian, they have a crushing heft that the English equivalent could never muster. The score instructs that the lines should be delivered like 'a scream into space'. When asked to explain its meaning, Ustvolskaya said this was the voice of a lonely person. 'He sees no way out. He falls with every step. He keeps falling and asks God for help.' She said that at the time she wrote it, the voice represented herself.

Thinking again of my grandfather, I wonder about the roots of all this soul-burden. I remember spending time in Moscow with friends who were incredulous when I made light of the sweet-sour melancholy in a particular Tchaikovsky waltz. 'You don't know about *toska*!' exclaimed one friend, appalled. Vladimir Nabokov wrote about the concept of *toska*, which translates roughly as 'lugu-briousness' or 'heart-sickness'. Nabokov claimed – and I'm sure he was right – that

> no single word in English renders all the shades of *toska*. At its deepest and most painful, it is a sensation of great spiritual anguish, often without specific cause. At less morbid levels, it is a dull ache of the soul, a longing with nothing to long for, a sick pining, a vague restlessness, mental throes, yearning. In particular cases it may be the desire for something specific, nostalgia, love-sickness. At the lowest level it grades into ennui or boredom.

Ustvolskaya did not bother with the lower levels of anything. Another of her fellow Petersburgians, Fyodor Dostoevsky, had a similar penchant for the deepest bleakness – an 'ability to submerge into darkness and remain there for a long time', as the philosopher Nikolai Berdyaev once observed of Dostoevsky's characters. Ustvolskaya's favourite writer of all was Nikolai Gogol, specialist in freewheeling absurdism and ardent believer in God, his stories enveloped by grimmer forces still. As the pianist and musicologist Elena Nalimova has pointed out, Gogol's very language is built on repetitions and distortions so extreme that the prose itself becomes grotesque. The novelist A. S. Byatt describes it as 'linguistic phantasmagoria'; Nabokov called it 'life-generating syntax'. It's a technique we find in Ustvolskaya's musical methods, too. In her final years, her strength failing, she would ask Konstantin to read to her from Gogol's unfinished novel *Dead Souls*, in which the questionable protagonist Chichikov roams across Russia, buying up dead bodies. The gist of it is ghoulish but there is a spiritual outcome. Just through reading out their names, through the act of sounding their identities aloud, Chichikov winds up breathing new life into these wretched deceased serfs.

. . .

The winter after my midsummer trip to Russia, I arrange to meet the composer and pianist Frank Denyer in a cafe in Oxford. Denyer was the first pianist to record Ustvolskaya's six piano sonatas and is one of the few performers who ever won her lasting approval for the way he played her music, so I suspect he is key to helping me unpick her esoteric secrets. 'Ah, but the thing is', he tells me as we take a seat, 'she was so damn extreme.' It is a cold morning and the windows of the cafe are steamed up. Ignoring the polite Oxford hush of tea and scones, Denyer proceeds to treat me to an animated re-enactment of some of Ustvolskaya's fiercest mannerisms. 'She was either over the moon or completely livid, nothing in between,' he says. 'She used to write triple exclamation marks that went right through the page. Like this!!!' He wallops the table, capsizing a milk jug.

Denyer first came across Ustvolskaya's music by chance in the early 1990s while he was staying with his trombonist-composer friend James Fulkerson in Amsterdam. Left to his own devices in Fulkerson's apartment one morning, he picked up a cassette tape with an unfamiliar name handwritten across the cover. 'I thought I would give it a whirl,' he recalls. 'It was the Second Symphony. It nearly took my head off.' Fulkerson and Denyer belonged to an ensemble called The Barton Workshop, which specialised in performing the furthest-out music they could lay their hands on. Ustvolskaya was a perfect project, given that, at the time, basically nobody had heard of her outside Russia, let alone tried to play her music. They tracked down some scores, took one look at them and exploded with questions.

'What we instrumentalists tend to do when we're confronted by something entirely different is we find ways of making it work in terms of what we know,' Denyer explains, setting the milk jug upright. 'Some performers might try to voice the chords in a way that would sound good in a piece of Rachmaninov while trying to convince themselves – *it's what the music needs. It isn't as bad as it seems.*' He replenishes his tea cup and takes a sip. 'We all try to understand the world in terms of concepts we recognise. Concepts we are comfortable with. But with Ustvolskaya . . . None of that works.' I think of *Hoy Mismo* and the fiasco with *Sonido 13* and the supposedly suicidal animals. How we tend to freak out when the familiar is skewed.

Denyer wrote to St Petersburg in hope of clues. He rummages in his briefcase and produces a clutch of typewritten pages, which he lays out across the table. These are letters written back to him by Ustvolskaya.

21 May, 1995

To Frank Denyer

I listened to the CD with the recording of my 4th Symphony, 5th Sonata, Grand Duet and Trio. I'm thankful to you and all your performers for your high inspirations, profound and with total understanding of my intentions.

Ustvolskaya always wanted performers to stick faithfully to her intentions, rather than risking their own interpretations. But then her letter turns to the matter of Denyer's sleeve notes.

You quote my words that I ask not to analyse my music but you yourself begin the sleeve notes with an analysis, and the analysis is very standard and ordinary. It's unclear how it is possible to

perform my music so loftily but write so routinely. If only you
would have written your own thoughts and feelings about the
music but instead you write ordinarily what everybody can see
on the page anyway.

In what might be technically classed as a 'shit sandwich', the letter
ends on a high.

You are a truly remarkable musician and feel my music very,
very well.

Denyer hoots with laughter as he relives the emotional pummel-
ling. 'Obviously, I threw away those sleeve notes immediately!'

He had been prepared for the vehemence. Ustvolskaya's manuscripts are similarly snared with inky outbursts. Drafts of her
symphonies and sonatas are crammed with furious instructions
to herself and performers, scrawled in a shaky hand, ideas circled
emphatically and finished off with exclamation marks. 'What do
you do with a passage that has five *fffff*s followed by a passage with
six *ffffff*s?' He demonstrates on the cafe table again. Loud – *pound* –
very loud – *POUND* – extremely loud – cups leap off their saucers,
and a waiter hurries in from the next room. Denyer shakes his
head, still chuckling. 'There should be some difference, but how?
I remember thinking, either she is overegging the pudding, or she
knows something I don't know about the piano. So I started practising the sonatas. I destroyed my piano. Over about six months,
many strings and keys got broken.'

The fifth movement of Ustvolskaya's Fifth Piano Sonata is the
nexus of one of her most vicious works. The pianist is required to
whack out a cluster chord nearly 150 times at dynamics of up to six
*ffffff*s. Meanwhile, a lone D flat sounds implacably at the eye of the

storm. Denyer remembers the literal rubble involved in learning this sonata. 'My piano went onto the junk heap,' he says. 'There was nothing whatsoever that could be recovered from it.'

Ustvolskaya warned us against analysing her pieces, but the questions keep circling. Why such determined wreckage? It seems the diametric opposite of the delicate processes Annea Lockwood sets in motion in her *Piano Transplants*, even if on the surface Lockwood's tactics of burning, drowning and burying are the more direct attack. Maybe the visceral totality of Ustvolskaya's performances has some kinship with Walter Smetak and his ethos of unplugged multimedia? Denyer points to 'the incredible physicality' of her writing, the fact that 'it's not just abstract sound. These are physical actions. A kind of scream at times.' A scream from whose lungs? And for whose ears to hear?

And why the wildly incongruous combinations of instruments in some of her ensemble pieces – combinations that make no logical sense, like piccolo and tuba (*Composition No. 1 'Dona nobis pacem'*), or trumpet, tam-tam, piano and contralto (the astonishing Fourth Symphony)? Just as Denyer cautioned, I can see the pitfalls of trying to understand these scores in terms of what is familiar. There is no use trying to make Ustvolskaya's music fit into conventional rules that suggest, for example, that instruments should blend together nicely. Her forces are not supposed to blend nicely. It's as though she's telling us: there is no way out of this self-exile, not even through companionship. Even when two or more instruments do find themselves together, they usually end up at war. They sound murderous, or else they try to get away from each other. In her Duet for violin and piano of 1964 – the piece that first got Rebecca Saunders hooked on Ustvolskaya – the two players hurl themselves across registers with nihilistic abandon. In the Third Symphony of 1983, the instruments begin in a nasty snarl-up and spend the rest of the piece dodging a gaping black hole created by the timpani.

• • •

'We often played four-hand duets together in Shostakovich's flat,' Ustvolskaya told the historian Sofia Khentova in 1977. 'He once gave me the complete set of Mahler's symphonies as a present.' She described the two of them listening to music – works including Stravinsky's *Symphony of Psalms*, which Shostakovich transcribed for piano four-hands so he and Ustvolskaya could play it together. 'Dmitri Dmitriyevich [Shostakovich] gave me many of his manuscripts, and often asked for my opinion about his works,' she continued in that 1977 interview. 'Our friendship lasted for nearly 14 years, until 1962. We spent much time together, walking, listening to music.'

Later, she scrubbed out all fondness from her account of their friendship. Nearly two decades after Shostakovich's death, she felt the need to set down in ink a revised version of events. 'Such an eminent figure, for me he was not eminent at all,' she wrote on New Year's Day 1994. 'On the contrary, he burdened me and killed my best feelings.'

The story goes – or rather, one of various stories – that Shostakovich had proposed to her, possibly more than once. Possibly, in one version, he invited her to his home in Moscow and introduced her to his children as his future wife, though he had not actually asked her first. In that version of events, she walked out of the building in tears. Decades later, she issued that caustic statement which severed any affectionate ties with Shostakovich for good. Why she felt the need to renounce him so absolutely remains unclear. What exactly went on between them – surely it is

none of our business, except that the shadow of their relationship
still haunts her reputation.

Early one morning, I visit a housing block in the Khamovniki
district of Moscow. I have been invited here by Andrei Bakhmin, an
Ustvolskaya enthusiast who has acquired her personal archive and
is currently writing her biography. It happens to be my birthday
on the day we arrange to meet, and although Bakhmin has no way
of knowing that, he has prepared a splendid breakfast of pancakes,
baked apples and cream. We talk for long hours about Ustvolskaya
and her riddles. He shows me her vinyl collection. Mahler and
Schumann, Bach's *St John Passion*, Rachmaninov playing his own
piano works, madrigals by Lassus and Monteverdi. This was the
music she loved best.

On my way home from Russia, I check my emails at Moscow
airport and find a long message from Bakhmin. 'Regarding your
question why she rejected DD with such a force,' he writes, picking up on a conversation we had over our breakfast of baked
apples. (DD is Dmitri Dmitriyevich = Shostakovich.) In the email,
Bakhmin goes on to share his own personal theory in enumerated
points.

1) We don't know the details of their relationships, but judging
by her late memoirs she was hurt by him. She knew him very
well and had full right to have her personal opinion here,
including calling him a coward. But even Julian Barnes called
him so.

2) She was critical towards his music at least from the end of
1950s. It's interesting to note that two of the most talented
students of DD – Sviridov and Ustvolskaya – were the most
critical of his music.

3) She rejected works of many composers, especially in the late years. Only Bach was left in the end. But the force of her rejection was the biggest in the case of DD. Because he was close to her in the past and now he was everywhere, he was an officially praised being and, to her opinion, hugely overestimated. It was politics more than music.

4) The last drop was, as I said, that she was repeatedly called his pupil (and still she's considered as his pupil). That was humiliating for her. In her memoirs she said that DD would leave the class to smoke when she was playing and she didn't know if she should stop. Then he would return saying: very good, until the next time. So did he really teach her? We cannot be sure to what extent.

Bakhmin concludes that Ustvolskaya 'had to be harsh' in order to be heard. 'Since then she is considered as a traitor by some of her colleagues, while DD was and still is like a saint for all of them . . . Do you know that he had friends in Cheka?' On the next line he copies a link to the Wikipedia page about the Soviet secret police. Bakhmin signs off: 'but enough. I should not criticise him so much! He was great, and times were hard back then.' It is an acerbic fatalism that I have learned to recognise from my friends in Moscow. Lately, they have been coaching me on the caustic wit required to stay sane while living under political regimes that might otherwise send us spiralling to inconsolable places.

What still intrigues me about the Ustvolskaya–Shostakovich business is that no matter how insistently she renounced him, no matter how emphatically she rejected their friendship in the end, the choice of how the relationship would be framed was apparently never hers to make. When Ustvolskaya died in 2006, the *Independent*

newspaper subtitled its obituary: 'Shostakovich's musical conscience'. The article opens with a Shostakovich quote and goes on to
introduce Ustvolskaya as Shostakovich's student and probable lover.
All of that in the first sentence. What chance does a composer have
to establish her own voice? Still in sentence one, the obituary goes
on to describe Ustvolskaya as 'a composer of prickly independence'.

Maybe Ustvolskaya recognised all of this typecasting and simply
chose to up the ante. She did not play ball. She claimed to be shy
but she could be also be rancorously strident. By some accounts
she was impish, bordering on plain rude. Her way of speaking was
similar to her music in its wild brusqueness. She issued strict orders
to musicians, dictating their every stage mannerism, even whether
to wear a shirt collar buttoned or open. These instructions were
ignored at the performer's peril. At least once she made a musician
audition down the phone to her before she gave permission to perform her works, and she could be cruel to any former champion of
her music if she felt him to be disloyal. And it was usually a him.
She preferred men to play her music. As for herself, she did not like
to be thought of as a woman at all.

Konstantin Bagrenin told the musicologist Elena Nalimova
that for Ustvolskaya everything was either 'genius' or 'sran' (shit).
(Genius: *The Night Watch* by Rembrandt plus basically everything
by Van Gogh. Most other things: *sran*.) Nalimova notes that 'optimistic and healthy people irritated her, as well as other forms of
"normality" such as students getting married and having children',
and details how Ustvolskaya would poke a finger into fresh loaves
at the bakery out of sheer malice. One former student, Sergey
Banevich, recalled her rolling down a taxi window and chucking ice
cream at a random pedestrian.

Her music might tell its message straight, but her words rarely
did. Myth, conjecture, mystique – it all clings so thickly around

her that it's hard to get a clear glimpse of the woman at all. With Ustvolskaya, the picture mists up with misinformation. She refused most interviews. She left no diaries and destroyed letters. She renounced former allies, disowned early compositions, wiped out entire sections of her life.

Why all the obfuscating? There are plenty of reasons why a Soviet composer might learn to speak in riddles, and hers have no neat solution that I can work out. Maybe that's the point. Maybe writing about Ustvolskaya was always going to be as darkly experiential as her music; maybe I was bound to get lost in a dank fog of half-facts and conjecture. Above all, she claimed that her music was her only valid biography, but even then she stymied any attempts to read between the notes and deduce meaning. As she stressed to Frank Denyer, she loathed analysis. 'It is better not to write anything at all about my music', she warned, 'than to constantly write the same thing over and over in a circle.' Maybe she was right, and her raw-scrubbed music is the only account we can trust.

Ustvolskaya is hardly the first or last composer to behave outrageously. Were she a man, she might have been slotted into the category of 'cantankerous artist' or 'genius prone to roguish eccentricity'. (Remember Smetak's fond monikers: Tak-Tak, The Old Wizard, Alchemist of Sound.) As it was, Ustvolskaya remains alien and unfathomable. Many of her acquaintances were concerned about the state of her mental health. She was formidable, but she was also fragile – that fragility Rebecca Saunders identified in her music. There were various reports of her instability, her volatile nerves, the cocktail of pills she took for decades to keep herself calm. According to the composer Valentin Silvestrov, her music is like a naked person standing on the street shouting: 'Don't look at me! Don't look!'

I ask Frank Denyer where he thinks Ustvolskaya fits in musical history. 'She doesn't,' he replies. 'And that's the glory of her. She doesn't fit with anyone in Russia, anyone anywhere else. She was an island of her own making. And she was an alter ego to the big beasts who were all around her.' In the end, I suggest, maybe that's how she staged her coup. Her isolation was greatest strength. Through sheer solitary aberration, she clung to her artistic freedom – Alejandro Madrid's point about composers on the periphery having a certain freedom from the politics of entrenched musical factions. Her peripheral state was less geographic, more self-imposed. Denyer nods in agreement. 'Being a Great Composer, a Genius Composer, all that came with its own restrictions,' he says. 'Especially in the Russian tradition. You had to write grand symphonies and concertos. You had to have a direct lineage to great traditions of the past with the godlike names that represent it. It's maddening to anyone who wants to do it differently. Then there's Ustvolskaya. She rages at the world. She writes a symphony for four players.'

. . .

When Ustvolskaya needed to think, she walked the streets of St Petersburg. Sometimes she headed out of the city, thirty kilometres south to the birch forests of Pavlovsk. So I make a sort of pilgrimage one bleach-skied Sunday afternoon in high summer. The centre of St Petersburg is still thronging with noisy teenagers. They mill about the train station buying sweets and cigarettes, then pile into my carriage just before we pull out of the station. The train line cuts through long miles of social housing blocks. Dostoevsky's novels swivel between the grotty and the grandiose of this city; today, St Petersburg keeps its slums at its edges. Buskers hop on and off the carriage between stops, rattling through gypsy tunes on accordions and fiddles. One woman sings a mournful ballad with enough verses to last for three stops.

We arrive at Pushkin, a regal country retreat with a palace and broad boulevards. Pavlovsk is one stop further, but I decide to walk the last five kilometres under the dazzling northern sun. The path wends due south, past a lake with beaches and past sunbathers who tan standing up with elaborate mirrors set up around them for an all-round bronze. There are families, groups of elderly friends, lone bodybuilders. One couple looks to be in the throes of a wedding proposal. At the enormous gates of Pavlovsk park there is a stall selling pies (mushroom or cherry) and a man renting bikes for 100 rubles. I hire one, fill my rucksack with pastries and set out through the trees.

These trees have a long history of providing escape and sanctity. The Russian royal family spent their summers in this forest in the eighteenth century. Catherine the Great made regular hunting trips here in pursuit of wild boar and deer. In the nineteenth century, Russia's first railway line was installed in Pavlovsk so that horse-drawn carriages could transport day-trippers out of St Petersburg. The grounds of the park are now strewn with replica Greek statues. There is a gaudy centaur by a pond and a bronze of Mercury that was lost during the Second World War, discovered in Austria decades later and returned to Pavlovsk in 1979. As I pedal along the avenues, black-headed gulls swoop at flies on a boating pond and toddlers run at trees to torment the red squirrels.

Pavlovsk is somewhere Ustvolskaya came to ponder her pulverising confessionals and hone her monastic discipline. I think of what Rebecca Saunders said about fragility being the brutality of what Ustvolskaya opened up, what she allowed us to confront. I think about the Sixth Piano Sonata. All that violence, then the sudden pianissimo chords. This was where she walked, where she watched the birds and found a spot by a lake in a grove of birches. Without paper, this was where she composed in her mind, among these golden meadows, these lakes and pathways. These shimmering birch trees.

Ustvolskaya lived in one of the cruellest cities through some of the cruellest acts of the twentieth century, and she channelled her experiences into sound without stopping to soften the blow. In that sense, her work provides us with the ultimate poetics of musical realism. In the thwack of the *Dies irae* or the onslaught of the Sixth Piano Sonata, we don't just get an account of the fear and isolation of Soviet life under Stalinism and the decades that followed. We begin to feel that fear and isolation ourselves – I mean feel it physically in the clenching of muscles and quickening of breath and doom-knot that takes hold in the stomach. Maybe she isn't so different from Annea Lockwood and her tactile techniques after all.

For more than half a century, the musical world has tried to unpick the cryptic politicking in the works of Ustvolskaya's teacher, Dmitri Shostakovich, as though his musical codes might contain some essential truth about what life was like behind the Iron Curtain. Meanwhile, Ustvolskaya's music tells its message straight, should we be brave enough to hear it. Relentless and ineluctable, scarred and scarring, dictatorial in her demands on performers and listeners – yes, Ustvolskaya leaves us with the sonic equivalent of augmented reality glasses. We should listen to her as reportage, as testimony. As one of her students put it: 'The winds of politics swirl around Galina, but she stays solid and true to herself.'

But it's not only that. Ustvolskaya's scores go beyond unfiltered personal response to the extremities of the life that she lived. If her works speak beyond their time and place, it's possibly because of their intense spiritual dimension. Three identical chords open her Fourth Piano Sonata: blasting back to bare truths, striking at penance for some earth-shaking sin, tolling like bells for an entire blighted population. She reveals an apocalyptic vision. Her monastic rigour, her religious awe, her white-hot anger – she wrote with a sort of blazing holy terror that sat uncomfortably with many of her contemporaries in the Soviet Union, and that still sits uncomfortably with many liberal modern listeners today.

Eight thousand kilometres to the south, another composer burned with intense spirituality. Both went to extremes of introspection, but their resulting music could hardly be more different.

Emahoy Tsegué-Mariam Guèbru

(b. 1923)

Waltz for Addis Ababa:
Ethiopia's piano royalty

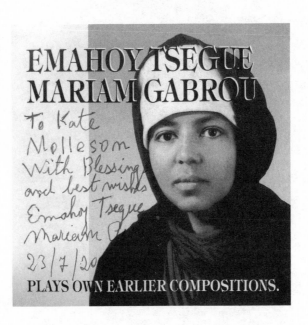

2016. One Sunday morning in Jerusalem, I visited the Debre Genet monastery early enough to catch the church service that gets going before sunrise. The first ritual of attending this service was blearily taking off my shoes before entering the building. Inside, the air was thick with incense. The smoke of frankincense and myrrh. It was all very lulling and soporific. The Orthodox priests leading the service were in no rush. They exchanged a lot of slow, low murmuring before the singing proper began. At first their voices were subterranean, more rumble than song, then they began rising in waves of overlapping pentatonic melodies, which the congregation followed in a sort of stretchy group response. I couldn't quite pinpoint where the beat landed or how the phrases moved together, but they did. More than an hour later, I emerged from the church blinking into the dawn that was now breaking over the courtyard. Breakfast *fatira* (a sweet pastry filled with honey and eggs) was being prepared over an open-air fire and fresh coffee beans were being roasted on little stoves, the traditional Ethiopian way.

Ethiopia's holiest tale concerns a woman and a journey to Jerusalem. Sometime in the tenth century BC, the Queen of Sheba paid a visit – was it a trade mission? – from her home in Axum to the Israelite King Solomon. Versions of the story are told in the Quran and the Bible, in Hebrew, Coptic and Yoruba legend, but the Ethiopian account is by far the most thorough. It details how the queen stayed at Solomon's palace in Jerusalem for nearly a year and refused his relentless attempts to seduce her. The night before she was due to return to Axum, Solomon devised a trick. He threw a farewell banquet of extremely salty food, and made the queen promise that when she left the next day, she would not be carrying anything belonging to his palace. If she broke the oath she would, he decreed, be obliged to submit to his will. Being no thief she agreed at once, but in the middle of the night, parched with thirst after all that salt, the queen reached for a glass of water. The liquid counted as property enough. Solomon forced her to go to bed with him, and the next day she left Jerusalem pregnant with the future King Menelik, founder of a dynasty that would rule Ethiopia for the next three thousand years. (Menelik later paid his own visit to his father in Jerusalem, and when he left he also took something with him: the small matter of the Ark of the Covenant, which is said – by some – to be housed in Axum to this day.)

For all the permutations of the story, it can be agreed that Ethiopians have had a presence in Jerusalem for a very long time. Scroll forward to 1936, when Italy's Fascist leader Benito Mussolini invaded Addis Ababa with chemical weapons and air strikes. The last of Menelik's ruling descendants, Emperor Haile Selassie, sought refuge in Europe. On the way he stopped in Jerusalem and was greeted as a messianic figure in exile. He headed to the elegant nineteenth-century Abyssinian neighbourhood just outside the walls of the Old City. Today, this is where you will find the Debre Genet monastery on Ethiopia Street. At prayer time, it is where you can still hear some of the most ancient religious music in the world.

Ethiopian Orthodox chants date back to the sixth century, and at the heart of these chants is a pentatonic scale system that forms the basis of nearly all Ethiopian music, traditional and modern. The pentatonicism is there in the yearning Amharic folk songs, and it's there in the shoulder-shimmying dance music. It's there in the intoxicating Ethio-jazz that emerged out of Addis Ababa in the 1960s and 1970s. Towards the end of the twentieth century, a French record producer re-released a series of classic Ethiopian albums that caught the ear of the world. There were compilations of slow, bluesy ballads and hot-tempo big-band numbers. The melodies weave around those pentatonic contours, but the music of one particular artist never quite fitted with the rest of the series. *Éthiopiques Volume 21* always struck me as uniquely beguiling. It features stately, featherweight piano pieces that lilt out of any definable time. The playing pivots on an impalpable kind of beat. The touch is intimate, refined, timeless. The pianist spins slow cartwheels, lands on both soles and takes flight again in airy, heat-loosed somersaults. On the cover of the album is a photograph of a nun with an enigmatic smile. Her name is Emahoy Tsegué-Mariam Guèbru, and she is the reason I went to visit the Debre Genet monastery on Ethiopia Street.

Jerusalem in July is dusty, nervy, loud. The tight-wound streets of the Old City are thronged with scooters, American tour groups, traders and soldiers. The place feels hot and intense, a pressure cooker, a fortress. Outside the walls of the Old City, the temperature changes. Step through the gates of Debre Genet and the air is suddenly sweet. The overheated sounds of the city are muted, replaced by the mellow clatter of cooking, cleaning, prayer, birdsong and chants. For the Ethiopian Orthodox community, one of the oldest Christian sects in the world, the gardens around a church are almost as holy as the church building itself.

This monastery is home to a few dozen monks and nuns. The nuns live in a row of extremely modest cells on one side of the compound, each room wide enough for a bed and not much else. After the service that Sunday morning, I ventured into those living quarters. The door to one of the rooms was propped open, and through it I could glimpse a wall covered in Ethiopian flags and photographs of Haile Selassie. Stepping over the threshold, I could see that the rest of the tiny room was crammed with hand-painted portraits of saints and priests. Stacks of old cassette tapes and audio equipment were piled precariously on an upright piano. There was a single bed, and in the bed, propped up on pillows, was Emahoy Tsegué-Mariam Guèbru.

. . .

Emahoy was ninety-three when I met her. She was dressed all in black with a veil wrapped tightly around her face and head. She wasn't well. She was hot and tired. She couldn't easily get out of bed, so our conversations took place in a necessarily intimate way, with me sitting on a stool at her bedside, leaning right in so she could hear what I was saying. Up close like that, I noticed how her eyes look as though they're naturally lined with charcoal and her skin is miraculously free of wrinkles. After a few visits, I plucked up the courage to ask what her secret is, which made her giggle.

We – my producer Peter Meanwell and myself – were making a BBC radio documentary about Emahoy's life and music. We had been told she has a sweet tooth so we brought gifts of ice cream, apricot jam and mangos. She received them happily and shared out the sticky treats, but before she would trust me with an interview proper, she put me through what I could only interpret as a series of character assessments. 'Play for me!' she instructed, her voice small, singsong and a touch imperious. She inclined her head towards the upright piano. On the music stand was a handwritten sheet, her latest composition. No sight-reading test had ever felt more daunting. On this particular page, Emahoy's handwriting was suggestive rather than specific, a flurry of notes written in faint pencil without time signatures or fleshed-out harmonies. I shifted the cassette tapes from the piano stool, sat down and picked my way through the tune with Peter at my back whispering, 'Three flats, Kate, three flats!' Of course my clumsy efforts sounded nothing like Emahoy's aerated, languid lyricism, but after I came to a fumbling finish she seemed satisfied at the attempt. 'Now,' she said. 'Sing for me. A song from your own country.'

Which is how I found myself in a cramped, sweltering bedroom in Jerusalem singing a Robert Burns song about lost love and melancholy. For some reason, 'Ae Fond Kiss' was the first song that came to mind. Outside, I could hear the cheerful chatter of women preparing *injera* for lunch, the clang of Jerusalem traffic in the distance. When I finished the verses, Emahoy let out a little sigh. She admitted that although she speaks eight languages, these particular lyrics were tricky to follow, so I offered a potted translation of the Scots dialect. Lovers meet, lovers part, lovers wonder whether the heartache was worth it in the first place. At that, she gripped my arm and fixed me with an intent gaze I would come to recognise over our several visits. 'We cannot always choose what life brings,' she whispered. 'But we can choose how to respond.'

Emahoy's room needed new light bulbs. There were dirty dishes stacked in the corner. She had CDs that she wanted to listen to, but the CD player sat in cellophane wrap, still needing to be unpacked and plugged in. It all seemed an extremely long way from this woman's upbringing in one of Ethiopia's most noble families. Matching the dignity and freedom of her music to this airless bedroom also felt a stretch. But after a life lived ricocheting from regal glamour to political exile to a decade of barefoot seclusion, she has her reasons for being here.

. . .

She was born Yewubdar Guèbru – Emahoy Tsegué-Mariam is the name she later adopted as a nun – on 12 December 1923. She grew up in Addis Ababa in one of Ethiopia's most privileged diplomatic families. Her mother, Kessaye Yelemtu, was a relative of the Empress Menen (Haile Selassie's wife) and played the Ethiopian harp, or *krar*. Her father, Kintiba Guèbru, was the mayor of the ancient city of Gondar and governor of several provinces. As a politician he travelled widely, including to the United States as part of the first official Ethiopian delegation across the Atlantic in 1919. Kessaye and Kintiba had twelve children, three of whom died as infants.

The Guèbrus believed in educating their daughters. Emahoy and her older sister Senedu were the first Ethiopian girls ever to be sent abroad for education. Eighty-seven years later, Emahoy could still tell me about that journey in detail. She was six; her sister was thirteen. She remembers her parents and siblings all gathering at the railway station in Addis Ababa to send them off. She remembers travelling north-east by train to the port city of Djibouti, and described how she hid her face when she boarded the boat to Marseilles because she didn't want her mother to see her tears. When the ship left the harbour, a fellow passenger distracted little Emahoy by rubbing sea salt onto her cheeks. She remembers not looking back, and the full moon that night shining brightly in a cloudless sky, silver glinting on the waves. She remembers lying beside her sister on the deck of the ship because the cabins were too hot. That particular memory would inspire a piece of music she wrote fifteen years later: *The Song of the Sea*, whose arpeggios trace the contours of a boat rocking on the waves, major-minor chords alternating serenity and trepidation.

Emahoy and Senedu were en route to a boarding school in Switzerland. It was springtime, and when they arrived in Basel there

were blossoms on the trees the likes of which they'd never encountered in Ethiopia. Emahoy was especially delighted by the cherry
blossom. She was by far the youngest in the school and she was
placed under the care of a nun called Sister Magda who helped her
learn how to wash and dress herself. Socially, she was on her own.
She kept herself company with dolls and flowers in the park, and
above all with music. When she was eight, she heard a concert given
by a blind pianist, and it moved her to tears. After the performance,
she wanted to show her appreciation to the pianist by giving him
flowers, but Sister Magda pointed out that it was winter and there
were no flowers to be picked in the park. Instead, Emahoy resolved
to learn to play herself. She started lessons on the violin, and began
making up little tunes on a piano that happened to be in her bedroom. When people asked what she was playing, she would answer
mysteriously: 'The storm.' She gave her first concert after two years.

Emahoy has spent most her life far from home in one way or
another. The musician Nadav Haber, who got to know her well in
Jerusalem, points out that a sense of homesickness permeates the
very grammar of her music. Whenever she writes a piece relating
directly to her family or her homeland, she uses distinctly Ethiopian
scales. *The Song of the Abayi*, for example, is inspired by the Blue
Nile where it tumbles out of Lake Tana in spectacular waterfalls. In
this piece, Emahoy's right hand forms playful, sparkling cascades
in an Ethiopian scale called *tizita* major. In traditional Ethiopian
music, *tizita* is usually used to convey longing – the word literally
means 'yearning' in Amharic. She uses the same yearning scale in a
piece that she titled plainly *Homesickness*. Here, the music toys back
and forth like the gentle strumming of her mother's *krar*.

When Senedu turned eighteen and finished school, it was decided that both sisters would return to Addis Ababa, where Senedu
would go on to set up a school for girls. Emahoy was now twelve

and her musical talent was starting to turn heads. She was sent to an elite Ethiopian boarding school, but life came to an abrupt halt just a year later when Mussolini, his eye on a colonial foothold in East Africa, invaded Ethiopia. Italian Fascist troops attacked from Eritrea and Somalia. Ethiopian soldiers were not equipped to stage much of a counter-attack, many of them armed with spears against Italy's modern artillery. Their desert clothes and sandals left no defence against the blistering poison of Mussolini's mustard gas. Still, it took the Fascist army seven months to get to Addis Ababa. On the way, they tore down the ancient obelisk at Axum, chopped it into five parts and shipped it via Naples to Rome as war booty. The UN ordered Italy to return the obelisk in 1947, but for nearly seventy years it remained in Rome where it was struck by lightning and used as a bargaining chip by various Ethiopian regimes. The obelisk was repatriated in 2005, and at long last reconstructed in Axum as late as 2008.

Haile Selassie fled in 1936. He went to the League of Nations and pleaded his country's cause in an address that became famous for several reasons. One was the fiasco whipped up by the Fascists. Mussolini's henchmen issued Italian journalists with whistles and instructions to deride Selassie on his arrival. A Romanian delegate leapt to his feet and called for the noise-makers to be removed. When the hall was finally calm, Selassie delivered an oration of such impassioned dignity that he became a hero to anti-fascists around the world. The League was broadly sympathetic but its actions were feeble, and Italy simply shrugged off the partial sanctions that were imposed. Some commentators have pinpointed the League's lack of proper response to the Ethiopian invasion as the precise moment it failed in its purpose.

Back in Ethiopia, several of Emahoy's close family members joined the resistance movement known as the Black Lions. Her sister Senedu worked as an informant; she caught pneumonia in the process and was eventually captured by the Italians. Her brother Meshesha was murdered by the Fascists in 1937 at the age of eighteen. Emahoy later wrote a grief-thick lament called *Ballad of the Spirits*. During the years of Italian occupation, the country's important families were forced into exile. The Guèbrus were key political prisoners, and they were sent first to Asinara Island near Sardinia then to Mercogliano near Naples. The family spent three years of tensely quiet political exile in Italy. Emahoy still remembers the strange hush of the place. The sense that time had been suspended. She came across an abandoned organ in a nearby monastery and taught herself how to play it. She got to know some of the locals, who told her she looked like the Black Madonna.

Haile Selassie spent his own years of exile in Bath, Somerset, in a house called Fairfield which he subsequently donated to the city and which is now used as a community centre. When Italy sided with the Germans in 1940, international support for the Ethiopian cause suddenly ramped up and forces from across Free France, Free Belgium and the Commonwealth joined together to reinstate Selassie to power on 5 May 1941. The Guèbru family was repatriated, and Ethiopian society life in Addis Ababa took up where it had left off.

By now, Emahoy spoke multiple languages. Her adolescence had been hijacked by the war and she was old enough to work. Making use of her family connections, she pushed for a job in government and became the first female secretary to work for the Ethiopian foreign ministry. She was adamant, she told me, that men and women should be given equal opportunities, and she talked admiringly about her sisters who founded schools and became doctors and politicians. 'We are', she smiled, 'a family of strong women.' I've seen a handful of photographs of her from this period. I love the strut and stylish confidence of her poses. Her wry smile, her bold sense of fashion. Emahoy moved in aristocratic circles, attending parties where, as she recalled, she would sing for Selassie and his guests. She remembers on one such occasion risking an Italian song – 'L'ombra del mio dolore' (The shadow of my sadness), whose melody she could still hum for me from her bed. She owned a car and raced a horse-and-trap around the city perimeters.

The post-war years were a heady time for the wealthy elite of Addis Ababa, but Emahoy was restless. There were ulterior motives behind her choice of job. She knew that with connections at the foreign ministry she had a better chance of taking off again – specifically, of travelling to pursue her musical studies. After two years she headed to Cairo for lessons with the esteemed Polish violinist Alexander Kontorowicz. Most serious musicians go through at least one period of development that involves practising with near-obsessive intensity. Cairo was that period for Emahoy: she practised for nine hours a day, learning music by Schubert, Mozart, plenty of Chopin, Strauss waltzes, Beethoven's *Pathétique* Sonata. She remembers it as a glorious period in her life. She was still learning the violin, but she focused on piano, she said, because it suited her taste for solitude. Ever since Switzerland, she had been in training to be content on her own. 'I couldn't play the violin alone,' she told me. 'But the piano, I could. I did not need anybody else. It is a *full* instrument.'

Solitude she can handle, but good health has not always been on Emahoy's side. After two years in the Egyptian heat and dust, Cairo's doctors sent her home to recuperate in the high-altitude temperate climate of the Ethiopian capital, which sits at 2,355 metres above sea level. When her body had recovered, Emahoy set her sights on a new destination – this time in more moderate climes. In 1946 she was offered a place at the Royal Academy of Music in London, and her future as a classical concert pianist looked promising.

What happened next remains a mysterious blank, a gaping question mark, which I've pondered repeatedly in the years since sitting with Emahoy in that bedroom in Jerusalem. It is the strange and tantalising hinge point of her story. For reasons she has, she said, never disclosed, and I suspect she never will, the Ethiopian administration refused Emahoy permission to go to London. The decision seems inexplicable. Surely it can't have been a basic bureaucratic glitch. Here was a woman accustomed to having doors opened and ambitions met; she was from a family of wealth and entitlement, with connections to the upper echelons of Ethiopian government and royalty. And yet, in 1946, Emahoy was told by a clerk at the interior ministry in Addis Ababa that she had not been granted a travel visa. She challenged the rejection but it held fast. Was it political? More probably personal? A spurned suitor? A jilted lover – possibly a member of the Emperor's own family? Of course I asked her about it, but the only answer she would give was her cryptic smile and that mantra which she repeated so often during our conversations. *We cannot always choose what life brings, but we can choose how to respond.*

At the time, the rejection nearly killed her. Desolate at seeing her dreams shattered – and for what reason? – Emahoy spiralled into deep depression. For a woman of such immense drive, the loss of agency felt unbearable. She gave up her hopes of becoming a concert pianist. She refused to eat. After twelve days she was hospitalised. She nearly starved herself to death. In hospital she was once more alone. A priest came to her bedside to offer communion and last rites, after which she fell into a deep sleep. That night her life took on a new direction – and this part of the story she was happy to tell. 'I slept for twelve hours,' she recounted. 'When I woke up, I had a peaceful mind. All I wanted to do was go to church and hear church music.'

. . .

A wedding was in full swing on the afternoon of my first visit to the Debre Genet monastery. The courtyard was transformed into a blaze of bright colour, guests dancing to the elliptical rhythms of drums and a choir singing uproarious call and response. Women were flinging their heads back to add descants of high, gleeful ululations while the whole gathering contributed percussion of hands and feet. The rhythms wove against each other in swirling threes-against-twos, sixes-against-fours. It was music that summons and takes hold.

The chants of modern Ethiopian Orthodox music, or *zema*, are attributed to a sixth-century Axumite priest called Yared, who is said to have learned music from the birds. Yared wrote his first hymnal in the ancient Ethiopian liturgical language of *Ge'ez*. In the fifteenth century, the Church developed its own system of notation called *melekket*, which follows a complex series of mnemonics to indicate pitch and rhythm. On celebration days, worshippers decorate their sacred songs with free-wheeling claps and flourishes that predate Yared's formalised hymnal by centuries. Even in devout worship, there is an intuitive, improvisatory looseness to the prayers, which, like Emahoy's piano ornaments, defies notation altogether.

. . .

Everything changed after that visa rejection. Emahoy checked out of her high-society life in the city and turned inward. She became a nun, though that didn't happen immediately. Once she had recovered sufficiently from her hunger strike, she looked again for government work and was given a position in the office of the imperial bodyguard. For a while she lived a sort of double life. By day she wore European clothes and worked in an office. In the late afternoon, she changed into traditional Ethiopian robes and headed for the Medhane Alem church. She didn't sleep much during those transition years, and she didn't play music at all. As her religious devotion intensified, she began to formulate a plan. After two years, she told her family and colleagues that she was taking a short holiday. She packed a small bag and travelled north to the sacred mountain of Gishen.

Gishen Amba is a tremendously holy place for Christian Ethiopians. 'Amba' means a steep-sided, flat-topped mountain plateau – the Ethiopian landscape has many of these formations, sculpted by volcanic rifts – and 'Gishen' is a naturally cross-shaped example. For centuries the mountain was used as a royal prison. Custom was that when a new Ethiopian emperor took the throne, his potential rivals (which included his brothers and even his own sons) would be interned on the mountain until his death. It seems a rather draconian precaution, but 3,000 years of near-unbroken stability was not built on trusting familial relations. Gishen has another claim to fame. It housed the treasures of the Ethiopian empire, including, it has been said, one of the country's most precious artefacts of all. The right-hand prong of the cross on which Jesus was crucified.

The presence of this most sacred piece of wood makes the soil of the mountain almost too holy to touch. When Emahoy joined the small community of nuns and monks who lived in poverty atop the plateau, sleeping on beds made of mud in small huts at an elevation of 3,000 metres, she removed her shoes as though she were entering a church. The way she explained it to me is that she did not

want to disrespect the earth that was so close to Jesus's own blood
by treading on it with shoes. 'At that time,' she said, 'it was finished
for me and music. I left it. I wanted only God and the music of the
Church, that was all. I was very happy on the mountain of Gishen.
It was like being a hermit. I took off my shoes and went barefoot
for ten years. No shoes, no music, just prayer.'

Emahoy had every intention of staying on Gishen until she died,
but her story does not end on the holy mountain. After a decade,
the archbishop passed away and the Gishen community began to
unravel. More pressingly, the soles of Emahoy's own feet needed
medical attention. After ten barefoot years at high altitude, her skin
was seriously cracked. She returned to her family home, where her
father had since died and her mother had herself been ordained as
a nun. The two women were now well matched as housemates.

Re-entry into urban society was gradual, and it happened only
through music. Emahoy had not played piano in the decade since
she left the city, but she found herself gravitating back to the instrument. She also discovered that something fundamental had shifted.
Now she tended to play her own improvisations rather than the
Chopin mazurkas and Beethoven sonatas that had previously been
her staple repertoire. Often she played in the middle of the night,
her mother waking to hear her picking out new melodies at four
o'clock in the morning. It was during this period that Emahoy
wrote a rhapsodic sort-of-waltz called *Mother's Love*. 'Everyone
knows how a mother's love sacrifices itself for the welfare and hap-
piness of her children,' she later added as a dedication. 'Indeed! A
mother's heart is a fortress of love.' She talked to me a lot about the
marvel of children, though she had given up the chance of having
any of her own.

Through these nocturnal meanderings, Emahoy's unique compositional voice started to emerge, and it spoke of all the lives she

had already lived. She wrote music for only herself to play, and sometimes to sing. Her pieces summon the prayerfulness of a nun and the unhurried isolation of a hermit. Her melodies trace the traditional pentatonicism and roaming ornaments of the Ethiopian chants she sang in church. Her delivery distils the virtuosity of her training as a classical pianist. Though it feels a cliché, she used the description herself: her music, she told me, alternates between East and West, simply because her references come from both directions. As José Maceda would come to achieve in his late instrumental works, hers is a multi-lingual amalgam with no hierarchy. In *The Garden of Gethsemane*, she opens by shifting between major and minor chords, then abandons diatonic tonality altogether and takes up the *tizita* minor mode.

She pointed out that she always channelled her feelings through the piano. 'My troubles, my joys, my spirituality.' How could a devout hermitic nun reconcile the act of public performance, which on the surface appears innately extrovert? Her solution was pragmatic. When her sister asked her to provide music for a theatre production at her school, she simply put up a screen to play behind. Certain members of the church didn't approve, but she understood that her music was its own form of worship. It also, she realised, gave her a platform for change. Troubled by the number of children sleeping rough on the streets, she resolved to make an album and donate the proceeds to homelessness charities. Once again she asked permission from Haile Selassie to leave the country so she could make her first record. This time she was granted it.

In 1963, Emahoy travelled to Germany. Her brother-in-law was the Ethiopian ambassador in Bonn and lived close to the house where Beethoven was born. Emahoy was thrilled to be so near to one of her musical heroes, and she later wrote a piece about exactly that called *Homage à Beethoven*. She spent a month in Germany preparing material for the album. When she was ready, she went to a studio in Cologne and sat down at a piano that had once been played by Mozart. The resulting record, *Emahoy Tsegué-Mariam Guèbru spielt eigene Kompositionen*, contains five pieces, from the tender swing of the *The Homeless Wanderer* to the dignified, stoic octaves of *The Last Tears of the Deceased* to the grand sweeping melody and rippling accompaniment of *The Mad Man's Laughter*. She would return to Cologne to record another record in 1972, but by that point the studio had bought a new piano and the connection didn't quite feel the same.

· · ·

Addis Ababa was in its golden age, buzzing with social tolerance and creative expression. With the exception of its brief Italian occupation between 1936 and 1941, the country had defied colonialism for 3,000 years and its cultural life had the swagger of resilient independence. After a failed coup and nascent student movement in 1960, an ageing Haile Selassie had loosened the reins and the city's nightlife was flying. Musically, new sounds were fomenting.

In the 1940s, Selassie had taken a trip to Armenia and been impressed by the pomp and pride of state police bands. Back home, he demanded bands of his own and imported Armenian musicians to train them. Talented players rose through the ranks of those police bands, playing Western instruments and improvising to their own traditional scales. A budding young scientist called Mulatu Astatke had been sent to school in North Wales by his wealthy family who wanted him to study aeronautical engineering. Instead he wound up in the jazz clubs of London and New York, testing out what might happen if he fused Ethiopia's slow cross-rhythms and traditional modal inflections with jazz forms and instrumentation. Emboldened by the models of Miles Davis, John Coltrane and especially Duke Ellington, Astatke became a bandleader himself and returned to Addis in 1969 with vibraphone, electric keyboards and wah-wah pedals in his suitcases. He was met with resistance from some purists who worried about preserving the integrity of the Ethiopian sound, but he also found camaraderie in the intensely expressive saxophonist Getatchew Mekurya and the soulful Amharic singers Mahmoud Ahmed and Alèmayèhu Eshèté. An enterprising young record producer called Amha Eshèté set up a studio in his back room and sent tapes to India for pressing. Ethio-jazz was born.

How much of that energy Emahoy soaked up is unclear to me. It seems she knew and respected Astake and Mekurya. When I mentioned their names she nodded fondly as though remembering valued friends and colleagues. But it would be a stretch to suggest she ever played any regular part in the legendary Addis jazz scene of the 1960s and early 1970s. She never released an album on Eshèté's home label. When the French producer Francis Falceto began re-releasing classic Ethiopian records in the 1990s with his sprawling series *Éthiopiques*, he included Emahoy's self-released Cologne album as his Volume 21. She herself is adamant that she's no jazz or blues musician. Her influences, she stressed to me, come directly from the classical music she studied in Switzerland and Cairo.

Do the labels matter? What Emahoy shares unequivocally with Astatke and Mekurya is that they all pioneered new ways of contextualising Ethiopian traditional music. The latter two turned to jazz forms and Emahoy turned to classical. Beyond that, the genres start to blur. Like José Maceda, Emahoy sought new ways to stretch time, bend place, span continents. To me, her truth-stamped melodies saunter like the blues, flit and meander like an arabesque. The ornaments are filigree, the chords rock gently like folk songs

– almost, but not quite. With Emahoy, nothing is regular. There is no strict metre, no pulse that can be fixed in notation, no adherence to any one scale system. Her music spins on its own axis.

· · ·

The golden age of Addis came to an abrupt end in 1974 when a Marxist-Leninist faction of the Ethiopian Army overthrew the empire and established rule by military junta, triggering a civil war that would last for nearly thirty years. The Derg, as the ruling council was known, imposed a strict curfew on the capital which shut down night life. The country waged war with its neighbours (Eritrea, Somalia) and pursued ruinous economic policies that caused devastation when famine struck in the 1980s. 1.2 million people starved and hundreds of thousands of Ethiopians became refugees, resulting in a new global diaspora. At home, artists were jailed and dissidents were executed. Many musicians fled the country.

Emahoy and her mother remained in Addis and sought inner exile with the Ethiopian community in Jerusalem. After some initial to-ing and fro-ing between Israel and Ethiopia, Emahoy settled in Jerusalem for good after her mother died in 1983, and she has not returned to her homeland since. She put her eight languages to use, becoming the first woman to work as a translator for the Patriarch of the Ethiopian Orthodox Tewahedo Church.

Only after twenty years did she move a piano into her room at Debre Genet. The church elders were confused by her playing, given the Patriarch does not accept organ or piano as part of church worship. They were unsure why a nun would want to release apparently non-religious albums under her own name, with her own photograph on the cover. 'I think they still don't understand it,'

Emahoy smiled, a mischievous sparkle in her eye. Whether they do or not, these days the little shop at the gates of the monastery stocks copies of her CDs.

. . .

A couple of years before I met Emahoy, she published her compositions. She enlisted the help of two musicians based in Tel Aviv – the fiery vocal improviser and multi-instrumentalist Maya Dunietz and the conductor, improviser and voracious musical polyglot Ilan Volkov. Emahoy wanted them to help her find a form of digital notation that could capture the unpindownable weft of her playing as closely as possible. She handed over a plastic bag filled with loose manuscript pages and they set to work.

Dunietz and Volkov had some tough decisions to make. Ruth Crawford had to balance accuracy and accessibility in her American folk transcriptions, trying to capture the nuances of real, fluid voices without straitjacketing them or making the notation too complex to read. Likewise, Dunietz and Volkov tried to retain the loose spirit of Emahoy's playing while recognising that no notation could really begin to capture her intangible lilt. The results, printed in a handsome volume comprising a dozen piano works, have made it possible for other pianists to wrap their fingers around her unique musical dreamscapes.

Now there is another urgency. Emahoy wants to share more of her music. She talked to me about her intention to release a new album, pointing at the cassettes and reel-to-reel tapes piled high on her piano. Tantalisingly, some of those tapes contain songs that she recorded in multiple languages in the late 1960s and that have never been released. She looked overwhelmed at the prospect of digitising the material, let alone negotiating record contracts from her bed. But it was clear that she wants the world to hear those songs.

Emahoy told me she never wished to be famous, that she wanted her name to be written in heaven, not on earth. She admitted that the connection people feel to her music does mean a great deal to her. 'Maybe I am like Tchaikovsky,' she said with a sad smile. 'He didn't believe in his music either. But people like it.' Before I left her bedside for the last time, she reached out for my hand. She didn't have a lot of strength but something about that grip was unconquerable. Go through life being strong, she ordered me. Don't be told no. Fight for equality. Those were her parting words.

Else Marie Pade

(1924–2016)

**Denmark's electronic music pioneer:
truth, trauma and fairy tales**

As a teenager, Else Marie Pade was thrown in jail for blowing up telephone boxes. This was during the Second World War and Pade was working for the Danish resistance. In her prison cell, she etched a tune onto the wall. She was punished for that, too, but she never forgot the snatch of melody which came to her during her internment, and she later turned it into one of her debut songs.

Sound was Pade's first and last, her sharpest sense. As a child in the 1920s she was frequently bed-bound with various illnesses, and she experienced the world via the noises that filtered through her window. When she was sent to an internment camp, she stayed sane by focusing her mind on the music she would write when she was free. And when she was free, Pade became Denmark's pioneer of electronic music. She worked as a producer at the Danish Broadcasting Corporation, and there she created some of the twentieth century's most daring and psychologically penetrating electronic works. She scored soundtracks for the darkest children's stories, crafting serrated voices for brutalised mermaids out of sine tones and warped recordings. She chopped up bits of archive radio to make symphonies of urban noise. She transformed pure electronics into shimmering nocturnal constellations.

What sets Pade apart doesn't have much to do with the technologies she used. Innovators around the globe were simultaneously landing on methods of *musique concrète* and electronic music. For Pade, the mechanics of tape machines and sound generators were never the point – in fact, she could hardly work the studio equipment. She wasn't allowed to, because she was never trained as a sound engineer. She had to rely on male colleagues to take care of that side of things. No: what set her apart was how vividly she imagined. How she used new methods to manifest the music that was in her mind. How carefully she listened, how candidly she rummaged around in her own visions and memories, and how many of those visions and memories she was prepared to share with us. Virginia Woolf wrote of being in touch with the thing itself, the 'atom', and not with the outer husk. That is what Pade's music does, tapping the innermost carnal and fantastic. Her sounds take on an indomitable life force, and the dark truths of her work leave her, and us, unmasked. She offers complete abandon. Nothing is held back. Despite the bleak demons that lingered in the recesses of her mind, Pade's music exudes a blithe enthralment that such sounds are even possible.

. . .

Making music was an act so internal, so natural and essential, that Pade claimed she could trace the instinct back to when she was three months old. She was born Else Marie Haffner Jensen on 2 December 1924 in the city of Aarhus on the east coast of Denmark's Jutland peninsula. Her father worked as a make-up salesman. As a child she was often ill, stuck in bed with a painful kidney condition called pyelonephritis. Intermittent bronchitis also added to her suffering. Her mother sang to soothe her, which worked well until she happened to land in a minor key. Pade would later remember the song 'Det er hvidt herude' (It is white out here) as one particular offender. When she heard it, little Else Marie started screaming. Her mother was intrigued and tried again, switching between major and minor, minor and major. Apparently the child cried every time the key darkened and smiled when it brightened. So the family story went.

Poor health lasted into her teens, as did the prolonged periods stuck inside. Like Robert Louis Stevenson confined to bed and compensating with a rollicking imagination, Pade began to fixate on the sounds that seeped into her bedroom from the rest of the house and from the world outside. She savoured every noise. She embellished their meanings in her mind. Her day began, she remembered, with 'sponges splashing and dripping in the washstand; the kettle whistling; the birds, also whistling if the rain wasn't pouring down; different footsteps, friendly words'. She began to categorise the sounds as music. She heard chords and cross-rhythms in the footsteps of passers-by on the street, Marstrandsgade, and in the cluck of a neighbour's chickens laying her eggs, and in the raindrops on the windowpane changing pace according to the season.

Later, she would describe it:

I learned very quickly that some of the sounds came at a particular time of the day in a particular order – every day. I also learned that during the day the sun could make the birds sing, while the moon could not make the stars say anything, although it looked as though they would like to. They twinkled. All that could be heard at night was bird calls and the moaning of the wind, cats miaowing and the sirens of ambulances now and then. So then I decided to give the stars some sounds of their own. I formed tiny little tingly sounds with my lips, and the Man in the Moon, whom I firmly thought I could see, laughed back at me – a deep, friendly laughter.

Reality fused with fiction in her imagination. The radio was a constant companion, and she internalised the voices of the presenters to the extent they started to narrate the fairy tales that played out

in her mind. This being Denmark, those fairy tales were not usually very comforting. Mermaids with severed tails and no voices.
Match-girls freezing to death on the street. Shards of glass working
their way into the hearts of boys and girls. Pade felt their fear. She
cried over *The Snow Queen*, *The Travelling Companion*, *The Red Shoes*.
'These and many other fairy-tale characters became my friends,'
she said. 'What they saw, I saw; what they heard, I heard; where
they went, I went too . . .'

Her mother taught her to love opera and books. Her father
brought her jigsaw puzzles and card games. Best of all was a game
involving a dimpled glass board and bright-coloured marbles that
could be arranged in intricate patterns. Pade had synaesthesia, that
neurological gift of cross-sensory association whereby harmonies
might take on colours and shapes might taste this way or that. When
she thought of constellations in the night sky, she heard voices.
When she saw the glass beads, she heard harmonies. 'I thought
they were saying something, these shiny marbles – or rather, that
they were singing. But what?'

Pade's kidney condition was cured when she was thirteen, and
she enjoyed a couple of vivacious teenage years. Her parents paid
for piano lessons with an inspirational teacher called Karen Brieg.
She got a job at the local library and met a lad who played in a band.
She bought jazz records and taught herself to play stride, New
Orleans-style. She joined a jazz quartet called The Four, which
later expanded into a six-piece called The Blue Star Band. They
played at school dances and youth clubs. Her parents despaired: all
those costly piano lessons, for stride?

She became politicised on 9 April 1940. She could pinpoint the
moment exactly: it was the day that Germany invaded Denmark,
Nazi tanks rolling across the flatlands to gain a staging post en
route to Norway. Pade was fifteen years old. 'It gave rise to a

righteous indignation in me that went beyond all bounds,' she said. 'I considered it incredibly cowardly that a giant country occupied a tiny little country that had done no one any harm.' She took to the streets. She spat at German soldiers and they chased her. She escaped by jumping on a tram and fleeing to the house of her piano teacher, who scolded her for being so careless. If you intend being a rebel, Brieg told her, at least do it properly. There is no glory in spitting. Brieg invited her to join an all-female resistance group under the leadership of an explosives expert called Hedda Lundh. And that is how Pade came to specialise in blowing up telephone boxes using sticks of dynamite.

An informant infiltrated the group. Names were turned in. Associated male resistance fighters were sent to concentration camps in Germany. On 13 September 1944, Pade, now aged nineteen, was arrested along with several other members of Lundh's group and locked up in a Gestapo prison in Aarhus. To conceal her family identity, she gave a false name: Wagner. She was interrogated and beaten until unconscious. When she woke up back in her cell, she heard noises she later described as the elves and trolls of her fairy tales arriving to keep her company.

What also came to mind during her time in the cell was a tune. Just a simple little thing, a line or two, but she took a clasp from her garter belt and etched four bars into the wall of her cell. Those four bars would become the opening of a song called 'Du og jeg og stjernerne' (You, me and the stars). It is a loping schlager, a pop song set to her own lyrics with a sweet-sour twist.

The day that went away, the night that's black
The prisoner's cloak of loneliness, the star that's soft,
the angel that's white, the voice close to my ears.

There's nothing inherently remarkable about those four bars, nor particularly about the pop song they became. What is remarkable is Pade's need to write them down, and what happened next when the vandalism was discovered. Pade would live and relive the moment aurally, the same way she had experienced much of her life. 'A sound collage of shouting and screaming, the tramping of boots, the rattling of chains, the slamming of doors and the ominous jingle of keys . . .'

She was punished for the vandalism of the cell, of course, but one of the Gestapo guards acted with secret kindness. He brought her pen, manuscript paper and cake. 'Ich bin ja auch Musiker,' the guard explained (I am also a musician). He told her that she reminded him of the daughter he had lost back in Hamburg. Pade described the arrival of the parcel: 'I stared at the label almost in a trance: in war and peace, compassion.'

She was eventually sent to an internment camp called Frøslev, a place run by the Danish state in an attempt to appease the Nazis and prevent Danes from being deported to concentration camps. Approximately 12,000 prisoners were held in Frøslev between 1944 and the end of German occupation in 1945. Most of the prisoners were suspected communists, homosexuals or resistance activists. Some were not saved, but sent south and never seen again. The conditions at Frøslev were not the worst. Detainees were fed. Garbled news filtered in. Pade's mother would write in code, offering cryptic updates on the Danish resistance movement. Pade later discovered that her father had travelled 175 kilometres from Aarhus to visit her, but had been sent back at the gates.

There was plenty of camaraderie among her fellow prisoners in the women's block H17. Her piano teacher Karen Brieg was there, and together they organised performances. They staged *A Midsummer Night's Dream*. Brieg arranged music for three-part choir and Pade composed songs and notated them on her manuscript paper. She gave them names like 'The Sailor, the Girl and the Little Cat', which would become a minor hit when it was released as a single after the war. On her twentieth birthday, the women of H17 clubbed together to set up a modest collection so that Pade could study music when the war was over. They asked how she was able to keep her mood so positive. 'Because', she replied, 'I am not really here. I'm in the future, writing music.'

· · ·

Else Marie met Henning Pade when they were both detainees in Frøslev. They married after the war in October 1946. And, true to her twentieth birthday promise, she did enrol as a piano student at the Royal Danish Academy of Music, but the Academy did not allow its students to be married, so she kept the relationship a secret and registered as Pade's housemaid. They had two sons, Morton and Mikkel, while Henning Pade rose through the ranks of the Danish Broadcasting Corporation (DR) to become head of programmes and Else Marie was hired as junior employee.

There is a tart irony in the fact that Pade was forced to masquerade as a housemaid: domestic work was never one of her fortes. 'Her sons were embarrassed,' I'm told by her biographer, Andrea Bak, whom I meet one bleach-blue-skied summer afternoon in Copenhagen.

> She didn't really care what they looked like. How they dressed. One son remembered how his underpants were often cut longer than his shorts so they would poke out the bottom. They were teased at school. It wasn't easy for them. They wanted someone who took care of them like a normal mother.

That said, it was a popular home for others kids because they were allowed to jump on the sofa.

She was an excellent pianist, but Pade did not enjoy performing. She suffered blackouts on stage. Instead, she wanted to compose, to pursue her interior worlds of sound, and she took private lessons with three figures of the Danish music establishment: Vagn Holmboe, Jan Maegaard and Leif Kayser. Tensions rose between her family life and her work. One teacher told her she had to choose between 'earth and heaven', which in a sense she did: heaven took it, the celestial sound of stars and merfolk. Interviewers in the 1950s took oblique digs at her. What about your sons? journalists asked. Are they getting fed every day? The newspaper *Aarhus Stiftstidende* demanded to know: 'How does art unite with the kitchen?' to which Pade replied that she did sometimes burn the potatoes. One interviewer concluded that he wouldn't want to taste her meatballs given what her music sounded like.

· · ·

To understand the backdrop of Else Marie Pade's music, I took a trip to the funfair. Specifically to a place called Dyrehavsbakken, or Bakken, which is the world's oldest amusement park. It is located in the woods north of Copenhagen, where natural springs were discovered in the year 1583. Crowds soon came for the waters, and entertainers soon came for the crowds. Over the centuries the trees were cleared and ghost trains and dodgems were built. Now there is a 5D cinema and stalls selling huge pitchers of Tuborg beer and bright red hot dogs. Pade lived close to Bakken in the 1950s and she loved the sensorial mashup of the place. She soaked up what she called its 'variegated, joyous and distinctive sound world', wandering the jangle of roller coasters and cabarets that made her think of the market scenes in Stravinsky's raucous ballet *Petrushka*.

In 1952, she heard a programme on Danish radio about the French composer Pierre Schaeffer and his emerging methods of alchemising daily life into compositional ingredients through *musique concrète*. 'Sound', as Schaeffer put it, 'is the vocabulary of nature.' The idea made obvious sense to Pade. She had been mentally shaping the sonic world around her into soundtracks for as long as she could remember.

On one particular visit to Bakken in 1953, her mind still ablaze after that encounter with Pierre Schaeffer on the radio the previous year, Pade was struck by the idea of making a film about the amusement park. The film would have an experimental soundtrack through which she could herself test out these *musique concrète* tape methods: cutting, splicing, bending. She pitched her notion to the newfangled television department of Denmark's state broadcaster and was given the go-ahead.

In the summer of 1954, she was told to meet with the technicians at the red gate in front of Dyrehavsbakken for the first day of recording. 'The big OB wagon came driving, full of people,' she later recalled, 'and I waved to them, but they did not stop. They just waved and drove on.' Pade looked very young. She was twenty-nine years old at the time but could pass for half that. She was small. She seemed girlish all her life. 'They had never in their wildest imagination thought that the little girl at the gate was the person they had to work with all summer. I ran up to them and we got to introduce ourselves to each other and smiled a little at the misunderstanding.' The story reminds me of working as a newspaper music critic in my early twenties, and the number of times an audience member would shake his head as I took my seat. 'Excuse me,' he would invariably say. 'That seat is reserved for the critic.'

Pade forged ahead, armed with cameras and camera crew, sound equipment and engineers to operate it. She set about making *En dag på Dyrehavsbakken* (A Day at Dyrehavsbakken) – a half-hour film that is, in essence, about a trip to the funfair. She and her team recorded through the summer and again early the following season. Sound must come first, she insisted, and visuals after, which was an unusual and audacious demand from someone who had never worked in television. They spent the winter months editing, speeding audio up and slowing it down, trying out how the recordings might sound if they were played higher or lower or back to front.

En dag på Dyrehavsbakken is no documentary. It's a darkly impish triumph of sight-sound dissonance, a glory of uncanny disconnect. Pade goes rogue. We see a carousel full of clowns and harlequins but we don't hear them. The sight of disembodied cabaret legs waggling above a doorway becomes doubly macabre when Pade scores it with a crying baby. Roller coasters dip and dive to delayed echoes of screams. People fall about on the moving floor of a funhouse, faces twisted in panic, to the sound of air-raid sirens. In a scene in the kitchens, cauliflowers are chopped, steaks sliced and lobsters plattered to a vocal drone, distorted and looped. A fat man swigs beer to the sound of jeering crowds. A gun fires but we hear no shot. A tin falls but we hear only cackling. When a clown closes the gates at the end of the day, we hear dejected mumbling. Pade laces every scene with jarring, macabre subtext – a deft experiment in sound play. She made *En dag på Dyrehavsbakken* at the dawn of the television age, and the work is a stroke of inter-sensorial trickery.

Sixty-five years later, I wandered the funfair at Bakken one cloudless late August afternoon. The plan had been to come here with Jacob Kirkegaard, an electronic music producer who worked closely with Pade at the end of her life and who suggested we team up and make a new Bakken montage in her honour. Early on the morning of our visit, Jacob texted me to say he'd woken up with a sore throat, so I went alone to Bakken and recorded a series of sounds that I later sent to him. Somehow the solitary trip felt apt, not unlike my solo pilgrimage to see Ustvolskaya's birch trees in Pavlovsk. This was Pade's equivalent, a variegated, joyous sound world. I gravitated to the corners of the funfair, or wherever I found especially extreme squeals and screams. I lingered by a pendulum ride that was shaped like a giant purple gyrating octopus and blasting out 'I Want It That Way' by the Backstreet Boys. I thought about how *En dah på Dyrehavsbakken* captures the weird menace of the place, that wilful abandon on the edge of fear. There is something wildly reckless about a funfair being open during a pandemic. Maybe there was something similarly perverse and perilous about Pade's generation voluntarily scaring themselves to oblivion within a decade of war. And that's entirely it: that's the searing disjunct that Pade clinches in her music.

• • •

Hans Christian Andersen is a complicated national icon. It's fair to say he was not quite the chaste man-boy that many history books would have us believe. Born poor in 1805, Denmark's most celebrated bard has traditionally been cast as purer than pure, whiter than snow, and it's true he never married or, apparently, had sex, although he would visit prostitutes in Paris if only to chat with them. He was probably bisexual, and he blurred gender norms in his stories by inventing adventuresome female characters and handsome princes with flaws and sensitive sides. A vein of stark social commentary runs through his work, making heroes of paupers and fools of haughty princes. Andersen published his stories under the title of plain *Fairy Tales*, soon abandoning the label 'for children' because he recognised that his savage, truth-studded fables belong to everyone.

Some of the tales – for example *Skyggen* (The Shadow), a proto-Jungian allegory in which a man's shadow enslaves and eventually executes him – are so dark that few parents would risk reading them at their own bedtime, let alone their children's. Maybe the most troubling of all is *Den lille Havfrue* (The Little Mermaid), first published in 1837. Torture, self-harm and deep existential melancholy hang over Andersen's tale of the mermaid who makes an ill-fated deal with a sea witch. The mermaid agrees to have her tongue cut out and her tail sliced into a pair of flimsy legs, all for the love of a human prince who hardly even notices her when she does get up on land. As a child, Else Marie Pade felt the mermaid's pain as though it were her own.

In 1955, the Danish Broadcasting Corporation asked Pade to score a new recording of six Andersen fairy tales, and she knew immediately what kind of tragic glimmer she needed to summon. She knew, she noted, exactly how to conjure the 'dwarfs and the giants, the dancing flowers and the quivering leaves of gold and silver trees'. And the darker stuff. When it came to making the soundtrack for *The Little Mermaid*, she knew she had to cut straight to the brutal heart of it. She wanted deep-scarred sounds that communicated dislocation and yearning, exile and butchered beauty.

In technical terms she divvied up the soundtrack into passages of *musique concrète* and pure electronics – a blended methodology that bypassed the ideological factions of the wider new music world at the time. Paris had Schaeffer's school of *musique concrète* (music made of manipulated recordings of acoustic events) and Cologne had Karlheinz Stockhausen's laboratory for *elektronische Musik* (music made entirely by synthetic means). But Pade was a

free agent. As Alejandro Madrid pointed out about composers of
the periphery having a certain freedom, as a woman operating in
isolation on the fringes of northern Europe, Pade was an outsider.
She was free to choose. Why not make use of both tactics? The
amalgam would later take off in Japan and America, in Russia,
Poland and elsewhere. At the same time, methodology cocktails
were being brewed by Bruno Maderna and Luciano Berio at their
Studio di Fonologia Musicale in Milan. But it was still a rare and
audacious blend.

To represent the mermaid's desired human world, Pade chopped
up fragments of archive radio. A drinking song from *The Tales of
Hoffmann*, a thirteenth-century Italian song, a snippet of Stravinsky's
Petrushka. She mixed in recordings of laughter and church bells.
For the underwater realm, she used rudimentary tape techniques
– reverberation, delay, loops – to make bubbles and gurgles, eerie
chords that seem to float in the drift. She experimented for eight
months to get the right sounds. Trying to summon a thunderstorm,
she noted her experiments in her diary: 'Production of lightning is
attempted: Paper tear, crunch from pick up. Ends up shorting the
microphone and making a tape loop of the sound.'

The hardest thing to get right was the mutilated voice of the
mermaid. For that she wanted a combination of the noble-voiced
soprano Elisabeth Schwarzkopf and the jagged edge of a saw. No
such sound existed in any archive recording, so she made her way
through the stately DR building to an upstairs room labelled
Lab. III. There she introduced herself to the station's top technician – a gentle-tempered sound engineer called Holger Lauridsen,
himself an important innovator in stereo microphone technology. After listening carefully to her request, Lauridsen stood up,
switched on an oscillator, twiddled some knobs – and 'NOW',
Pade would remember, 'the mermaid sang as mermaids should.'

The resulting sound is exquisitely sad. It is an eerie voice, human and not human, infused with doomed beauty. Pade filed it in the archives of DR under H for *havfruesang*: 'mermaid song'.

. . .

Here's a list of the technical equipment in Lab. III of the Danish Broadcasting Corporation, formerly Statsradiofonien, in 1955:

Modulated sweep generator with web modulator
Sawteeth wave and square wave generators
White noise generators
Frequency or speed generator
Pulse generator
Cross modulator
Ring modulator with feedback
Octave and one-third-of-an-octave filters
Filter used in radio plays for the distortion
    of human voices, etc.
Reverberation machines
Reverberation plate
Reverberation chamber
Reverberation spring
One- or two-track tape recorders
Record player

. . .

When James Joyce's *Ulysses* was first published in Danish in 1949, Pade read the novel in three days flat. The carousel of characters, the devious tangents, the twitches and yo-yoing registers between grot and grace – Joyce's tactics made a lot of sense to her. She, too, wove her own experiences in between the sonic contours of a city (her Copenhagen to Joyce's Dublin). She, too, transgressed lines between public and private, elegant and crass, real and half fantasised. Like Joyce, she tells it all with emotional truth and wit. Like Joyce, she lets us all the way in, uncomfortably far in.

The novelist Ali Smith describes Joyce's lexical Dublin symphony as 'making an epic forever out of a single passing ordinary day'. Using chopped-up bits of radio archives and various recordings of her own, that is exactly what Pade does in her *Symphonie magnétophonique* of 1958. The work is a daring jolt of sound collage distilling twenty-four hours in the Danish capital into a capricious twenty-minute tone poem. It is an aural romp around the city, a mischievous, frightening, bleary and lionhearted portrait of a day in a life. Copenhagen provides the cool and swaggering centrepiece of this movie for the ears. We are given a backstreet walking tour in sound, a postcard in noise.

The piece opens in a dream. It sounds almost blissful, maybe a bit heartsore. In the distance we can hear bells ringing at the town hall. An alarm clock yanks us into the bright morning. Yawning in harmony. Brushing in semiquavers. Rinsing, spitting, vocal warm-ups in the shower, the screech of a boiling kettle. Coffee slurped, door slammed, feet hammering down stairs. The street outside is noisy with trains, trams and bicycle bells. The office clatters with typewriters and phone calls. There are crows in the park at lunchtime, a barrel organ and a mangled news bulletin. Afternoon shopping is followed by tea, kids in the playground, rush-hour traffic. Evening restaurants to the soundtrack of calypso records and fireworks at Tivoli Gardens (the second oldest funfair in the world, after Bakken). Then comes darkness, and now the world doesn't feel quite so friendly. We hear flashbacks of bombs, soldiers, sirens, screams. At last the breath slows and the heart beats. We can feel a breeze, the song of a lark, and around we go again.

Edgard Varèse did something not dissimilar when he infiltrated an orchestra with sirens and foghorns in his trailblazing *Amériques*. Audiences hated the piece when it premiered in 1926, Leopold Stokowski conducting the Philadelphia Orchestra at Carnegie Hall. There were boos and catcalls. Critics declared it a riot, which was exactly the point, because modern life felt like a riot and Varèse made it his business to embrace that, saying his goal was to 'blow wide open the musical world and let in sound – all sound'. *Symphonie magnétophonique* bypasses the orchestra altogether and goes straight to the source.

What grabs me most about Pade's masterful sound collage is not the recording mechanics: that had been done before, not least in Cairo by Halim El-Dabh when he borrowed equipment from the Middle East Radio station and recorded women at an ancient religious ceremony, then manipulated the sounds to create his breakthrough 1944 tape work *The Expression of Zaar*. It was the first piece of *musique concrète*, predating Schaeffer by four years and Pade by a decade. What is most extraordinary about *Symphonie magnétophonique* is its intimacy. There is, extremely palpably, a protagonist at the heart of this urban thrum. The brusher of teeth, the singer in the shower. She who takes us by the hand and shows us her daily haunts and wounded memories. She who brings us so close to her beating heart and slowing breath that we start to wonder if they might be our own. Where *Amériques* turned floodlights on the brazen cacophony of New York, and *The Expression of Zaar* prised open a collective ritual in forensic detail, *Symphonie magnétophonique* personalises the story. The subject is not really Copenhagen at all but a woman who lives her troubled, open-eared life there. Like Ustvolskaya, Pade holds nothing back in her musical reportage. Both confront us with their own brutal fragility, and so insist that we consider our own.

· · ·

In 1958, Pade set out for Brussels with three colleagues from the Danish Broadcasting Corporation: Erik Schack and Mogens Andersen from the music department and Sven Drehn-Knudsen of technicals. They were on their way to the world fair, Expo 58, for a scandal-hit bumper edition during which:

a) someone vandalised the original manuscript of Mozart's Requiem, ripping off the corner where Mozart supposedly wrote his last ever words
b) the Soviet Union blamed the Americans for stealing a facsimile of Sputnik
c) the host nation's planning committee somehow thought it appropriate to stage a human zoo as part of their Belgian Congo pavilion, importing actual people to pose as 'primitives' in a *village indigène*
d) the Mexican ambassador pulled strings to find a proper platform for Julián Carrillo's fifteen metamorphoser pianos

Else Marie, Erik, Mogens and Sven made their own routes around the exhibitions. At the famous Philips Pavilion they heard Luciano Berio's *Omaggio a Joyce* and Varèse's *Poème électronique* diffused through hundreds of loudspeakers that had been specially installed by the architect Le Corbusier and the composer/architect Iannis Xenakis. Pade met Pierre Boulez and Karlheinz Stockhausen and struck up a lasting friendship with the latter. What thrilled her most during her visit was the planetarium, where she could lie back and listen to music played through surround-sound speakers. As she gazed up at the twinkling cosmos, she felt as though there must be a speaker hiding behind every star. When she was a child she had already worked out the chatter of the constellations. Once again, it felt to her as though the material world was only just catching up with her imagination.

Back home in Copenhagen, Pade drew seven circles on a sheet of graph paper. Each circle is studded with a constellation of seven notes. This is the score. The notes are played in order, on loop. After the first circle's notes have been heard once through, the second circle is sounded, but twice as fast. The third circle is twice as fast again – and so on, circles layering up, together forming patterns that strobe and flicker. The music lands as it takes off, one by one the circles starting to fade until the sky is dark again. Pade called the piece *Syv cirkler* (Seven Circles), and said she wanted the music to move like the stars. Mysterious and clear-sighted, meticulous and – as ever – very personal, *Syv cirkler* was Denmark's first piece of purely electronic music.

· · ·

When she finished it, Pade put *Syv cirkler* in the post to a planetarium in San Francisco where the prankish sound artist Henry Jacobs was staging multimedia shows in his Vortex 'theatre of the future'. She also submitted the piece for broadcast in a series called *Music in the Atomic Age* – a sequence of experimental programmes inspired by Expo 58. Pade was part of the organising group, and they programmed music by Schaeffer, Boulez, Stockhausen, Nono, Cage, Xenakis, Kagel, Takemitsu and Berio. She herself contributed three of her own breakthrough works: *Syv cirkler*, *Symphonie magnétophonique* and all forty-two minutes of

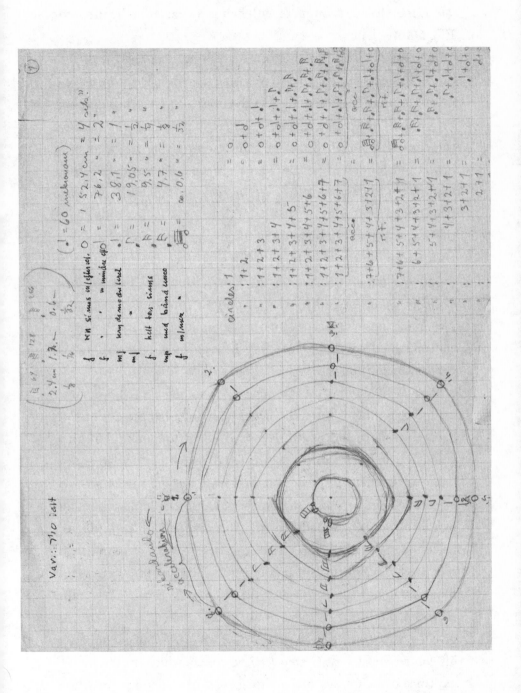

The Little Mermaid complete with haunting narration by the actor
Ellen Gottschalch.

It was a landmark moment in Danish musical history, though
not all listeners felt inclined to welcome this so-called atomic age if
it was going to feel anything like the noises coming through their
radio sets. The series triggered 'a deluge of phone calls', Pade later
remembered. 'Panel discussions, reviewers giving it the thumbs
down and hordes of people who aired opinions exhibiting their
literary understanding of *The Emperor's New Clothes*.' Knudåge
Riisager, composer and at that point director of Pade's alma mater,
the Royal Danish Academy of Music, responded to *Seven Circles*
with particular outrage. In a scathing critique he wrote that he
found it *nauseating*, claiming the work made him feel *physically
uncomfortable*. Worse: there was, he posited, something *dangerous* at
play in the music's mechanism, which reminded him, he wrote with
alarming tactlessness, of Hitler's speeches during the war. Remember *Hoy Mismo* and the scandal of the suicidal fish.

Pade never did find much camaraderie among her fellow Danish
composers, though she did with certain sound engineers at DR.
Several of the technicians recognised her vision and did all they
could to help her realise it. She treated them with respect in return,
knowing that her voice relied on their craft. But she missed a broader creative circle. When she got back from that mind-expanding
trip to Brussels, she and the sound engineer Holger Lauridsen
co-founded a study group called Aspekt with the aim of making a
safe space to discuss avant-garde ideas. They hosted experimental
film screenings and absurdist theatre productions. They talked about the future of radio drama. Pade invited Stockhausen to
give a presentation to the group – which he did, bringing along
his controversial mass *Gesang der Jünglinge* in which the disembodied voice of a choirboy melts into an aura of sine tones, the whole

of sacred musical history dissolving into Stockhausen's new *elektronische* mantra. Above all, Stockhausen endeared himself to the Danes by complimenting their studio, pretending that it matched the facilities of his famous WDR headquarters in Cologne.

It seems that Pade always had lukewarm feelings about her home country and its default cultural conservatism. DR never fully supported a radiophonic workshop, though Pade was given permission to experiment after work hours. Her position away from the European centres of tape music and electronic experimentation allowed her to sidestep doctrine and make her own composites, but the biographer Andrea Bak told me how Pade once described Denmark as 'a small place for the mind' and encouraged Bak to move to New York to 'set her mind free'. Pade herself took off to the Darmstadt Summer Course and stayed in close touch with Stockhausen even as his star rose until it orbited the earth. In 1991, he sent her an improbably cute Christmas card with hand-drawn musical staves arranged in the shape of a Christmas tree. 'To lovely Else Marie Pade,' he wrote, drawing a heart in place of the word 'lovely', 'with electronic sympathies.'

· · ·

The Pades' marriage broke down in 1960. Henrik Marstal, a musician and prominent Danish columnist who has written a detailed book about Pade's work, surmises that the relationship didn't last partly because of what he describes as 'a mismatch' in domestic expectations. 'Henning came from a rich part of the city; Else Marie couldn't or wouldn't keep a neat house,' Marstal told me. 'She had a hard time remembering to cook. Instead she composed, threw parties and had love affairs, apparently with her teacher Vagn Holmboe and later possibly with Stockhausen, although this assumption is based on pure conjecture. She was living like a bohemian, and that didn't exactly match the expectations of an upstanding Copenhagen housewife at the time.' Two years after the divorce, both sons were sent to boarding school.

Accounts of Pade from those who really knew her paint a portrait of an introverted and acutely imaginative person, someone of rare perception whose mind operated at a remove from prosaic matters like potatoes left frying on the stove. In company she could be nervous and reticent, with a loud and sudden laugh. An operation for throat cancer in the 1970s left her with a strangely small, squeaky voice. She often wore yellow. Andrea Bak describes her as

> a very unusual person, very light. Different from anyone else I've known. She would make connections I didn't understand because of her synaesthesia. She was very intuitive about other people. She would never judge a person on what they said, but on how they looked her in the eye. I think she was clairvoyant. Her son described her as an alien.

. . .

Das Glasperlenspiel (The Glass Bead Game) is the final novel by the German writer Herman Hesse. It was published in Switzerland in 1943 after Hesse was denounced in Germany for being anti-fascist. The novel is a chronicle of a better future. Hesse imagines the year 2400 and an educational institute working to salvage decent values from the wreckage of the twentieth century. The 'glass bead game' itself is a sort of intellectual ceremony, like an intricate form of chess or Tetris, a Smetakian utopia that interlocks all human knowledge and nature into some sort of glowing universal harmony. (Hesse had taken a shine to Theosophy in the early 1900s.) Let us overlook the fact that in the story this notional game leads to fatal consequences, and that its masters are all men: Pade loved the novel, particularly the interweaving of music and philosophy, sciences and arts. As a synaesthetic child, she had blurred street sounds with her interior narratives of fairy tales and radio plays. With her own glass bead game, the one her father gave her when she was sick in bed, she had a universe of intricate patterns and associated harmonies literally on a plate. 'When my sonic experiments began to cohere and become compositions,' she reflected, 'I was struck by the second déjà vu of my life: it was the tone colours of the glass beads of my childhood game that were emitted by the speakers. My mental sound picture had become reality.'

The year Else Marie divorced Henning, 1960, she returned to that favourite childhood game. Inspired by Hesse, she wrote *Glasperlespil I* and *II*, a pair of works that are mercurial, gentle, mystical, spacious. There are twelve notes. Each one has its own sound quality – some piercing, some wan, some aquatic, some hollow, some gong-like. Think of them as individual marbles, and think of the music unfolding as though differently coloured marbles are being shifted into patterns, one by one, row by row, until the glass plate has been filled up. 'Serialism' is the term for music constructed out of a pre-determined series of notes. It earned a reputation for emotional frigidity thanks to some of its dogmatic early headliners. Varèse, never a fan, called total serialism a 'hardening of the arteries' and considered it 'a great tragedy that Schoenberg, having freed music from tonality, subsequently sought refuge in a system'. But Pade's *Glasperlespil* is serialism at its most bewitchingly celestial. It spins us into her fantastical orbit, her intuition that each colour has its own secret voice. Stockhausen understood the wonder of it. In lectures he would use *Glasperlespil* as an exemplar of how downright kaleidoscopic electronic serialism could be, in the right hands.

So much of Pade's music has to do with stars or fairy tales or colours. *Lyd og lys* (Sound and Light) is a work from 1960 in which she imagines a note hurtling through space like a comet. She described it, rather magically, as a 'ballet for searchlights and speakers'. Her viscerally demonic score for a school radio play of Goethe's *Faust* (1962) is thirty-one minutes of ghostly palimpsest. Multiple worlds are conjured by piling up very high frequencies on top of very low ones. There are astral leitmotifs for the lovers and – a stroke of sublimely emasculating subversion – a warped recording of a whining poodle for Mephistopheles. The witches flying to their annual gathering at Brocken are depicted with almighty stereo swooshes panning from hard left to hard right. As for the love scene: all is suddenly tender, soft blankets of mid-range pulsations and whispered commentary. The gorgeous huskiness of the analogue oscillators adds to the sense of eroticism. This is electric romance, blissfully dilated and unhurried.

In fact, that unabashed sensuality is present throughout Pade's works. It's there in the dreamscapes of *Symphonie magnétophonique*. There in the damaged ecstatic of *The Little Mermaid*. There in a 1964 television ballet called *Græsstrået* (Blades of Grass), scored for percussion, prepared piano, violin and electronics. Pade herself played the prepared piano part of the recording, which was televised in 1965 on Nordvision with dancers from the Royal Danish Ballet. The narrative follows a blade of grass waking up and gambolling around in a bacchanalian celebration of the joys of nature. Birds, mosquitoes and butterflies join the dance. If it all sounds suspiciously pastoral, just wait. This is no skip through a spring meadow. Pade treats the instruments electroacoustically with emphatically abrasive effects; nature is savage and threatening, laced with biting teeth. In a classic stroke of Pade sorcery, she saves the pure electronics for the love dance, a fleeting Elysian *pas de deux* under the stars.

· · ·

In 1970, Pade created her final masterpiece. *Se det i øjnene* (Face It) is the last in a set of four works called *Fire radiodigte*, eight minutes long and brutally cathartic. In a very fragmented way it sets a ferocious political poem by Orla Bundgård Povlsen read by the actor Peter Steen, featuring the constantly repeated line: 'Hitler is not dead.' Pade scores the words to an implacable marching drum. Chillingly, we hear distorted recordings of Hitler's own voice, snippets of the dictator blurted out in rapid fire. Pade loops the sounds relentlessly. She stares down her demons. As the poem breaks apart and eventually stalls on the word 'Hitler', the dictator's own voice begins to gather force. She gives the last word to the crowd, turning the gaze on us all.

Around the same time she wrote *Se det i øjnene*, Else Marie Pade suffered a form of breakdown. She could not sleep at night. Triggered by television images of the Vietnam War, she experienced palpitations and feelings of panic. She spoke to a psychologist and was told that she was experiencing a post-traumatic condition called 'concentration camp syndrome', which had begun surfacing in many survivors of the Second World War.

There was a common attitude in Denmark after the German occupation, Henrik Marstal tells me. 'Keep a lid on it. Let it be. Don't mention it.' He is referring to what he says is Denmark's collective approach to dealing with trauma. 'Maybe', he continues, 'it isn't considered dignified to admit that things are painful. In the 1970s, there hadn't been a lot of reconciliation here in Denmark.' Pade's son Morten told Marstal that he could not remember a single time during his childhood that his parents – who had both been detainees at Frøslev – had ever talked about their experiences of the war.

Pade's psychologist told her she should resign from her job at the radio, which eventually she did in 1976. She moved into a form of sheltered accommodation and converted to Catholicism, attracted by its doctrines and mysteries. She lived a secluded life. She wrote a handful of pieces devoted to Mary, scored for voice and electronics. In the final decades of the twentieth century, she produced only a small number of works, including a church play called *Syv billedsange om Teresa af Avila* (Seven Picture Songs about Teresa of Avila) in 1980 and *Efterklange* (Reverberation) *I*, *II* and *III* for percussion (1984). She wrote prose and poetry, sometimes under the pseudonym Christian Sand; she wrote religious texts and librettos. In 2008, she completed a songbook, *Pas på os*, subtitled 'A picture book of prayer and meditation – for children of all ages.'

. . .

Henrik Marstal 'rediscovered' Pade at the beginning of the twenty-first century, together with the musicologist Ingeborg Okkels. Marstal is careful to put air quotation marks around the word 'rediscovered' when he says it. We are talking in his garden in a small town outside Copenhagen. He and his family moved here from the city only a fortnight earlier and there isn't yet much furniture in the house, so we sit outside at a picnic table in the sun, drinking coffee and eating cinnamon pastries, Marstal balancing an uproarious infant on his arm while recounting the chronology of his meetings with Pade.

In 2001, he was working on a book about the history of electronic music and he happened to meet Pade's granddaughter at a
dinner party. The encounter led to an interview published in *Dansk
Musik Tidsskrift* (Danish Music Review), which led to an article,
which led to a radio documentary, which led to re-releases and
remixes of Pade's music. She developed a niche but enthusiastic
following. A select number of younger-generation electronica and
avant-garde musicians seized hold of her story: they considered her
a lost icon, this 'sweet old lady with a funny little voice', as Marstal
mocks the stereotypes. Articles hailed her as the 'grandmother' of
electronic music or, in the words of a 2003 headline in the Danish
tabloid *Ekstra Bladet*, 'Technogranny'. The music producer Thomas Knak, a prominent Danish artist who has worked with Björk, felt
that a forgotten heritage had been excavated. 'Turns out', Knak said
in 2002, 'she is the grandmother of all of us electronic musicians.
But it's kind of funny, because none of us knew until recently that
we actually had a grandmother.'

Marstal isn't surprised by the way Pade has been typecast. He
suggests Danish electronic musicians want to invest in her because
she lends a certain heft and credibility to what they do. 'Things
had started happening in the electronica sound world during the
1990s,' he argues. 'It started to be taken seriously – artists like
Underworld or Aphex Twin were considered "serious" artists by
the mainstream. So people like Daphne Oram, Éliane Radigue,
Else Marie Pade – they came in handy as outsider intellectual ori-
ginators of the genre.'

He points out that Denmark is the country that adopted Hans
Christian Andersen's story of the ugly duckling as integral to its
national psyche. 'That is the story everyone wants to hear all the
time,' he shakes his head. 'How we have such a hard life but our
inner goodness will shine through in the end.' The story of Pade,

with her sick childhood and her role in the resistance, then her years of near silence only to be 'rediscovered' in old age – 'It's so good', he says, 'that people who never even intended to listen to her works still wanted a piece of the saga.'

Marstal himself has listened deeply to Pade's works, and he considers many of them to be a form of *Trauermusik*. Funeral music. 'She had a lot of humour,' he says, 'and there is a lot of humour in the music. But the deep trauma underpins it all.'

Pade died on 18 January 2016 at the age of ninety-one, dementia having occupied her marvellous mind towards the end. Her funeral took place in Sankt Andreas Kirke in Ordrup, north of Copenhagen, on a bitterly cold winter afternoon. The wake was at a nearby Chinese restaurant. Over coffee and spring rolls, someone had the questionable idea of playing Pade's recordings as background music. When *Se det i øjnene* came on, an office worker ran down from the estate agency upstairs. He complained they could hear the music through the floorboards and had mistaken the repetitions for techno.

Earlier that day, during the funeral itself, Pade's son Morten sang some of the songs his mother had written in Frøslev. When the microphone suddenly stopped working in the middle of the liturgy and strange noises started emerging from the church's speaker system, many in the congregation glanced at each other in wonder. 'It sounded like someone had taken the microphone and thrown it in an aquarium,' says Andrea Bak. She smiles at the memory. 'We all thought: that's her! She's waving to us from heaven.' Marstal refers to the incident as Pade's last gesture of electronic wizardry. It was as though only then, in that moment, days after her death, did she finally wave her farewell and hang up her boots as a musical illusionist.

Pade's story is about an artist dealing with damage by turning to sound for solace. It is about an innovative mind harnessing new music technology for reportage and release, to tell the most frightening fairy tales, to pray. Her music was resistance. She wouldn't be contained by existing sonic parameters. Like all the women in this book, she would not be restricted to making the kind of sounds that women were supposed to make. Her memories flecked with deep wartime trauma, she turned the role of composer into documentarian, conjuror and confessor. Her experiences ring true for so many of her generation, and she speaks them in a troubled and truthful voice. That's why we need to hear what she has to say.

Across the Atlantic: another composer who made music as an act of resistance. But while Else Marie Pade turned inward to express the grief and the glory, Muhal Richard Abrams threw the doors open wide.

Muhal Richard Abrams

(1930–2017)

**Tradition wide as all outdoors:
an awakening on Chicago's South Side**

It's the opening event of New York's Composers Now Festival in 2017, and Muhal Richard Abrams is invited to the stage. He wears a brown velvet jacket and brown trousers. He ambles his way to the piano but doesn't sit down. Instead, he ducks behind the instrument, circles it and inspects a recording device that is pointing inside the lid. 'Just a moment,' he tells the audience, no hint of hurry. He is eighty-six years old. He will die later the same year. He looks at his watch and makes his way back to the keyboard where he finally takes a seat. He inspects his watch again then strikes a low note with unceremonious and exacting conviction. Eyes closed, he listens to the note decay, checks his watch yet again, then sets off.

What unfolds is an improvised piece called *Four+*. Abrams plays with his head bowed, his body still, only his shoulders occasionally lifting a little while his hands stalk the keys. The lines come in spurts, the articulation jerky and decisive. He lingers in the bottom octave and erupts upward. His fingers clamber around the keyboard as though speed-scaling a cliff face. He keeps returning to that bass note. That kernel. The pianist Jason Moran, who studied with Abrams, has described how his teacher would encourage him to *go all the way* with an idea. If you start a gesture, why stop? Follow it. Pursue it. See where total commitment will take you.

Those late Abrams performances could be trance-inducing. They could last close to an hour. On this particular occasion he keeps it to a brief eleven minutes, but still he magics up what feels like a complete rocky massif from that single starting note. For all his methodology – and he had fierce methodology – there was always a spirit of grand, rugged adventure about his playing. 'He was a basket of curiosity,' is how one of his lifelong friends puts it to me. 'A basket of curiosity.'

Abrams wrote fearsomely exploratory orchestral works, chamber works, electronic and piano works. He released dozens of solo and ensemble albums as a pianist and bandleader. His phrasing tends to have a lurching gait and his melodies are often all elbows, giving a sharp angularity to his sound. You might notice I've been avoiding the word 'jazz'. That's because he did. Abrams could definitely play hard bebop and blues when he wanted to, with a sense of swing that was tart, tight and jolting. He also wrote music that sits within the classical lineage – a lineage that encompasses his fellow African-American composers Olly Wilson and Hale Smith just as much as it does Chopin, Rachmaninov and Scriabin.

What is shared between all the work that Abrams made is the way he would take an idea – sometimes it was just one single note, sometimes an unlikely little pattern – and *go all the way* with it. In that regard he shared the total commitment of Galina Ustvolskaya, though his ethos was as intensely communitarian as hers was solitary. But yes: he would follow an idea, nurture it, coax it out or, if necessary, hunt down its core potential. And it had to be original. 'No licks,' he would tell his band members. That was one of his only creative dictums. No clichés, no hackneyed defaults, no smart-arsery. 'I don't want anyone playing no licks.'

. . .

'He was not – how would you put it – he was not one of those *huggy* people.' This is Leonard Jones, telling me about the first time he met Abrams. The year was 1964, and Jones, then a young bass player recently discharged from the US Army, showed up at a Monday night music session on the South Side of Chicago.

In the early days, the Experimental Band met at the C&C Lounge (owners: Chuck and Claudia). Later the meetings moved to a chunky red-brick social-services centre – the first building designed by Frank Lloyd Wright. The rolling line-up of musicians included some of the most creative minds ever to come out of the Midwest, out of anywhere, and on other nights of the week you could find the same players headlining jazz clubs and blues bars across the country. But this particular Monday configuration never performed or made any commercial recordings. They met for themselves.

Jones remembers walking into the rehearsal room and having no clue what was going on. Eight or ten musicians were earnestly discussing matters of harmonic structure and motivic development. He recalls being introduced to the band's leader: a lean, serious-seeming man called Richard Abrams ('Muhal' was the one-name moniker by which he would come to be known, but that was later). Abrams was thirty-four at the time, Jones thirteen years younger. The two men soberly shook hands. Not the huggy type. After a few rehearsals, Abrams invited Jones back to his apartment which, Jones quickly discovered, was a gateway into new modes of thinking.

Abrams and his wife Peggy lived in a tiny basement flat on South Evans just off Cottage Grove Avenue, the epicentre of the explosively creative South Side neighbourhood. The rooms were painted purple and crammed with books, scores and musicians. There were always musicians at Peggy and Muhal's. Saxophonist Roscoe Mitchell, ten years younger than Abrams, had been brought into the fold by drummer Jack DeJohnette, who would call round regularly after high school for informal music theory lessons. Saxophonist Joseph Jarman, who later joined Mitchell in the Art Ensemble of Chicago, has described Abrams's enthusiasm for painting, astrology, herbology, and all manner of music. 'It was like I had found a teacher,' Jarman said.

Jones soon became a regular. He eyes me quizzically as he describes the scene. 'You know horehound?' he asks, leaning on the word with a slow stress. I do not. 'This extremely bitter herb. Muhal would brew it up and we would sit there in his kitchen sipping horehound and discussing everything. All kinds of ideas evolved.'

At the time, none of these musicians – not Abrams, not Mitchell, Jarman, DeJohnette or Jones – had access to a formal experimental music studio. There were no courses in jazz, improvised or electronic music in the United States in the early 1960s. With the Experimental Band, Abrams and his peers effectively organised their own Monday night laboratory where they tested out, tried out, ventured new sounds in front of no audience at all. Each week the musicians would bring along new compositions, stand in front of the rest of the band and explain the ideas behind their work. If certain members couldn't read the dots, they developed alternative notation so that everyone could understand. Even if someone didn't think he was a composer, in the Experimental Band he soon became one.

The Monday night workshops grew directly into the Association for the Advancement of Creative Musicians, and the AACM – officially founded in 1965 by artists who just happened to live in the same neighbourhood – grew into one of the most significant collectives in musical history. The AACM's Chicago South Side vanguard wanted to take charge of their own music. They wanted control of how they made it, what it sounded like, where they played it, how they labelled it. They refused to allow their expressive selves to be limited by racial stereotypes, refused to be told that a black musician holding a saxophone could exist within only one stylistic genre called 'jazz'. The AACM challenged the policing of borders between jazz and classical music, its members defying reductive racial attitudes around style and form, instrumentation and reference. For doing so, they were often dismissed from all sides. Too black to be classical, too avant-garde to be black. They kept making their genre-confounding music anyway.

For the members of the Experimental Band, composition was a radical statement. Which is to say: it wasn't just the music they were making that was radical – though it was very – but the fundamental process, the act of composing. Writing challenging music was a defiant gesture. An equaliser, an assertion of the right to choose one's mode of expression. Creating the particular sorts of far-out sounds they did was a racial leveller. On Monday nights, this group of pathfinders sidestepped the exclusivity of genre simply by equipping themselves with the technical tools to get stuck in.

There was a wild, paradoxical synergy that existed between this bunch of intensely headstrong personalities who came together to ensure that they could all be themselves. And the man at the heart of them all – the man who started nothing less than a movement – refused to play the guru. If someone wanted to be in Muhal's band, the thing he had to contribute above all was himself.

. . .

The twentieth century had plenty of new-music gurus. Iconoclasts. They founded schools and institutions, studios, venues, festivals, ensembles and theoretical methods. These men – and they were always men – had magnetic charisma, supercharged gravitas and orbiting devotees. We can name them, the likes of Schoenberg, Boulez, Schaeffer, Cage, Britten, Cardew, Glass. Some of them, the Stockhausens and Sun Ras, evangelised cosmic spiritualities, diets and dress codes. Their mark on musical history has been indelible. Their stories have been told and retold.

Muhal Richard Abrams made his mark in profound and expansive ways, and he too had all the ingredients to play guru had he wanted. The quiet authority, the occult spirituality, the herbal tea. He had a school, a devotion to a dense pedagogical treatise, a commanding gift for rhetoric. He practised yoga and vegetarianism in Chicago in the 1960s and he taught himself to interpret star signs and tarot cards. He investigated astrology, numerology, the secretive mystic sects of Rosicrucianism. 'Everyone wanted to talk to him,' says George Lewis, the Chicago-born trombonist, composer and academic who has written a monumental authoritative history of the AACM. 'You're sitting in his house, and Muhal's phone is always ringing. People wanting advice, ideas, whatever.' The trumpeter-composer Taylor Ho Bynum describes meeting Abrams in later life, how the older musician would come backstage at gigs and offer fellow musicians 'some kind of benediction'. By the end, Bynum grins, 'He had a total sage vibe.'

Intrepid composition already had a foothold in the Midwest. There was Ruth Crawford, her mind opened when she moved to Chicago in the early 1920s and discovered Scriabin and Theosophy via the bohemian gatherings hosted by her piano teacher Djane Lavoie-Herz. There was Florence Price, who had left her home state of Arkansas in the late 1920s when racist attacks, including regular lynchings, made daily life impossible. Price settled in Chicago where her First Symphony, premiered in 1933 under the open-eared conductor Frederick Stock, was the first work by an African-American woman to be played by any major orchestra.

There was Herman Poole Blount, aka Le Sony'r Ra, aka Sun Ra, who flew the spaceways into Chicago in 1946. He claimed to have been the first black man in space, reaching orbit before any rocket ships did; while out there he had, he said, experienced an extra-terrestrial happening in which aliens from Saturn told him how urgently us earthlings needed his music. Sun Ra produced hundreds of uncategorisable records testing everything from early synthe-sisers to cosmic big-band improvisation. He was a blazing futurist who was rooted, like Abrams, in jazz – but there was a key differ-ence between them. If you were in Sun Ra's band, his Arkestra, you submitted head, heart and aura to Sun Ra's vision. Abrams insisted on the opposite. He was an exacting leader, a searching composer, a ferociously fine pianist in his way, an investigator of alternative spiritualities. But he refused to act the grand master. 'It wasn't like being in some groups,' Lewis chuckles, 'where you had to at least try to be mystical if you wanted to be in the band . . .'

It's an intriguing contradiction, this preaching of emphatically autonomous thought. But that's exactly the ethos that produced some of the most progressive musicians in modern America. Roscoe Mitchell, Amina Claudine Myers, Anthony Braxton, Joseph Jarman, Henry Threadgill, George Lewis, Wadada Leo Smith, Nicole Mitchell – the list of AACM associates heaves with indi-viduality. It is an anti-hierarchy, an antithesis to the conventional orchestral set-up that positions conductor as god, principal leaders as his messenger and rank-and-file as his flock. According to Jack DeJohnette, 'Muhal was the inspiration' – because 'he helped us to be ourselves.'

. . .

Richard Abrams's mother, Edna, was from Tennessee. His father, Milton, was from Alabama. Edna and Milton were among the mil-lions of African Americans who turned their backs on the former confederate states in hope of finding work and equality in the industrial north. They brought with them truth-soaked songs from the sun-baked south. 'While segregation created the blues,' writes Mike Rowe in his survey of Chicago's iconic blues sound, 'migration spread the message.'

By the 1930s, the South Side of Chicago was an almost exclusively black neighbourhood, so much so that the tight grid of streets around Cottage Grove Avenue was nicknamed Bronzeville. Saxophonist Henry Threadgill remembers Bronzeville being 'ablaze' with culture. It was the cross-section of immigrant communities all across Chicago that really opened his ears, he says: Polish, Italian, German, Irish, Appalachian, Serbian, all tastes catered for by local radio stations. For others, it was the concentration of various walks of black society that made Bronzeville so vibrant. According to the bassist Malachi Favors, the neighbourhood had 'the greatest entertainment section in the world'.

Richard Lewis Abrams was born in Bronzeville on 19 September 1930, the second of nine siblings. He was a tough kid, lithe and streetwise, watchful and quick. He was good at sports. His first school was a place called Forrestville, which if nothing else taught him how official narratives could easily wipe out an entire people. 'Forrestville was a standard public school,' Abrams told George Lewis, 'based on white history. There was no mention of black people in history at all, not even George Washington Carver. You studied about Columbus, Amerigo Vespucci. They had the music of Gluck and people like that.' Abrams got kicked out of Forrestville for truancy and fighting and was sent to a reform institute where the kids were even tougher but at least the black teachers taught a version of history that included themselves. At home, Edna Abrams demonstrated the power of self-education, fostering in her son a love of painting, cinema and literature. Every week she would take herself off for piano lessons at the YMCA with young Richard in tow to keep him out of trouble.

Abrams could not escape music. It was there on every street corner in Bronzeville, through every window left ajar. On hot summer nights, the jazz clubs of 43rd Street would throw open their doors and Abrams, still too young to venture inside, would linger on the threshold. He eavesdropped a musical education via Dinah Washington, Nat King Cole, Muddy Waters, Howlin' Wolf, Sun Ra and his Arkestra. Chicago was the crossroads of America. Everyone who toured the country came through town, and every black artist who came through town played in those bars on the South Side.

By sixteen, Abrams had caught the bug irreversibly. He worked a job in a printing company uptown to save enough money to buy himself a piano. He taught himself how to tune it, and enlisted lessons from a piano-playing woman he knew from church. He enrolled at the Metropolitan School of Music, but for the most part he learned on the job: blues clubs, church socials, stage shows. His most regular apprenticeship took place at all hours of the night and day at the Cotton Club, where there were fast and furious bebop sessions every night and into the small hours. Later in life, there was one particular story that Abrams liked to tell about a teacher at the Metropolitan School. This teacher knew that young Abrams was already turning heads at the Cotton Club. Looking to glean intel from his talented student while retaining his own status, the teacher invented a scenario about a 'friend' who didn't know the chord changes to the jazz standard *April in Paris*. How would Abrams play it, the teacher asked? Abrams quit school soon after, and put his faith in mentors on the scene.

The earliest known recording of Abrams dates from when he was in his late twenties: a 1957 album with the band MJT+3 featuring trumpeter Paul Serrano. On a three-minute track called *No Name*, co-written with the pianist Walter 'King' Fleming, the Abrams sound is already unmistakable. Those tangy chords, that angular strut. The way his introduction holds the tension for eight po-faced bars then, when the tune finally breaks out, how the left hand adds biting chromatics while the right hand strikes like a cobra. Abrams always played like this, with poise and stylish proportion. He always rode his flair so that it felt on the edge of exploding.

. . .

The astrophysicist Neil deGrasse Tyson has joked that the good thing about science is that it's true, whether you believe in it or not. Abrams subscribed to the scientific rigour of music, but he wanted the expressive stuff, too. 'We are dealing with something that is intuitive *and* scientific,' he said, in reference to what he believed to be the essence of musical composition. 'It's a combination of both.'

Among the towering early influences on Abrams was a firebrand Ukrainian-born polymath called Joseph Moiseyevich Schillinger (1895–1943). Mention that name to a room of music graduates nowadays and next to nobody will know who you're talking about, but in the first half of the twentieth century, a compositional methodology called the Schillinger System opened many an American musical mind. Schillinger – a composer, theorist, teacher, inventor, anti-establishment rogue thinker – taught Benny Goodman, George Gershwin, Glenn Miller. In the early 1930s he worked with the inventor Leon Theremin and the composer Henry Cowell on promoting the first ever drum machine, the audacious Rhythmicon, which had the power to summon various complicated rhythms all at once. Schillinger thought of music as pure process. He suspected that technology would eventually replace human performers, and for a while his theories were extremely popular – he even had a school named after him, the Schillinger House School of Music in Boston, until his legacy there fell out of favour and the institution rebranded itself as Berklee.

Schillinger could be a grouchy iconoclast. He was prone to heckling at lectures. He had little patience for the orthodox music canon, calling Beethoven 'crude', Chopin a 'failed contrapuntalist', Bach the nadir of 'so-called European classical music'. He enjoyed humiliating respected academics by making them guess who had written a certain work and then revealing that the work had in fact been written by him using his system. What I find particularly interesting is how he proposed an antidote to the myth of genius. Forget any romantic image of a high-brow composer seized by inspiration, music pouring out of him as if through divine alchemic intervention. Schillinger advocated methodical planning, geometrics and preordained modular building blocks (think Lego), which, if selected wisely, should produce logical rhythms and narratives. He thought of his scientific approach to art production as *engineering*.

B. B. King was a devotee, as was Charles Stepney, who was a house arranger at Chicago's Chess Records and worked for Muddy Waters and Earth, Wind & Fire. It was Stepney who introduced Abrams to the Schillinger System in 1957. Abrams had recently dropped out of music class and was looking for a theoretical framework through which to develop his writing. He was gripped by this idea of a rigorous methodology, which, Schillinger argued, could be learned by anyone and applied to any music. The idea was that whatever material the composer chose, no matter how humble, it could generate more material. The composer Earle Brown was a convert, impressed by Schillinger's reach not only across musical genres but across artistic disciplines. The system could apply to visual arts, cinema, literature, dance, to electronic as well as acoustic music. For Brown, it went right into contemporary multimedia. That interdisciplinary scope appealed to Abrams, too, as he was already a painter and soon to be an explorer of electronic music.

Schillinger's complete theory manual was published posthumously in 1946 as two gigantic volumes under the title *The Schillinger System of Musical Composition* (SSMC). There were sceptics, of course. Some decried this tutorial for advocating mechanical modes of reproduction: where was the soul, wherefore the future of artistic genius? But Abrams was enthralled by its promise of permission. He bought himself a copy of the hefty SSMC, all 1,640 pages, and studied it faithfully. According to George Lewis, 'Everywhere he went over the next four years, Abrams kept those two massive tomes at the ready.'

The key thing about the Schillinger System is that it worked as an equaliser. It gave Abrams a science to prove that composition belonged to anyone who was prepared to learn the techniques and apply them – to prove that there was no innate right, no inherited gift and therefore no inherited exclusion. For the composer Henry Cowell, the Schillinger System offered possibilities. 'A positive approach to the theory of musical composition [. . .],' he wrote, 'instead of the rules hedged round with prohibitions, limitation and exceptions.' The societal parallels resound.

What Abrams learned in those books would remain at the heart of how he composed, played and taught for the rest of his life. The drummer and composer John Hollenbeck – who references Abrams as a major influence – emails me with a memory of his first encounter with Abrams at the Banff Centre for Arts and Creativity in the Rocky Mountains of Canada. The year was 1988. 'The big moment that changed my life was this lecture that Muhal gave,' Hollenbeck recalls.

It was mostly based on a small dot that he drew on the
board. He asked EVERYBODY what that dot was until he
got the answer he was looking for: that dot was or could be
anything . . . and that dot was or could be the beginning of a
piece. The point being that you can start writing a piece with
ANYTHING and you only need that ONE thing to start and
complete a piece!!! This compositional philosophy opened
up my idea of composition forever and that is why I speak of
Muhal every time I give a lecture or workshop on composition.
This has been my main mode of composition ever since!

One bewitching example of that lasting effect on Hollenbeck is
his tribute to Abrams, a beautiful work for eighteen-piece ensemble
titled *R.A.M.* It begins not with one dot but with five. A simple little
theme, just the outline of a major triad, which various instruments
join and develop to make an elastic tangle. They twist and stretch
and enmesh, then explode into something between swing and earth
shout. The piece reminds me of a wonderful George Lewis phrase
describing the AACM as an 'unstable polyphony of voices'.

. . .

The Black Power movement gathered force through the early
years of the 1960s. Its activists called for decisive solidarity and
self-sufficiency. They believed equality was going to take a lot more
than polite integration tactics. On 21 February 1965, Malcolm X
was assassinated as he prepared to address the Organization of
Afro-American Unity in Manhattan's Audubon Ballroom. Three
months later, the AACM was founded around the kitchen tables of
Chicago's South Side. George Lewis has written about the initial
meetings in engrossing, often minute-to-minute detail.

Abrams, [Jodie] Christian, [Philip] Cohran and [Steve] McCall
sent postcards to the cream of Chicago's African-American
musicians, announcing a meeting to be held on May 8, 1965,
at Cohran's South Side home on East 75th Street near Cottage
Grove Avenue. Abrams recorded this and subsequent meetings
on his Sony portable reel-to-reel recorder, and the discussions
on the tape made it clear that the aim of the meeting was the
formation of a new organisation for musicians.

Lewis stresses how the act of organisation was itself an act of
resistance, a straight-up rebuff to 'the conventional wisdom that
casts improvisation in general, and the products of black music in
particular, as both lacking in structure and insensitive to historical
or formal concerns.' Abrams chaired the first meeting according to
an agenda laid out on those postcards, and like the conscientious
bandleader he was, he made sure all voices present had a chance
to be heard. There were dissenting opinions. There were spats. Of
course there were: this was a gathering of fiery-willed individuals,
and over time there were walkouts, fallouts, resignations. 'Don't
make the early years of the AACM into a utopian garden of Eden,'
Taylor Ho Bynum warns me. 'There were a lot of very brilliant,
occasionally very ornery people. That's what made Muhal's role
all the more important. To be able to bring together a community
with so many strong personalities and aesthetics, and to understand that all of their work would become stronger by playing
together.'

By the end of May 1965, the new collective had given itself a
name. Abrams, keen on numerology, was especially pleased that
the initials AACM resolved on nine ($1+1+3+13=18$; $1+8=9$), which
in numerological terms is the top possible result. 'That's a high
vibration to live up to,' he mused.

Was the AACM open to black members only? The matter was raised at one of the early general meetings. Some musicians argued for colour-blind membership. Others argued the opposite. Abrams notably spoke up, explaining his support for a black-only organisation in a tone that Lewis likens to that of a revivalist preacher. Three years later, *DownBeat* magazine asked Abrams directly whether the AACM had anything to do with Black Power. 'Yes,' came his reply. 'It does in the sense that we intend to take over our own destinies, to be our own agents, and to play our own music.'

By August, the AACM had agreed a nine-point charter.

To cultivate young musicians and to create music of a high artistic level for the general public through the presentation of programs designed to magnify the importance of creative music.

To create an atmosphere conducive to artistic endeavors for the artistically inclined by maintaining a workshop for the express purpose of bringing talented musicians together.

To conduct a free training program for young aspirant musicians.

To contribute financially to the programs of the Abraham Lincoln Center, 700 E. Oakwood Blvd., Chicago, Il., and other charitable organizations.

To provide a source of employment for worthy creative musicians.

To set an example of high moral standards for musicians and to uplift the public image of creative musicians.

To increase mutual respect between creative artists and musical tradesmen (booking agents, managers, promoters and instrument manufacturers, etc.).

To uphold the tradition of cultured musicians handed down from the past.

To stimulate spiritual growth in creative artists through recitals, concerts, etc., through participation in programs.

Note that at the heart of the AACM mantra is *composition* – or, as it's written in the first point of the charter, 'creative music'. There were long debates about what that meant, exactly, and some members felt peeved that players might not be taken as seriously as writers. 'No one's excluded,' Abrams assured them. 'You may not be Duke Ellington, but you got some kind of ideas, and now is the time to put 'em in. Wake yourself up. This is an awakening we're trying to bring about.'

The point was this: the AACM was composing itself into a historical narrative. By placing written music at the core of its manifesto, its members were forcing their voices to be heard and held within the lineage of avant-garde composition. As Lewis puts it to me, 'What you're trying to do is open up a space where you exist. Really it's your right to exist that's at stake.' In 1967, a group of artists including Jeff Donaldson emblazoned Chicago's Wall of Respect with African-American heroes. Donaldson would later write in his AfriCOBRA Manifesto: 'It is our hope that intelligent definition of the past and perceptive identification in the present will project nation-full direction in the future – look for us there, because that's where we're at.'

The year 1967 saw the AACM officially open its South Side school, with Roscoe Mitchell as the first dean. In preparation, Abrams instigated a rigorous training regime for all the would-be teachers. They gathered on Wednesday afternoons and went through theory exercises together. When the school opened, it taught the Schillinger System at ten o'clock on Saturday mornings.

There, leading a classroom of ten-year-olds, was Leroy Jenkins with his violin. There was Lester Bowie with his trumpet, teaching a brass class. There was Anthony Braxton going through the basics of harmony, Amina Claudine Myers training voices, Roscoe Mitchell marshalling the woodwind. And Abrams introducing students to the art of making music out of the most humble ingredients. AACM performances might encompass face paints, masks, dance, theatre, spoken word, free improvisation and sprawling ensemble compositions. Some critics were scandalised by what they lamented as the 'death of chord structures', because AACM performances didn't tend to involve many standard chord changes.

This was also the year that Abrams adopted the name Muhal, adjusting his given identity to associate more with black culture. And in the same way 'AACM' was charged with numerological energy, his choice of new name had a particular significance.

$$M = (13; 1+3=) 4, U = 3, H = 8, A = 1, L = (12; 1+2=) 3$$
$$4 + 3 + 8 + 1 + 3 = 19$$
$$1 + 9 = 10$$
$$1 + 0 = 1$$

Number one. The pioneer, the eternal beginner.

A year later, Abrams released *Levels and Degrees of Light*, his first record as a bandleader. On the cover was his own painting: a desert landscape, a red-limbed woman carrying a Venus symbol, a patchwork staircase descending into the earth through a gateway of Rosicrucian hieroglyphs. 'Muhal Richard Abrams, the name commands respect,' the sleeve note declared. 'He is wise beyond his years.' The recordings were done in two sessions flat, one day in July and another in December. *My Thoughts Are My Future* is a foreboding incantation followed by a yowling duet between saxophonist Anthony Braxton and drummer Thurman Barker. *The Bird Song* is an expanse of cosmic spoken word (poet David Moore) and long immersive minutes of spacey harmonics led by Leroy Jenkins on violin. The galactic strings meld with birdsong – an early trick of studio production, Abrams already using subtle electronics to fuse his music with the natural world. The album's title track opens with a wordless vocalise sung by Penelope Taylor over washes of cymbals. Then in comes Abrams, not on piano but with a wailing lament on clarinet. He was not a brilliant clarinettist, but that wasn't the point. Inherent in this multi-instrumentalism is the idea that learning is never done, that music is always a work in progress. Abrams strove for excellence his whole life, but he never lost touch with what it was to be a beginner. In the liner notes he typically refused to explain his music, but he did offer this: 'What is here is what we are and what we hope to be.'

. . .

Abrams began exploring electronics properly in 1972. He signed up to study at the new Governors State University, which had founded a jazz course in the suburbs of Chicago. Richard McCreary, a composer who eventually became a Pentecostal minister, kitted out a studio with a new ARP 2500 – as it happens, Éliane Radigue's modular synthesiser of choice – and Abrams taught himself the newfangled computer programming as it developed: BASIC, Forth, Max. Technology creeps into his recordings in ways that are sometimes subtle, other times front of stage. Take the psychedelic twang of *Think All, Focus One* – a 'technology-laden sonic uncanny valley', as the pianist and Abrams scholar Marc Hannaford describes it. Hannaford points to the way that Abrams plays man off machine in this piece: how he sets up a gleefully quantised polyphony then infiltrates it with the defiant humanity of improvised flux and flow. As ever, Abrams refuses to be caged either way. *Think All, Focus One* is very deliberately neither fully electric nor fully not. It is a dialogue with the digital present and future.

I ask George Lewis about why Abrams and many other AACM members took to electronics so keenly. Lewis himself spent time at the Parisian music technology epicentre IRCAM and has done decades of pioneering work in computer music and AI. 'Oh yeah,' he nods. 'Pay attention to the electronics in Muhal's music, all right. There's a reason he went there.' On the surface, there are factors such as timbral exploration, colour play and extended sonic palettes. Maybe electronic sound builds bridges to an unearthly realm – maybe that uncanny valley Hannaford refers to. But Lewis suggests a broader significance, too. 'He was resisting the idea of the Afro-diasporic being essentially, in its nature, non-technological. So as part of your mobility practice, you ignore that.' Once again, Abrams was resisting simply by doing.

That choice around what kind of sound production one is societally allowed to partake in comes with weighty historical symbolism. In his book *Listening to Nineteenth-Century America*, Mark M. Smith looks at how the control of sound has a long precedent in American power structures. 'Masters went to great lengths to discipline plantation soundscapes by insisting on quiet-ude and trying to delimit slaves' sounds,' Smith writes. 'For the most part, antebellum planters got what they wanted from slaves: songs sung and sounds made at appropriate times in appropriate places.' And yet the essence of slave resistance, according to Smith, 'resided in both the singing of songs (important information could be conveyed in words) and slaves' ability to control their own sounds'.

Abrams was determined to control the sounds he made and how he made them, including extensive work using electronics. Still, when he died in 2017, the *Washington Post* obituary insisted that 'Mr. Abrams did relatively little experimentation with electronic music, preferring the traditional acoustic sound of the piano.' Like Ustvolskaya, the choice of how he was framed even in death did not seem to be up to him.

. . .

Abrams was socially radical, certainly. His openness to occult spirituality, his dogged resistance to the status quo of what an intellectual composer could look like. Across dozens of albums he was constantly reinventing his sound – but that was only in keeping with the spirit of innovation he had inherited from Duke Ellington, John Coltrane, Ornette Coleman and multiple others who had been challenging constrictive notions of jazz for decades. In the early 1990s, on the album *FamilyTalk*, Abrams included a blazing zinger of a track dedicated to his groundbreaking bebop idols. He called it *DizBirdMonkBudMax (a Tribute)*. And his vision for collective empowerment only built on a legacy of black American jazz leaders – mentor figures from King Oliver to Jelly Roll Morton, Charlie Parker to Count Basie, all of whom brought up apprentice musicians by insisting everyone needed to shoulder his part of creative agency.

Maybe Abrams is best considered a radical traditionalist. He shared with José Maceda a deep respect for the past and belief in a deep-rooted future. His radicalism was not about ripping things up and starting again, but about honouring several deep heritages that all involved experimentation of sorts. Actually, it was more essential than that. Experimentation *was* the way of honouring his heritage.

He loved the classic ragtime and stride pianists. Leonard Jones tells me with some reverence about the time he and Abrams made a pilgrimage to meet the ragtime pianist Eubie Blake in 1979. 'We went along to a book signing and there sat Eubie. The man had the longest fingers of anyone I'd ever seen! We both shook his hand. He was nearly a hundred years old.'

Abrams had notably spidery fingers himself, fingers that could explore and hunt, weave contrapuntal webs and dart out to opposite ends of the keyboard. His heroes included romantic piano titans: Sergey Rachmaninov, Vladimir Horowitz, Sviatoslav Richter. He also loved the dexterity and athleticism of stride: Art Tatum, Phineas Newborn, James P. Johnson, Willie 'The Lion' Smith, Luckey Roberts. Jones remembers Abrams at home in his late years, always sitting at the piano playing standards to amuse himself. The drifting *Oh! Look at Me Now* was a particular favourite. 'And he wore out his Hank Jones records,' Leonard Jones smiles. 'He played those 78s until there were no grooves left on them.'

In 1975, a full decade after forming the AACM, multiple complex ensemble albums already under his belt, Abrams released a solo record called *Afrisong*. Here we get his lateral musicianship in all its holistic idiosyncrasies. *Infinite Flow* is a spiritual haze that lapses into romping boogie-woogie. *Peace on You* is a minor-key invocation. *Roots* is a spry homage to past stride masters in classic Abrams herky-jerky swing. The last track on *Afrisong* is *The New People*, the name a nod to 'newcomers' on the South Side scene (including George Lewis). It is a thrillingly dissonant and fractured study that sounds as jagged as ice shattering on metal. And all this is contained under the heritage-highlighting title *Afrisong*. To borrow a resounding phrase from the saxophonist Julius Hemphill, 'Tradition in African-American music is wide as all outdoors.'

Taylor Ho Bynum explains it to me like this, referencing the 'neoconservative' attitude of trumpeter Wynton Marsalis, who has positioned himself as gatekeeper of jazz historiography. According to Marsalis, jazz stops where swing stops, denying more experimental practitioners the right to their own heritage. 'Everyone talks about the neocon movement – Wynton Marsalis and his guys – as being the first to go back to early jazz,' says Bynum.

> But Muhal and the AACM were already going back in the 1960s. They were digging Joplin rags and Jelly Roll Morton. They were going all the way back. They investigated the history and the pre-history of their music. They were looking at it to learn, to ingest and to keep expanding, not to preserve it in aspic. That's the depth of their reverence for the past, present and future.

Abrams felt permitted to plot his own reference points through that past, present and future, through a miscellany of traditions, all honoured, all progressive. 'Basically,' he said, 'we're musicians. It's music. You appreciate your roots and you express them, but you're not limited by them.'

· · ·

4 February 1977. The *New York Times* reports that:

> The New York City Board of Estimate voted last night to approve a controversial plan to use most of the troubled Manhattan Plaza apartment development near Times Square as housing for people in the performing arts.

That simple statement heralded one of the most exciting housing developments New York has ever witnessed. Two forty-six-floor apartment blocks had been built in Midtown between 42nd and 43rd Streets and Ninth and Tenth Avenues. They were intended initially as prime real estate for middle-class aspirants, with sweeping views over the Hudson, airy balconies and spacious bedrooms. The complex contained its own tennis courts and an Olympic-sized swimming pool in what was then known as Hell's Kitchen – real-estate agents today will tell you it's 'Clinton', but back in the early 1970s it was still one of the roughest neighbourhoods of Manhattan. The swish new apartments did not sell. What happened next should be a case study for urban renewal across the world.

The unwanted blocks were bought by the federal government and designated as subsidised accommodation. Local businesses were horrified, assuming a new influx of working-class residents would bring the neighbourhood to its knees and scare audiences away from neighbouring Broadway. In the end it was the Broadway producer Alexander H. Cohen who came up with the solution. If Manhattan Plaza is going to be for the poor, he said, 'let's make it *our* poor. It should be the actor's bedroom.'

Seventy per cent of the accommodation was reserved for artists, with rent set at 30 per cent of their income. Manhattan Plaza became a haven for musicians, dancers, actors and comedians. Samuel L. Jackson worked there as a doorman in the early years while he auditioned for plays at the Negro Ensemble Company. It was, he reflected, a 'very vivid New York education working from 11 o'clock until 7 o'clock in the morning in Manhattan Plaza.' Alicia Keys grew up in one of the blocks. Larry David dreamed up *Seinfeld* with Kenny Kramer who lived on the same floor. At various times you might meet Charles Mingus, Dexter Gordon,

Tennessee Williams or (later) Marin Alsop walking through the Plaza's revolving doors.

Muhal Richard Abrams moved to New York in 1976, following a general eastbound direction of travel taken by many of the Chicago AACM members. Henry Threadgill, Julius Hemphill, Amina Claudine Myers, Steve McCall, Lester Bowie, Kalaparusha Maurice McIntyre, George Lewis – they all decamped from the Midwest around that time. Artistically, they wanted to keep pushing. They could not resist the pace, punch, interchange and perhaps above all the earning potential of New York City. Leonard Jones helped Abrams move his piano eight hundred miles east. 'The two of us hauled this piano from Chicago to New York,' Jones tells me. 'Just the two of us. We loaded it into a trailer and drove it to New York.' The *Village Voice* heralded the arrival of Abrams, who went on to found a New York chapter of the AACM, as 'a crest on the wave of immigrant musicians recently arrived from St Louis, Los Angeles and especially Chicago'.

Abrams and his family moved into Manhattan Plaza when the complex was brand spanking new in 1977. According to trumpeter Lester Bowie, the AACM crowd 'knew about it before the New York cats did, and that's what pissed New York off'. When Jones needed a place to stay, the Abrams family took him in until he managed to secure his own Manhattan Plaza apartment. Jones remembers it as a buzzing place. He remembers routinely running into the actor Gloria Grahame in the elevator, and how 'the musicians came together and had the Manhattan Plaza Big Band. Chico Freeman, Muhal, Walter Bishop Jr . . . It was our own rehearsal band for musicians in the building.' He got to know Russell Procope, clarinettist in Duke Ellington's orchestra, and frequently breakfasted with Roger 'Ram' Ramirez, one of the composers of 'Lover Man'.

Jones and Abrams were early risers. Even when they were gigging regularly at the Greenwich Village club Sweet Basil – it might
be a trio with Steve McCall, a quartet with George Lewis, a quintet
with Henry Threadgill – they would be up by six the next morning.
'Muhal found out that Vladimir Horowitz would take early walks
around Manhattan. So we would get up early too, head up 42nd
Street, grab a cup of coffee and a doughnut, head over to Lexington
Avenue and see if we could meet Horowitz on one of his walks.'
They never did, but they stuck to their routine. 'Yeah,' says Jones,
'those walks became our thing.'

One night while they were gigging at Sweet Basil, Leonard Jones
noticed that a power of bass players had congregated at the back of
the bar. Lisle Atkinson and Reggie Workman were among them.

We stopped playing this one piece and Muhal said, hey Jones.
I said, what Richard. He said, look over there at the back. He
said, you see all these bass players? I looked and saw all those
bad cats. I mean – they were *bad* cats! He said, Jones, they came
to hear you. Play your stuff, he said. Don't play anything you
can't play. They came to hear *you*.

A few days after we talk, I receive an email from Leonard Jones.

One aspect of Muhal I would like to say something about which
I don't think got enough mention in our conversation was his
relationship to family. He was in every sense of the word a
family person. I would think that this part of him evolved out of
his own family relations being that he was one of nine siblings
growing up in the 1930s, which is to my imagination difficult
for any family but even more so for a Black family in the
United States. Although I never met most of his family,

I knew the bond was very strong, and most likely in this respect that bond carried over when he established his own family. As I said before, I was fortunate enough to have experienced what it was like to be a part of his family for a short period of time, and it was a lesson in how to be humane that I have not forgotten.

· · ·

Taylor Ho Bynum, now a teacher at Dartmouth College in New Hampshire, credits *The Hearinga Suite* for changing the course of his life when he was introduced to it aged twelve by an especially ear-opening mentor. *Hearinga* was the album Abrams released in 1989, just over a decade after he left Chicago. The eighteen-piece ensemble is a resplendent meeting of musicians from the AACM and the New York scene, straight-ahead players and free impro-visers, black and white, uptown and downtown, all there in the mix. So much for the city's supposed great divides. The suite forms a surprising and multi-layered manifesto. A swirlingly chromatic ballet, a psychedelic sorcerer's apprentice of reedy, warm, warbly and sinewy ensemble exchanges. There are nods to the breadth and vistas of Charles Mingus and the expansive chordal arrangements of Gil Evans, but nobody had ever written big band music quite like this. Abrams also includes a private moment in the second track, *Conversations with the Three of Me*, which opens with mysterious piano chords, Messiaen-like in the way they summon mystical realms through dense clouds of harmony. Then he cuts to twink-ling, gurgling synthesiser. It is a knowing wink at his own plural dimensions, none of whose edges he felt he had to curb in order to fit with the rest.

The 'classical' works that Abrams wrote starting in the 1980s were no great leap of style or form from the rest of his music. They use the same building blocks, the same methods that he had been exploring since the 1960s. The only practical difference was the kind of ensembles that played them, now orchestras instead of big bands, string quartets instead of improvising jazz quartets. He wrote three string quartets, a quintet for voice, piano, harp, cello and violin, a formidably arresting, quasi-expressionist atonal work for baritone and strings. He wrote an extraordinarily high-octane, tight-meshed saxophone quartet (it was recorded by the group Rova in the late 1990s: search it out) and a string trio called *Strings and Things*. He wrote for symphony orchestra – works including *Transversion I* op. 6, which was performed by the Detroit Symphony Orchestra, and *Folk Tales '88*, which was performed by the Brooklyn Philharmonic Orchestra. He composed for the sensationally named zoomoozophone, an instrument described by its inventor Dean Drummond as 'a thirty-one-tones-per-octave, just-intoned metalophone'. Carrillo, eat your heart out.

Abrams himself never had any qualms about bringing together the improvisational and the compositional sides of himself. After all, he knew he was only doing what others had done for centuries. 'The great composers did a lot of improvising,' he told the journalist Frank J. Oteri in 2016. 'All of them. When you play their music, you can tell. It's not just mechanical. Rachmaninov sat down and played ideas at pianos. I'm sure he did that. Then he said, Well, I'll make this a piece.'

Abrams improvised and composed every day. His former student Jason Moran talks about the filing cabinet stuffed with new ideas that his teacher kept in the room where he taught lessons in his Manhattan Plaza apartment. 'Oh yeah, he was a man who composed all the time,' Leonard Jones confirms. 'You'd be watching television and he would disappear. He'd go to the piano. Whatever he had just heard on the television – he would go to the piano and all of a sudden he would play that little figure, start to develop it. Days later it would be a whole composition.' John Hollenbeck, who incidentally also lived in Manhattan Plaza, remembers seeing Abrams walking through those storied revolving doors. 'Whenever I saw him, he seemed to be lost in thought and I imagined he was composing,' Hollenbeck tells me. 'I figured I shouldn't bother him.'

I haven't found it easy to pick out which Abrams pieces to highlight here. There are too many points of entry. I should mention his Étude op. 1 no. 1 with its lacerated walking bass line. I should mention *Piano-Cello Song*, featuring the double bassist Dave Holland playing a raspy cello elegy to a backdrop of muted, musky piano chords. I should mention the whole panoply of styles we get on the album *Think All, Focus One*, and the astral visions of *Mergertone*, a recondite work for orchestra and electronics that has been recorded by conductor Petr Kotik and the Janáček Philharmonic.

I should mention *Piano Duet #1*, premiered by Ursula Oppens and Frederic Rzewski, a piece of compressed and nocturnal majesty. It reminds me of Béla Bartók and the earthy magic of his night music, but there is something unmistakably Abrams about how the music feels as though it is being improvised in and out of synch by the two players. How their hands twist in gnarly configurations and land on snarl-ups, then extract themselves and set off in stealthy pursuit. There's an urgency in the way the four hands explore, a restlessly searching instinct. The writing is consumingly chromatic – it's as though Abrams wants to squeeze the notes of the piano together to make the polyphony even tighter, even more distilled, then suddenly he turns a corner and brings us to a place of sparse and ravishing mystery. Abrams said the unison double octaves in the third part of the piece are a nod to the last movement of Chopin's Second Piano Concerto. Now, whenever I go back to the Chopin, I hear Abrams in the blithe cascades and rhapsodies, in the swaggering dexterity and the rondo form that keeps circling back like the blues.

All of these pieces by Abrams deserve to be better known. They deserve to be performed for their originality, their forensic craft and expansive spirituality. They deserve recordings that do them justice. But while Abrams is highly revered in the jazz world, his name remains unknown within the infrastructure that would provide such recordings and performances. It is exactly the divide he fought against all his life.

. . .

George Lewis tells me an apocryphal story about a time Duke Ellington offered a cautionary word to Dizzy Gillespie. Dizzy, said Duke. The biggest mistake you made was to let them name your music bebop, because from the time they name something, it is dated.

Lewis writes about the racial significance of labels and genre with enormous depth and dignity. I would urge you to read his AACM history, *A Power Stronger than Itself*, and Chapter Nine in particular, for a detailed account of contemporary music politics in 1970s New York, where labels really mattered. Labels determined who was called what, who did the gatekeeping, what the implications were for everything from funding opportunities, venue access and press coverage to a musician's right to claim a cultural history. As we talk, Lewis recalls a particular example. He was on faculty at UC San Diego and he invited Abrams to California to work with his students. 'We got the new music ensemble in the department to play one of Muhal's pieces, and someone in the group commented cheerfully that it was the first time they'd ever played jazz.' The thing was, the piece was not jazz. If the same music been brought in by another composer, a white composer, it would not have occurred to this student that the music belonged to a genre called anything other than 'new music' or 'contemporary classical' or 'avant-garde' or 'modern'. 'That's the thing about race,' says Lewis. 'It can make you deaf.'

Abrams had no problem with jazz. He loved and celebrated his jazz roots to the end. He resisted labels mainly because there was only one label available to him. Marc Hannaford writes about Abrams and his refusal to be pinned to binaries. Low/high, Dionysus/Apollo, electronic/acoustic, improvisation/composition, jazz/classical, beginner/master, individual/collective – maybe Abrams's greatest legacy is that he found a way to have them all at once. He ate up those contradictions. The eternal student, the scientific spiritualist, the evasive ringleader.

History does not tend to headline the enablers, the team players, the behind-the-sceners who facilitate community. To be clear: this story is by no means just about how Abrams supported others, but his lasting influence has as much to do with how he exemplified an attitude as with the gripping music he made. Actually, the music and the attitude are inextricable. It's all one. Abrams sits between strands, eluding definition. He embodies individual and collective thought – an admixture of the intensely inclusive ethos of José Maceda and Walter Smetak and the intimate, personal aspects of Else Marie Pade, Éliane Radigue and Emahoy Tsegué-Mariam Guèbru.

Leonard Jones sums it up like this. 'The thing about Muhal', he tells me, 'is his individuality had a hook. He brought others with him.'

Éliane Radigue

(b. 1932)

**Occam Ocean:
in search of sound within sound**

One of Éliane Radigue's favourite phrases is borrowed from the French symbolist writer Paul Verlaine. His poem 'Mon rêve familier' describes 'une femme inconnue' – a mysterious woman – 'qui n'est, chaque fois, ni tout à fait la même / ni tout à fait une autre' (who is never quite the same and never quite different).

Radigue is all about that perpetual transition. She loves a long modulation. Her music exists in a state of quiet and constant flux, the slower the rate of change the better. She is not interested in arriving somewhere so much as in unearthing whatever subtle riches there might be along the way. She is master of transience, queen of the in-between. She will claim with a shrug that her technique boils down to a simple continuum – a recurring process of 'fade in, fade out, cross fade'. She applied that process to her majestic early electronic works. She still applies it to the series of instrumental collaborations she has been making since the turn of the millennium.

Hers is the most deceptive kind of simplicity. Radigue writes awesomely gradual music that is always on the move. Her art is full of paradox. It is music that flowers in some enchanted hinterland where sounds are sparse and mercurial, spiritual and grounded, narrative and abstract. She works intuitively, and her intuition has always drawn her to meticulous procedure, finicky electronics, the innate physical properties of sound production. She says she is always on the hunt for sound within sound – a realm of partials, harmonics and subharmonics. Which is to say, not any ordinary, fundamental note you might strike on a piano, but the intangible cloud that makes up that note's aura.

Radigue first found these illusive inner-sonorities in the 1960s via the dark arts of *musique concrète*, tape manipulation and speaker feedback. In the 1970s, she turned to the husky thrum of analogue synthesisers, which beguiled her for the next three decades. Now she allows a select bunch of instrumentalists – she calls them her *chevaliers d'Occam* – to search out secret sounds alongside her, and from her performers she requires a level of precision and long-form patience that is physically and mentally extreme. Imagine holding your arm just so, moving it only ever so slightly, for an hour or more. Most of us would start to hurt or lose focus after a couple of minutes. Not Radigue's band of spectral knights. In her total-body demands she shares an intense immersive instinct with Ustvolskaya, but with music that is as subtle as Ustvolskaya's is brutal.

Maybe most thrilling of all is what Radigue can do with time. In her *Trilogie de la mort*, an immense meditation on death and transcendence, she telescopes three hours into an instant. Somehow it feels both now and infinite. Her pace of transition is glacial, but the action shimmers once you start to hear it. Rhodri Davies, a wonderful improvising harpist and one of Radigue's most trusted *chevaliers*, has talked to me about performing her music, and the feeling of suddenly 'waking up' while playing it – not dissimilar to the story about the pianist who forgot where she was while playing Pascale Criton on a Carrillo piano. Davies told me that he suddenly becomes aware of the room and the audience only at the end of a Radigue piece. He often has no sense of how long he's been 'out'. Somehow time has both imploded and exploded.

None of this really works if your attention flits. Listening to Radigue's music means slowing down to its pace and *genuinely* listening. If you can and do sink in, you're in for an engulfing ride. Maybe it's something like letting your eyes rest on an inconspicuous spot in the darkest night sky then suddenly catching a glimmer of the Northern Lights.

. . .

The first time I visited Radigue, she opened a bottle of champagne and I smashed a glass. We had just finished a long interview ahead of some performances of her work hosted by the BBC Scottish Symphony Orchestra. She went through to her kitchen to fetch some crystal flutes and a bowl of pretzels, though at eighty-three she didn't feel quite strong enough to shimmy out the cork with her own hands – 'Who knows where it might go!' she grinned – so she passed over the bottle for me to deal with. This was when the interview really got going. Or rather, this was when it changed direction and she started asking the questions.

We were in her apartment on Rue Liancourt in the 14th arrondissement of Paris, a neighbourhood of charcuterie markets and stationery shops around Montparnasse. She has lived in this same block since the 1970s. Through the windows, the winter sky was the colour of slate. Inside, the studio was all bright silk scarves and family portraits, Radigue pictured surrounded by children, grandchildren and multiple great-grandchildren. The walls were hung with resin pieces made by her ex-husband, an artist called Arman.

The overwhelming singularity of Radigue's sound world made a new sort of sense after I met her and learned her story. Here is a woman who has always seemed to know what she wanted in her music and in herself. The crucial bit: a woman who had the conviction to spend months or years or even decades practising patience like an extreme sport in order to get it. For thirty years she worked alone on electronic music. She likes to joke that her cat was her only studio assistant, and that he was pretty discerning. 'There was music I wanted to hear,' she says, 'and to hear it I had to make it. It was as simple as that.' Another thing I've noticed about her is that she does a deft line in understatement.

· · ·

Éliane Radigue was born in Paris in 1932 and grew up on Rue de la Lingerie around the old market halls of Les Halles. She didn't especially enjoy the inner-city hustle – she unfondly remembers being whistled at as a girl – but she is, she smiles, *toujours Parisienne*. Her family was not musical, but an astute great-uncle gave her a subscription ticket to afternoon concerts at the Châtelet where she would crane her neck from the cheap seats on the highest balconies to develop a lasting love for the works of Mahler, Beethoven and Ravel. These are still the composers she chooses to listen to most: don't be fooled by the fact her own music sits at the remote margins of form, sound and silence.

She always had her own way of listening. Like Ustvolskaya, she loved to sit under a piano when someone else was playing; like Walter Smetak, she loved to ingest the full resonance of the instrument through her body. As for playing it herself – there was no piano in her family home, but she took after-school lessons from a kindly teacher called Madame Roger who lived in the apartment block next door. Radigue never had any intention of being a professional pianist, but the thing Madame Roger passed on above all was a love of the way music is constructed. Radigue learned the lives of composers (Beethoven, Mahler), the inspirations behind their scores, the basic methods of building music out of constituent parts. Even when her mother put an end to the lessons because they were too expensive (or possibly because she was jealous of her daughter's devotion to her beloved teacher), Madame Roger kept up the lessons in secret.

Things at home were tense. Radigue's parents were concerned about the free-spirited direction in which their daughter seemed to be heading. When she finished high school in the summer of 1950, she was sent south to the Riviera to spend some time 'improving her character' with an appropriate set of family friends. What Radigue was definitely not supposed to do was fall in love with a radical art student in Nice, and even less was she supposed to get pregnant. She was still a teenager and, worse, she was unmarried: not an easy predicament to navigate in a conservative French family in the early 1950s. But she did not retreat to Paris with her tail between her legs. Here is another of Radigue's guiding wisdoms: 'Always in life, when it comes to the important matters, things go well when you make a real decision.' She stayed in the south and married Armand Fernandez, who would go on to drop all but the first five letters of his name as his artist's moniker. Together, Radigue and Arman had three children in as many years, and motherhood became an essential part of her being.

The French Mediterranean had been the playground of film stars and literati before the Second World War. 'A sunny place for shady people,' as W. Somerset Maugham described it. Bertolt Brecht, Aldous Huxley, Jean Cocteau and Vladimir Nabokov were all regulars; Pablo Picasso motored around in a yellow Hispano-Suiza until his 1939 painting *Night Fishing at Antibes* signalled the end of an era. Eleven eviscerating years later, Radigue arrived on this post-war coastline, which now had scant avant-garde artistic action. She was determined to eke out whatever music she could, so she joined a choir and enrolled at the local music conservatoire where she learned to play the harp. She took to swimming in the sea at night, because pregnant women were not to be seen on the beach during the day.

Arman was busy fomenting ideas with a small set of Niçoise intellectuals that included the painter Yves Klein and the poet

Claude Pascal. These were Radigue's kind of people. In 1949, Klein had staged a twenty-minute chord followed by twenty minutes of silence and called it his *Monotone-Silence Symphony*. He became god-father to the Arman-Radigue children. On Sunday afternoons, they would all congregate at the Parc de la Californie and debate how artists might perceive and represent the everyday. Years later, the set became known as the École de Nice; later still, the Nouveaux réalistes (New Realists).

Radigue and Arman lived in a small apartment near the Parc de la Californie, which also happened to be near the airport. Radigue often found her ears wandering. At home looking after three very young children, she tuned into the rumble of air traffic. Six flights a day came and went from Nice airport at that time, and she punctu-ated her hours by focusing her listening on the distinct timbre of each model of plane. She started hearing music within the whir of those propellors: drones, counter-drones, cross-rhythms. 'The sonic landscapes of the Nice region were inexhaustible,' she described years later in an essay called *Le temps n'a pas d'import-ance* (Time is of no importance), and she was not talking just about Provençal crickets and birdsong.

And then came the epiphany. 1952. It was, in fact, the very same epiphany that happened to Else Marie Pade in the very same year, which is perhaps not surprising: both women heard sonic wonders in the everyday, so of course they were equally thrilled to discover a method of making that everyday into music. One ordinary morn-ing in her kitchen in Nice, Radigue was minding the children and listening to Radio France. From the radio she heard unexpected clangs, screeches, puffs and pistons. It was Pierre Schaeffer's *Étude aux chemins de fer* – a symphony of railway noises. Wheels on track, whistles, bells, hammers, squealing breaks – this *Étude* was an eman-cipation of noise. It was music made out of modern street sounds, all of them now up for grabs as ingredients to be layered and looped and spliced together into a work of sonic art. Radigue remembers her precise reaction that morning. She recalls exclaiming to herself: '*Alors, voilà!*' The notion made perfect sense to her. The permission to take anything and find sonic value within it – she had already been doing it when she listened to planes flying overhead. Hearing Schaeffer's *musique concrète* on the radio only confirmed that she could legitimately harness those sounds and call the results music.

Not long after that kitchen revelation, Radigue met Schaeffer at a concert in Paris. She told him about the way she listened and explained to him how she felt about the inner life of sound. He invited her to his Club d'Essai on the Left Bank in Paris. The studio had once been a hub for wartime resistance radio activity and was now a burgeoning electronic music laboratory frequented by future heavyweights of the genre including Luc Ferrari, François-Bernard Mâche and Pierre Henry. And Éliane Radigue. Still living in Nice but willing to make the 700-kilometre commute to Schaeffer's HQ on Rue de l'Université, she was soon a Club d'Essai regular.

These were Radigue's apprenticeship years. She became assistant to both Pierres – Schaeffer and Henry – taking on the painstaking intern work of cutting and splicing vast reels of magnetic tape. She learned the techniques of sonic montage and mixing. After long days wielding scissors, she would stay on extra hours at the studio and test out the machinery late into the night. Her own creative visions went deeper, longer, lower and higher than anything her bosses were doing. When she shared her experiments with them, they didn't always seem impressed. She continued, undeterred. The pursuit of new sounds galvanised her. In 1956, she switched back to using her maiden name for the first time since her marriage and began giving lectures on the techniques and philosophies behind *musique concrète*.

Home life was vying for attention. When her children were very small she could pack them up and deposit them with her parents in Paris while she was in the studio. Now that they were school-age and more tied to Nice, the juggling became trickier. Being away so much was not without cost. She felt the stretch of leaving her children so often with Arman and a young au pair. One obvious solution was to continue her sonic experiments closer to home, but for that she needed access to a studio and, despite a letter of introduction from Pierre Schaeffer, she was refused permission to use the Maison de la radio Niçoise. The reasons can be explained only as misogyny, as Radigue later reflected with cool detachment. 'The director', she surmised, 'patently assessed my anatomy much more than my potential talent.'

The two Pierres had an infamous falling out in 1958. Henry was resentful about the work he did for Schaeffer without being given due credit; Radigue sided with Henry, and Schaeffer severed contact with both for nearly a decade. The reunion of the Pierres was ultimately Radigue's doing – a dinner party she hosted in 1967 – but in the meantime, the rupture put a kibosh on her ability to pursue her experiments anywhere at all. Caught in a clash of electro-acoustic egos in Paris, and with no studio access in Nice, she was now cut off from the machinery she needed to pursue her sound within sound. Stumped by Crawford's 'career vs love and children battle', she stopped working for nearly a decade and turned her attention to playing the piano and raising her kids.

. . .

During one of our early conversations, I ask Radigue what it was like to be a woman working in the overwhelmingly male environment of French experimental music in the 1950s and 1960s. It is relevant to note that she was, she is, a natural beauty. There is one particular photo from the mid-1950s which sums it up. In the photo, she's on a beach wearing a lime-green sleeveless dress and holding a conch shell to one ear. She is tanned, blonde, intent. The atmosphere is everything that Godard and Truffaut wanted to bottle in their New Wave films, but the magic is in Radigue's totally uncontrived absorption in the moment. She always loved listening to shells. 'You hear the noise of the blood,' she points out. 'Sound is perceived by the body as well as the ears. The deaf know it well.'

She says she never dwelled on either her beauty or her talent. She told me that while she was married she considered herself 'Arman's wife' rather than 'Éliane Radigue, composer'. She remembers getting her hair done to go to his gallery openings, but otherwise she wouldn't tend to bother. I think of Peggy Seeger despairing over her mother's clunky footwear at the awards ceremony. Radigue was no vocal feminist, no overt activist of any political stripes. When protests erupted in Paris in May 1968, unleashing an energy with global repercussions, Radigue was on a boat in the Mediterranean, preparing to perform a work of experimental tape music.

So when I ask about being a women at the Club d'Essai, she responds with a classically Gallic shrug. Then she tells me a brief and infuriating anecdote about a technician who commented that it was nice to have her in the studio because she made the place smell good. 'Those men?' she raises an eyebrow. 'They were all very macho.' It's a raised eyebrow that doesn't so much suggest amusement or resignation as a lifetime of prioritising other ways to expend her energy. She does, though, acknowledge that she was only ever accepted by Schaeffer and Henry as an assistant. If she had revealed her full ambition as a composer, she would, she suggests, have been a lot less welcome in their studios.

Radigue is nothing if not determined. She knew full well that confronting what she calls these 'machos' would have absorbed her energy, derailed her focus, jeopardised her access to studios and the equipment she needed to make her music. So she navigated the dynamics in whatever way felt to be the least disruptive at the time. An important clue here lies in another of her guiding principles. It is a philosophy known as Occam's Razor, named after the fourteenth-century Franciscan friar William of Ockham who argued that, faced with multiple options, the simplest choice is usually the best.

For Radigue, Occam's Razor has been a survival tactic as well as an aesthetic credo.

· · ·

In 1963, Arman was offered work with a gallery in New York and Radigue and the kids went with him. The city was an awakening for them all. They landed in a community of kindred spirits: the pianist David Tudor and the composer John Cage, the choreographer Yvonne Rainer, the visionary musician James Tenney, through whom Radigue discovered a radical new world of loft concerts and Fluxus happenings. It was in New York, in the company of these rule-rewriting artists, that she first realised she could be taken seriously as a composer herself without her looks or her creative ambition getting in the way. As Arman's career took its own upwards trajectory, Radigue recognised that she was done with playing the artist's wife. She ended the marriage in 1967, though she and Arman remained friends until he died in 2005.

Radigue loved those first four years in New York, but even so she returned to Paris every three months just to plant her feet on home turf. She is, remember, *toujours Parisienne*. After the break-up of her marriage, she moved back to France with the children. At this point she had been away from any tape work for nearly a decade, but she reconnected with Pierre Henry and he asked her to assist in his new studio APSOME (Applications de Procédés Sonores en Musique Électroacoustique). Radigue's work there consisted of fourteen-hour days of unpaid technical minutiae helping Henry put together his epic *Apocalypse de Jean* (1968) – an oratorio-scale amalgam of narration, electronics and *musique concrète*. It was also the year that Henry met his second wife, and that meant his attention was often elsewhere. Radigue found herself alone in the studio for long hours. She was able to take up where she had left off with her own sonic investigations.

After a year at APSOME, she told Henry it was time for her to work alone. The kids would come home from school and find their mother concocting wild loops and lapses with tape machines in the hallway. When her oldest son, Yves, announced he was giving up the harp, Radigue made him a valedictory piece called *Étude pour Harpe* (1968), which, in an Annea-Lockwoodian act of instrumenticide, involved placing a microphone inside the body of the instrument and, as a final flourish, performing a glissando with a razor blade. She would later worry about having inflicted too much violence on an instrument she loved, but as a closing statement it was triumphantly conclusive.

These were exploratory years for Radigue. She probed the ephemeral potential of electronic feedback, testing the precise point of interference between speakers where beautiful sounds emerged from the white noise. Speaker feedback was usually an out-of-control domain of din and abrasion, but she trod gently and managed to tame the beast. She also became a dab hand at manipulating magnetic tape, and she made a series of breathtakingly delicate electronic pieces. The first was a game of gently dilated beats called *Jouet électronique* (1967). The second was *Elemental I* (1968), made from a personal archive of recordings (sea, wind, rain, landslides) collected in Nice using a little Stellavox tape recorder. In the beguiling maze of *Labyrinthe sonore* (1970), listeners unspooled their own Ariadne's thread by physically wandering among six different sources of sound. It was twenty-eight years ahead of its time: *Labyrinthe sonore* was finally staged in 1998 at Mills College in California, with participants including two luminaries of American experimental sound, Pauline Oliveros and Maggi Payne.

Making music the way Radigue did, equipment could literally blow up at any moment. 'When I started with electronics,' she tells me, 'before I had access to a synthesiser with feedback effect, I just respected the behaviour of moving very slowly, not going too near to or too far from the loudspeaker because that would make it explode. I loved testing the limits. Believe me, there was only a hair's breadth to play with.' Again, a paradox: such delicacy out of such danger. She learned how to listen, how to understand the language of feedback, how to 'open up a conversation with it'. The approach she honed in those seventeen pre-synthesiser pieces ended up defining her life's work. She had found her sound within sound.

In 1970, thanks to the advocacy of the composer Steve Reich, Radigue was offered her own year-long residency at New York University. This time she moved into a loft on the Bowery in the East Village – avant-garde heartland at the time. Reich asked her to help him out with some vocal parts but she turned him down. She had her own work to do. She staged annual performances at The Kitchen, a hotbed of experimental sound on Mercer Street near Washington Square Park. She performed at centres of cutting-edge music across the country. At Phill Niblock's loft on Centre Street, and at CalArts and Mills College in California. She was friends with

Terry Riley and Maryanne Amacher, Laurie Spiegel, Philip Corner, Charlemagne Palestine and Robert Ashley, all of them seeking to repurpose sound and the way we hear it. She hung out with Reich and Philip Glass, who in those days were still working with each other. She attended Max Neuhaus concerts in outdoor swimming pools and performed at ambulatory happenings where performers and audiences dressed entirely in white.

Radigue recalls one particular conversation she had with Philip Glass, during which he told her that he was interested in arpeggios. 'And look!' she laughs. 'All his music ended up being made out of arpeggios! Well, I was interested in modulations, and all my music is made out of modulations. In the same way that I didn't choose the colour of my hair, I didn't choose the music I was drawn to.'

What is it with Radigue and slowness? She has never written a single fast thing. Slowness does not mean stasis, and she has always objected to her works being categorised as drone music: the label is too reductive, too static, too concerned with fundamentals. 'Of course, we need fundamentals in order to produce harmonics, but they are just the base' – she pats the sofa beside her – 'like something to sit on.' It's up above, where you can move your arms and incline your head, where the action happens. 'A piece is all right when a listener forgets about the fundamentals,' she says. 'My pieces start very quietly in order to give listeners and performers time to adjust their ears. To lay down the fundamentals solidly enough that we can then forget about them completely.'

In her essay *Le temps n'a pas d'importance*, she likens her music to a plant. 'We never see a plant move, but it is growing continually.' I ask her about that thing she does with time – her temporal sorcery, how time in her music feels both contracted (in the way it focuses on tiny details) and elongated (in the way it unfolds over many hours). 'By nature,' she says, 'slowness is expansive, yet it allows us to hear up close.' She quotes the Romanian conductor Sergiu Celibidache, who said that when an orchestra was running well he could slow his beat right down, but when things were going wrong he needed to speed up. She bemoans the fact that tempos in classical music these days are generally faster than when she was young. She singles out the second movement of Ravel's Piano Concerto in G as a glory of slow writing, its right-hand melody unfurling note by simple note over stoic chords in the bass. 'It always has this ambivalence,' she says. 'It is exquisite because the melody spins on and on. Always moving, always in transition.' *Ni tout à fait la même, ni tout à fait une autre.*

She tells me about travelling in her youth. She used to pride herself on being able to navigate almost any city in the world without a map. 'Except for Venice,' she smiles. 'Venice was the only place where I ever got lost, and that was an incredible feeling.' Modulation as a musical equivalent to submitting to the deliciously tangled backstreets of Venice – it's an enchanting thought. So what happens at the end of one of her pieces? Does the feeling of dislocation disperse after the music has ended, that moment Rhodri Davies described when the room comes back into focus? 'I suppose that it does,' she allows. But the transition, she stresses, can feel limitless.

· · ·

In the early 1970s, Radigue made three pivotal discoveries. The first happened when she was introduced to a synthesiser in New York. This was a Buchla analogue modular synthesiser, to be precise, which had been installed by the electronic music pioneer Morton Subotnick at New York University and which Radigue shared with fellow experimentalists Laurie Spiegel and Rhys Chatham. She likes to call that meeting with the synthesiser 'the beginning of a great

love affair'. She spent months getting to know the instrument inti-
mately, honing in on what made it click, what made it purr, finding
its purest sounds and how those sounds worked in a certain room.
She knew about La Monte Young, his long-form music stretching
sustained tones to their limits and arguably beyond. She knew that
Alvin Lucier was busy bouncing sound around space in landmark
works such as *I am sitting in a room*, which turns any acoustic into a
sonic playground. For her part, she always worked alone.

It was for the Buchla that Radigue wrote a piece called *Chry-ptus*
featuring two tapes played with a time lapse to produce tiny palpitations. The sound is subtle and deadpan, the rhythm steady, the
sonic equivalent of an Agnes Martin painting. The premiere took
place at the New York Cultural Center in April 1971, on a day so
rainy that the Mets played a shortened home opener. Spiegel and
Chatham came along to the performance to see what Radigue had
managed to summon from the machine they were also testing out.
Chatham rang Radigue the next day and told her he had attended
the performance just to be polite, but that he had been blown away.

The synthesiser was Radigue's new right-hand man, and would
remain so for the next thirty years. She shipped one across the
ocean when she returned to Paris in 1971, sharing her cabin with
the innards of the instrument. Not the Buchla this time, but an
ARP 2500 analogue modular synthesiser, which she loved for its
special voice, its hiss, its hazy potential, for the fact it was less direct
and metallic than a Moog or a Buchla. She didn't bother bringing the keyboard: she was interested only in the inner workings
of the machine, which she could mess around with 'like a plate of
spaghetti'. With the ARP she found she could make noises that
were warmer and more enveloping than anything she had done
with tape. When a friend in Paris asked her to make a sound 'like
the silence of the stars' – a commission Else Marie Pade surely

would have relished – Radigue happily obliged. At first she felt almost shy of the temperamental machine and she addressed it as 'Monsignor', a term once reserved for the highest clergy of the Catholic Church. Later, as they became friendlier, she fell into the habit of calling the instrument 'Jules'.

The second of those pivotal discoveries happened inside her own head. In 1974, Radigue was visiting her son Yves, himself now a budding art curator in New York. Chatting with her daughter-in-law, Radigue leaned back on the sofa and propped herself up with one hand over one ear. Suddenly she realised that although she could still see her daughter-in-law's lips moving, she could no longer hear what was being said. It turned out that her hearing had been impaired in one ear since birth, and she was nearly half deaf. Radigue did not panic: the condition was not degenerative. And besides, she had unknowingly accommodated for her partial deafness all her life. In fact, she framed it as an advantage. Her hearing has shaped the acute way she listens, the way she internalises sound and the magnifying care and attentiveness that she devotes to a note's interior life.

The third discovery happened that same year, 1974, at a concert in California. A French couple approached her after a performance and said they heard an affinity between her music and their own spirituality. They were Buddhists. Radigue has never aimed to write meditative music, even if she doesn't dispute the idea that others might hear it that way. But after that encounter in California, she connected a spiritual framework to her instinctive hunch that everything is impermanent. Back in Paris, she paused her performance schedule for the next few years and devoted herself to studying the religion, spending six days a week at a Buddhist centre in Belleville. Remember, she doesn't do anything by halves. *When it comes to the important matters, things go well when you make a real decision.*

Is it trite to hear Radigue's music as a form of meditation? She herself is reluctant to be drawn on any overt spirituality in her works – 'Meaning', she insists, 'always comes from the life of the sound itself.' Instead, she describes music and spirituality as train tracks, never meeting but connected by the vehicle (presumably us) which is travelling upon them.

There are a few notable exceptions. A small collection of works in which Radigue deals explicitly with Buddhist subjects. *Les Chants de Milarepa* (1983) builds a capaciously lush backdrop under the voices of Tibetan Lama Kunga Rinpoche, who sings hypnotic chants, and composer Robert Ashley, who intones spiritual teachings on patience and humility in a cool, soporific drawl. In the low thrum of *Jetsun Mila* (1986), tones emerge and fade from an enthralling sonic cross-hatch to represent the eleventh-century yogi Milarepa and his ten stages of life. In 1974, Radigue had just finished the first part of her mighty *Trilogie de la mort* when her son Yves was killed in a car crash in Spain. Deep in grief, she retreated to a Buddhist centre in the Dordogne. She would return to the second and third parts of the *Trilogie* slowly, the music's expanse resonating with unspeakable loss as she incorporated Buddhist texts of pilgrimage and the transcendental.

Radigue wrote her electronic masterpieces for Jules, her ARP synthesiser. The *Adnos* trilogy (1974–1980–1982), the *Chants de Milarepa*, the *Trilogie de la mort*. As her tempos grew slower, her music became less static, constantly in flux like a shimmering aurora with all the time in the world. Her final electronic piece (to date) was *L'Île Re-sonante* (2000), name borrowed from the French Renaissance writer François Rabelais. The piece imagines the Lac du Bourget at the foot of the Jura mountains. It is the deepest lake in France – in some places as deep as the mountain next to it is high. Accordingly, *L'Île Re-sonante* plunges to the depths with frequencies so low you feel rather than hear them. Above ground, the sweeping vistas are vast and romantic. Somewhere in the ether hovers a high overtone, a wisp of cloud forming around the peaks.

. . .

These days, Jules is nowhere to be seen in Radigue's apartment in Montparnasse. Their divorce – which is her word for it – occurred in the first decade of the new millennium. She stopped writing for the ARP, or for any synthesiser whatsoever. She dismantled Jules and stored him away in a basement. As mentioned, she never does do anything by halves.

But she did not stop working. It was the French bass player and noise artist Kasper T. Toeplitz, introduced to Radigue by Phill Niblock, who instigated her next body of work. Toeplitz convinced Radigue to write something for him to perform on electric bass, and the result was a piece called *Elemental II* (2003). It seems fitting that her next chapter would open with a sequel to one of the very first pieces of electronic music she wrote. Having spent a lifetime working alone, collaboration 'changed everything', she says. 'It is strange, all of this interest in me all of a sudden. Years ago some musicians asked to play my music. I said no. I wasn't ready to open up. And I thought, I will never be asked twice. I was wrong.'

After Toeplitz, the cellist Charles Curtis came calling. Long an advocate of avant-garde music, he encouraged Radigue to abandon electronics altogether and go totally acoustic. Which she did, setting to work on what became a grand trilogy for cello and two basset horns. She named it *Naldjorlak*: *naldjor* meaning a kind of unity, *lak* being a term of respect. *Naldjorlak I*, for solo cello, homes in on the 'wolf tone' that is normally the bane of string players. It is the place on a string where the physics of the instrument are out of whack, or maybe too in whack – the resonance of the cello's body and the resonance of the string amplifying each other out so the sound goes wild. *Sons sauvages*, Radigue calls them, and, like her work with volatile speaker feedback, she is once again tiptoeing on the edge of the volcano. When *Naldjorlak I* was performed, she realised this was the music she had always wanted to hear, but could never fully achieve with electronics. 'What a strange experience,' she reflected. 'After so much wandering, to return to what was already there, the perfection of acoustic instruments.'

In 2008 she launched a series of works under the title *Occam*. It has since grown to include dozens of collaborative solo pieces and small ensemble configurations. Occam Rivers, Occam Deltas and the open-ended orchestral iteration *Occam Ocean*. She likens the series to Felix Mendelssohn's collection of songs without words. 'There are no lyrics, but those pieces tell deep stories,' she explains. 'And me too. *Je me raconte des histoires*.'

There is a story behind every one of her pieces. Every new piece in the Occam series begins with Radigue and a performer sitting down in her apartment and talking about water. They talk about oceans, seas, lakes, rivers, waterfalls. This is the starting point. It might be just a corner of some pond – it has to be a place that has meaning for the performer. 'Music inspired by a huge torrent won't sound the same as music inspired by a little mountain spring,' she points out.

I like the musician to choose an image from his or her own country: we all have a special place associated with water. Who hasn't meditated in front of an ocean, a river or a waterfall? For example one musician was interested in the image of an underground river coming out into a cave, forming a deep fountain and rising into the sea. That became the score of the piece.

We'll never know which piece that is, because Radigue is not one for telling. She keeps the images secret because she doesn't want listeners using up their mental energy wondering what is supposed to be happening next. 'The best audience', she says, 'is one that makes up its own images while listening.' Once she and the performer have agreed on an image, they write it down to provide a structure for the music that she calls a 'living score'. Her notation is verbal and her language is pictorial. It is not quite like taking a photograph because the image keeps moving. Maybe a hologram. And the works are for specific instrumentalists, not instruments. Radigue doesn't want them to be played by musicians other than those she has worked with personally, unless the music is passed on orally from one player to another. Even if that means the works might be lost over time – so be it. Integrity is worth more to her than longevity.

Writing for orchestra might have presented a conundrum when it came to this kind of one-to-one working, but Radigue began *Occam Ocean* with a gathering. Food, drinks and thirty musicians crammed onto cushions on the wooden floor of her studio apartment. After that first meeting, she instructed every player – not just the conductor or section leaders, but every single musician – to visit her again so they could devise their parts collaboratively. It is the only way she is prepared to work. 'The first question I asked all of them was: please, make some waves. Just waves. With some of them I knew it would be all right after about three minutes. With others it took more time.' Altogether the process took two years. She doesn't know if she will write another orchestral piece. 'Maybe a sea,' she contemplates. 'And hopefully many more rivers. But I think there can be only one ocean.'

. . .

Back to that visit in her apartment in Montparnasse. We'd done a long interview but Radigue still wanted to talk, and she'd had enough of talking about herself. She poured out the drinks and leaned back to listen. She didn't bother with minutiae. First thing she wanted to know was whether I was happy in my work. At the time I was mainly employed as a music critic and I explained that actually I found the whole thing fairly stressful and conflicting. I confided in her about my lurking suspicion that the years of voicing critical feedback had started to shape my own personality in ways that weren't entirely positive. She looked at me quizzically. She asked about my family, about my relationships, whether I had children yet and whether I planned to.

She asked what I considered important in life, assuming that (like her) I would have a clear and ready answer. She was tired after speaking English during the interview so she flitted into French and I found myself summoning phrases I had last used when I was a music student in Montreal. I've noticed this phenomenon before: that speaking French makes me more frank – by necessity, I suspect, because my grasp of the language lacks any of the nuances required to be guarded. Or maybe it's because I associate the language with a more cavalier period in my early twenties when subtlety wasn't high on the agenda. My dad used to say the same about my Irish grandmother and how language could change her in a flash. In English she was demure, an immigrant struggling to survive in wartime London. But in the 1920s she had lived an altogether more glamorous existence in Paris, and for the rest of her life, whenever she spoke French, she became vivacious, sophisticated and glorious.

In any case, there I was telling Radigue blunt truths as she asked her clear-gazed questions. The sudden candour was a shock to the system and somewhere along the way I dropped my glass, champagne forming a fizzy puddle around my socks. 'Now we're getting somewhere!' she laughed, handing me a cloth.

This is what Radigue's music does too. It prises into the best-defended recesses.

Eventually our conversation that night was cut short. I had a ticket for a concert across town at the new hall, the Philharmonie de Paris, and I headed off under strict instructions to report back on the acoustics. Due to frail health, Radigue doesn't leave her apartment much these days, and I found it heartbreaking not being able to bring her with me, this woman who has spent her whole life investigating sound and spaces. Buildings are, she says, like conch shells, in which the audience is placed 'as if inside the body of an instrument'. Of course she wanted to know what it was like to be inside the shiniest new shell in Paris. As I pulled on my coat, she ordered me to come back. 'There is much more to talk about,' she said.

The second time I visited her in Montparnasse, a photographer was in attendance and Radigue seemed embarrassed. She wasn't enjoying the photoshoot. She gestured at a Zimmer frame pushed into the corner of the room. 'It's so ugly,' she whispered. 'Don't you think it makes me look old?' Nah, I assured her. In a sky-blue silk scarf that matched her eyes, she looked electric.

There is one more important concept behind Radigue's Occam pieces. It's a sort of dizzy expansiveness that comes if you try to fathom the infinity of magnetic wavelengths. Radigue describes it as some kind of cosmic sonic bathing pool, and for her it defines the spirit of the whole series. 'A kind of vertigo,' she says, explaining how she first experienced it years ago when she had an epiphany standing in a museum and imagining all the wavelengths bouncing from the earth to the sun and onwards between galaxies. 'It was too much to comprehend. I imagined how we are all bathing in a galactic ocean of sound waves.' I love the immersive hugeness of that prospect, which I suspect is what Walter Smetak wanted to achieve in his *Estudio Ovo*. It's the exact effect of sinking into Radigue's music. I picture her back in Nice while she was pregnant, secretly swimming the Mediterranean at night. Now she swims this great ocean in her mind, where sounds are a shoreline constantly reshaped by the lapping waves.

Radigue is no lone wolf of slow-fi quietude. In terms of her private spirituality, she shares the intensity of Ustvolskaya and Emahoy, of Sofia Gubaidulina and Arvo Pärt – not because her works are so explicitly defined by faith, but because her boundless attention to musical process is intricately informed by her meditation practice. She is an original deep minimalist, an exemplar of close and concentrated listening. In a world increasingly polarised by voices who shout the loudest and dogma that sticks its heels in the staunchest, we might do well to calibrate to such lessons in subtle wonder. Such pursuits of sound within sound.

. . .

There is another composer who hunts down subtle sounds with virtuosic patience and playfulness. A composer ready to relinquish control and let her ears and the elements transport her places. A composer who up-tips conventional compositional practice, that act of organising and pinning down sound, and becomes – well, let's try calling her an anti-composer.

Annea Lockwood

(b. 1939)

New Zealand river crossings:
hung up on serenity

The piece begins on a walkway lined with cedars, leading to a small clearing in the forest. In the clearing are two hammocks. Sound bounces all around the trees and dangles from the branches. Sub-woofers boost the lowest frequencies. We hear bats, tiger moths, earthquakes, hydrothermal vents, the sun, but it isn't obvious which source is making which sound. The trees themselves are joining in. Listeners fold themselves into the hammocks – the hammocks are important, because the more relaxed we feel, the better we can really hear. The piece is called *Wild Energy*, made by Annea Lockwood together with the sound designer Bob Bielecki, and it's typical Lockwood in her knack of connecting places, ears, bodies, breath and the natural world.

Lockwood is one of the world's great listeners. She is one of the world's great devotees of tactile sound. The way she thinks about sound is playful, elated, specific, subversive, up-close, hard-hitting and soft-moulding. Since the late 1960s, this New Zealander has been staging mischievous and meticulous situational dramas in sound. Sometimes her works involve the slow decay of instruments. Sometimes they involve placing us in the torrent of gurgling rivers. Always she considers how sound is formed by nature and by our own bodies, and what sound can do to nature and our bodies in return. Sound is a transfer of energy, she says. It can carry us, imprint upon us, awaken, attune and attend us. Sound can make us feel. Sound can make us care.

The first time Lockwood performed one of her *Piano Transplants*, she gave a clapped-out old upright a beauty makeover. She dangled an empty Chianti bottle against the strings: it made tinkling glissandos. She glued a pair of vaudeville eyes onto the body of the instrument and applied mascara to the lashes. When she played a trill, those lashes would blink seductively. A little train ran vertically up and down the bass strings, operated by tugging a thread, and when Lockwood pressed the soft pedal, bubbles would emerge from plasticine lips at the side of the keyboard. She stipulated that whoever was in charge of this permanently prepared piano must choose one tune and stick to it like a cranky bar singer. For her own part, she settled on 'Lili Marlene' and played it on loop.

Her next transplant involved burning. The year was 1968 – 'We were burning American flags, political effigies, the status quo,' Lockwood later recalled. She had been commissioned to write a score for the choreographer Richard Alston. That particular dance piece, *Heat*, never actually materialised, but Lockwood took the brief at its word and set out to capture the essence of immolation. She tried recording bonfires and fireplaces but nothing felt, well, hot enough. She wanted a sound that scorched, a sound that was 'really sonically interesting'. If an emblem of female domesticity happened to combust in the process, so much the better.

At the time, the Wandsworth Borough dump in south-west London had a special area reserved for defunct parlour pianos. A lot of pianos were being chucked out in those days to make room for incoming television sets. Lockwood went to the dump, picked out one of the doomed instruments and dragged it to the embankment of the Thames where the performance poet Bob Cobbing was hosting an arts festival. She set to work, wrapping a bunch of old microphones in asbestos so they might withstand the flames as long as possible, wiring them up to a reel-to-reel Uher tape machine and burying them inside the belly of the instrument. Then she added a dash of lighter fluid and struck a match.

A crowd gathered and chattered so excitedly that the recording – the whole point of the exercise – was wrecked. Eventually the spectators fell silent as they gazed, mesmerised, into the flames. Strings twanged, wood creaked and various glues and varnishes melted. The piano burned for more than three hours. When the last embers had died down, Lockwood and a group of fellow artists retreated to a tent and performed a seance to summon the spirit of Beethoven. They asked him what he thought of their act. His answer was not articulated very clearly in the tent that day, but apparently some strange affirmative blurp did emerge on the tape recording when 'Ludi' was summoned for the third and final time. I like to think he was grunting his ghostly approval.

Annea Lockwood has drowned pianos in cattle ponds in Amarillo, Texas (*Piano Drowning*, in which a $100 white parlour instrument with gilt ornamentation gets submerged). She has planted pianos in genteel English gardens in Essex (*Piano Garden*, in which various instruments are set among laurel saplings and foxgloves). She has invited the sea to lap around the legs of a grand piano which she marooned on a beach at the high tide line. That was her work *Southern Exposure*, which she dreamed up in 1982 but finally managed to stage only decades later in Fremantle, Australia. The piano in question mysteriously disappeared just a day after it was installed, triggering an SOS call-out complete with reward in exchange for a tip-off on the piano's whereabouts. A group of backpackers turned themselves in. They had earnestly 'rescued' the instrument, which they thought had been abandoned, and had carried it back to their hostel and set about restoring the bodywork. The misunderstanding was cleared up and the piano was reinstated on the beach, where eventually a storm dismembered the legs and filled the body with sand and seaweed. The notes, played by the wind, rain and birds, rang on.

Instrumenticide was all the rage when Lockwood began her series of transplants. Keith Moon was exploding drum kits and Jimi Hendrix was smashing guitars. In 1968, a piano was dropped from a helicopter in front of 3,000 spectators in Washington State. Four years later, students at MIT inaugurated what is still an annual 'piano drop' from atop their dormitory roof, gleefully obliterating what they saw as a symbol of tradition-bound music making. For Lockwood, herself a talented pianist, that sort of pulverising vandalism was never the point. She wasn't interested in violence and she found the most brute sounds of destruction uninteresting.

Her pursuit was the opposite: she wanted to see where close listening and attention to process might get her. Above all, she searched for sounds that were rich and complex enough to trigger a wake-up call. Her hunch was that if we allow ourselves to listen properly, if we start to really feel a sound in our bodies, we might also start to take more notice of the thing that made it. If that thing is a river, or a cat, or a neighbourhood, or a fellow human being, we might start to care about the source in new and deeper ways.

With her *Piano Transplants*, Lockwood explored what it might mean to let natural elements – fire, water, wind, plants, earth – work their unbiddable stuff on an instrument that had been built for maximum control. She works with an impish, considered abandon. I don't mean to suggest she isn't precise, because she is, extremely. But she knows when and how to let go and just see what happens. In 2007, she made a piece called *Gone!*, in which she attached helium balloons to a tiny piano-shaped music box. The mini piano lifted off from inside a grand piano and floated around the concert hall, wayward, roaming free.

Here is the score for Annea Lockwood's three *Piano Transplants*, to be read left to right. The last instruction is my personal favourite because of that understated but complete surrender to the elements: *do not protect against weather / leave pianos there forever.*

PIANO BURNING

set piano upright in an open
   space
with lid closed

staple inflated balloons
   all over

spill a very little lighter fluid
   here
and light

play whatever pleases you
   for as
long as you can

PIANO DROWNING

find a shallow lake in an isolated
   place
lake should have a clay or other
   solid
form of lake-bed

slide piano into position,
   vertically
just off-shore

anchor it (by rope to a stake
   for instance)
against storms

take photographs every month

as it slows sinks (a few inches
     per year)

the Pacific Coast just off-shore is also
a good location   in this case, use only
a concert grand piano and anchor
very strongly

PIANO GARDEN

dig a sloping trench and
   slip piano
in sideways so that it is   set piano down amongst
   half-buried   young trees

plant fast growing trees and   do not protect against weather
   creepers
underneath and around   leave piano there forever
   the piano

Womens Work, 1975

. . .

Annea Lockwood is sitting in her kitchen in Upstate New York. She is eighty-one years old. Her hair is cropped short, the same crop as Peggy Seeger's. She wears a sweatshirt of blue and white stripes. She is long and lean, her movements springy, her eyes shining. She loves conversation, loves the excuse to find exactly the right words to articulate a certain line of thought. She always speaks with a smile, even when she's raking through painful memories or thorny concepts. She laughs a lot. Judging from filmed interviews with her in the 1960s, this is how she's always been. Behind her seat at the kitchen table is a pinboard crammed with useful phone numbers and train schedules into New York City (a journey of about an hour). In prime position on the board there is a snapshot of mountains. The Southern Alps of New Zealand. Home turf.

Her given name was Anne. Anne Lockwood, born in Christchurch, New Zealand, in 1939. As a child she changed the 'e' at the end of her first name to an 'a' in an early gesture of self-

determination. Later, living on the other side of the world and feeling homesick, she became increasingly aware of what the Māori
people would term 'Pākehā', which is to say her light-skinned roots,
and she regretted not having more connection with the indigenous
population of her islands. 'Oh yes,' she sighs. 'I would love to have
had that richness.' She found a reference to a female spirit of the
Pacific whose name was 'Ea', pronounced 'é', so she conflated this
aquatic deity with her former selves, the Anne and the Anna, and
became 'Annea'. Anne-é-a.

Lockwood's mother, Fergie, was a strong and adventuresome
woman born in 1899 in Southampton, England. Fergie learned
piano and the Dalcroze movement method, took a history degree,
taught physical education and wrote theatre pieces for women living in deprived areas of Southampton. She moved to New Zealand
on a teaching exchange in her thirties, met and married George
Lockwood and gave birth to two children in quick succession just
before she turned forty. Fergie taught her daughter Anne to read
musical notation as early as she taught her to read words.

George Lockwood was a lawyer who loved the mountains. In the
early decades of the twentieth century, he and his friends purchased
little huts in the Southern Alps and set up mountaineering clubs
and ski schools. They pioneered routes through the mountains,
where Annea and her brother spent summers and winters camping
out by the rivers, learning to identify the birds and listening to
the water. Those were serious rivers, fast and forceful and multi-
currented. George taught his children how to cross them safely:

1) observe the weather conditions
2) tie a rope between you, as though traversing a glacier
3) be strong and be bold

The family home in Christchurch was full of books and music. Records on frequent play included Schubert chamber music, Tchaikovsky's *Romeo and Juliet* Fantasy Overture and Kathleen Ferrier singing Mahler's *Das Lied von der Erde* in her rust-toned contralto. On warm spring and autumn evenings when they weren't camping in the mountains, the Lockwoods would jump in the car as soon as George knocked off work and drive to the coast to swim in the Pacific Ocean. Christchurch was, says Lockwood, a wholesome place to grow up. 'Politically conservative,' she adds, but a city passionate about its music, with two decent choirs and an active music department at the university. Her piano teacher was a kind and diligent woman by the name of Gwen Moon, and Gwen's viola-playing husband, Ron Moon, led a string ensemble, which he encouraged Lockwood to write for. Nobody around her seemed to question the fact she should be composing little string ensemble pieces at the age of twelve. 'My mother took my composing seriously,' she says. 'So I also took it seriously.'

Gung-ho, humble, straight-up Annea Lockwood moved to London at the beginning of the 1960s, part-funded by a master's scholarship to the Royal College of Music, part-funded by the New Zealand government on the condition she would come home when she finished her studies and become a teacher. She never did. After a few years in the British capital, Lockwood decided to cut free and repay the New Zealand government instead. To raise enough money, she worked for a year in a psychiatric hospital where she remembers spending most of her time encouraging troubled young women to write poetry.

Her early student compositions were well behaved enough. She studied piano with Edgar Kendall Taylor and composition with Peter Racine Fricker, who himself wrote knotty contrapuntal symphonies and string quartets. Fricker guided Lockwood through post-Mahlerian sound worlds where she tried her hand at composing Sappho settings for soprano and flute; a violin concerto that was performed by Frederick Grinke and what was then the BBC Welsh Orchestra; a set of songs based on twelfth-century letters between the French abbess Héloïse and her lover Peter Abelard which were performed by soprano Noelle Barker at the Society for the Promotion of New Music. These were no small successes for a student composer, but her passion for writing concertos and song cycles was already dwindling.

This transition intrigues me: the musical and conceptual distance Lockwood travelled in the early years of the 1960s. How does a diligent young student walk up the august steps of the Royal College of Music only to emerge a couple of years later writing pieces that literally smash apart conventional mechanisms and leave the wreckage wide open to the elements? 'My parents,' she offers when I put the question to her. Of course! Those river crossings. That instinct to question and venture – it had always been there, she says, inherited from her father who trailblazed new routes through the mountains and her mother who took it as read that a girl of twelve should commit her own music to manuscript paper.

'Thing is', she expands, 'I've always liked *exploring*. I wasn't drawn to continuing to work in the styles I was hearing around me. They were well known to me. There was nothing distinct there that I wanted to probe.' She stops herself mid-thought and laughs, throwing back her head. 'Wait, isn't that an absurd thing to say? There was plenty to probe! I suppose a better way of putting it is that I wasn't hearing the inspiration there that I found in other sounds.' Any known-ness, any well-trodden-ness, was increasingly uninteresting to her. It was wilderness that enticed.

Lockwood got caught up in the countercurrents, discovering there was more to sound than could be straitjacketed into

conventionally notated music. To his credit, Peter Fricker recognised that his gently spoken but fiercely enquiring student
needed broader perspectives, and he pointed her in the direction
of the Darmstadt Summer Course, where in adjacent classrooms
of a concrete education block she could attend lectures by Luciano
Berio, Olivier Messiaen, Pierre Boulez and Karlheinz Stockhausen.
She witnessed La Monte Young pushing furniture around a room
in his *Poem for Tables, Chairs, Benches, etc.*, and befriended Franco
Evangelisti, a progenitor of aleatoricism, which is music made
using elements of chance. There's a photograph of the two of them,
Annea and Franco, her in heels and neat skirt, him in oversized
leather jacket and shades. In those days, Darmstadt was a playground of iconoclasm, a battleground of ideologues. Lockwood
says she 'loved that there was a vital push and pull going on' over
the direction that new music should take in the fractured post-war
landscape. The stern rigour of serialism, where notes and other
factors are pre-ordained, versus the deliberate freedom of chance
operations – 'The sense', Lockwood sums up, 'that all parameters
could be consciously designed in serialism, and on the other hand
an openness to parameters taking unexpected swerves.' She found
that stylistic tug of war 'totally exhilarating'.

Lockwood was not the only woman at Darmstadt in the early
1960s (Else Marie Pade, as we know, was there honing her electronic techniques during the same period) but she seems bemused
when she reflects on the fact she was one of relatively few. 'Do you
know, Kate, it just wasn't something that struck me at the time,'
she shakes her head. 'But definitely something which I became
increasingly aware of. By the time I went to Bilthoven [the CEM
studio in the Netherlands where she studied electronic music with
the composer Gottfried Michael Koenig], I found myself the only
woman in the group. Then I was very much aware of it.' How

did it feel? She pauses for a long while, considering the question with great scrutiny. 'No,' she eventually replies. 'No, I don't want to comment on that, because I can't do so with clarity. My many subsequent years as a feminist would colour my response. I know how I would feel about it now, but truly, I can't remember how I felt about it then.'

This is classic Lockwood. This frank self-forgiveness. Like Peggy Seeger, she won't project, refuses to backdate her contemporary feminism. She reminds me of my own Canadian mother, who regularly shakes her head at the astounding acts of misogyny she accepted as 'just part of the job' when she was a young teacher in 1970s Toronto. When I rage at the fact she put up with it, my mum just smiles. 'I didn't know better then,' she tells me. 'I didn't know what you know now.'

'I will say this,' Lockwood interjects. 'As I kept working with electronic resources over the years, every now and then I would find myself questioning my own technological capabilities and under-standing. At times I was susceptible to assuming that my abilities weren't as sharp as they should be. And yet I have kept producing work, and it has kept being OK. But yes, there is a long history of doubt about how proficient I am technically, and I do think that comes from the male dominance of the tech world in those days. And – well, it's still a pretty male world.'

Lockwood's feminism emerged gradually, propelled by what she describes as 'moments of acute revelation'. She befriended the radical multimedia artist Carolee Schneemann, who released a film of herself and her boyfriend James Tenney having sex in order to reclaim the lens on female desire. She met the video-art pioneer Nam June Paik and the performance-art cellist Charlotte Moorman, who was famously arrested mid-performance for playing topless in Paik's *Opera Sextronique* at the Film-Makers' Cinematheque in New York City. Lockwood observed how hard Moorman had to work compared to Paik in order to get noticed and achieve her creative vision. 'How much she struggled. How absolutely neces-sary it was for her to assert what she wanted, and how easily it came to Nam June.' There's a lightness in the way she talks about all this, as though she is simply sitting back and observing the times she lived through. Like Éliane Radigue, she doesn't become consumed by the injustices. She doesn't waste her time with resentment.

Here's a point that strikes me as particularly telling. 'Because I was a woman,' Lockwood reflects, 'and there weren't as many of us working in composition then as there are now, maybe in a way it became more enticing for me to explore, rather than to try to hue a career path against some considerable odds.' This seems to me a masterclass in reframing – turning obstacles into incentives to do things her own way. She didn't bother vying, but instead side-stepped the male-dominated world of orchestral commissions and went off-piste. Was it the only way she could keep going? 'Ah,' she grins mischievously. 'I was going to keep going anyway.'

. . .

Anna Lockwood's glass concerts began with a half-hour black-out. This was in late 1968, and the venue was a hippy haven called Middle Earth in London's Covent Garden. Submerged in total enveloping darkness, dressed in polite skirts and knitwear, hair elegantly clasped back, Lockwood shattered stuff. She brought mallets down on panes of glass: crash! She toppled whole glassy stacks: a spectral splintering! Mainly, she found the basic sound of breaking glass a bit crude, so she made delicate clinking mobiles and rubbed cello bows along the edges of large wired-glass panes. She set huge sheets of glass gently swinging against each other, and, when the lights at last came up, those sheets glinted as they twisted and twirled.

Her glass concerts gathered a cult following. The likes of Pink Floyd's Richard Wright, Soft Machine's Kevin Ayers and composer Michael Nyman counted themselves as devotees. Nyman, who was working as a music critic at the time, reviewed a Lockwood performance for the *New Statesman*, calling the concerts 'more astonishing, rare and enchanting' than most contemporary music that was being created electronically. 'A studio full of elaborate equipment is not necessary,' he concluded, which was precisely Lockwood's point: she did not need the sine-wave oscillators or the ring modulators, the reverb chambers or the modular synthesisers. She found more than enough sonic intrigue within natural sources.

Lockwood called her glass works 'anti-composition' because she felt the process was more about discovering, uncovering and revealing than imposing any grand design. Like her *Piano Transplants*, this was no gimmick or exercise in destruction. It was the intricacy of the sounds that enthralled her. 'The sounds were interestingly complex,' she explains. 'And varied. And fun to work with.'

She listened intently to the effects of bowing, rubbing and shattering. She zoomed in on the cross-section of sound, aurally delineating lines and angles like a meticulous architectural sketch.

> I was thinking: usually, in most music, a listener doesn't have time to absorb all the delicate details of a timbral structure before we move onto the next sound. And we're always combining sounds to create more and more complex timbral structures. The inherent detail of any one sound tends to get buried. I was thinking: I need to learn to hear each sound.
>
> I need some ear training.

After honing her methods late at night in a church in north London with the help of audio engineer and producer Michael Steyn, she recorded her debut album. *The Glass World of Anna Lockwood* is part meditation ritual, part tactile sound laboratory, part dance, part abstract song without words.

During this period of glassy revelation, Lockwood was living in Essex and married to a larger-than-life American character named Harvey Matusow whose backstory is colourful indeed. Matusow seemed to live multiple lives. Born in the Bronx, he became a communist actor then turned FBI informant. By the time Lockwood met him, he had recanted, quit the USA, moved to England and reinvented himself as an avant-garde arts entrepreneur. He would go on to reinvent himself several times again – as a clown, as a television executive, as an Aquarian Age mystic, as a Mormon convert and, under the name Job Matusow, as a maker of chimes using reformed ammunition and bomb shells. His reserve lives ran out in

2002 when he died in a car accident, long after he and Lockwood had parted ways.

During that period in the late 1960s, Matusow lived with Lockwood in the Essex village of Ingatestone. Now it's affluent commuter belt within easy reach of London, but at the time it was an unlikely enclave of radical artists – home to the French sound poet Henri Chopin and to Penny Rimbaud and Gee Vaucher of the punk band Crass. Matusow, never slow to foment action wherever he landed, formalised the Ingatestone alt-culture scene when he organised a festival in the village which he titled the International Carnival of Experimental Sound. The festival opened with John Cage's multimedia piece *HPSCHD*, for which he recruited a harpsichord and an illustrious rota of musicians to play it – including the avant-garde pianists David Tudor and John Tilbury, the communist composer Cornelius Cardew, and his own wife, Anna Lockwood. While they played Cage's music for harpsichord and computer-generated sounds, Matusow projected films onto oversized balloons, which bobbed around in the background.

Lockwood, meanwhile, was changing the Essex landscape in subtler ways. Ingatestone is where she planted her original *Piano Garden*, setting three pianos among the laurels just off Station Road. Occasional passengers walking home from the London train would venture through her gate and test out the earthy keys.

. . .

In 1970, Lockwood made a piece called *Tiger Balm*, mixing BBC archive recordings of mating tigers with sounds of tree frogs, volcanoes, earthquakes, a heartbeat, an airplane, her own voice and a purring cat – specifically Carolee Schneemann's cat, Kitch, who even sneezed on cue. *Tiger Balm* is a hyper-sensual ensemble piece, an erotic elegy, sounds of feline and woman so intertwined that the tiger becomes a sort of wild, glorious avatar.

1970 was also the year that Lockwood started writing letters to San Diego. On the receiving end was a forceful and gregarious accordionist-composer called Pauline Oliveros, who was busy shaking up the musical climate of the American West Coast. Oliveros was a founding member of the San Francisco Tape Music Center and she, too, was digging deep into the connection between music and the body. Oliveros and Lockwood exchanged ideas and shared scores. Oliveros posted Lockwood her *Sonic Meditations* – exercises in sound and mindfulness – and Lockwood organised groups to perform them in the gardens of Ingatestone. Their first in-person meeting took place in California in 1972 and was captured in a live radio conversation on Berkeley's KPFA FM. It's fascinating to listen back now to that rambling interview. Oliveros holds court, recounting her dreams. Lockwood is the more unassuming and inquisitive of the pair, an astute and gentle listener, less assertive but clearly sure of her own mind. When Oliveros asks what music is floating her boat at the moment, Lockwood confides: 'I'm really hung up on serenity-inducing sounds.'

Lockwood's centre of gravity was being tugged west. She was increasingly beguiled by the work of American artists whom she encountered as they passed through London: David Behrman, Robert Ashley, Alvin Lucier, Carolee Schneemann, Nam June Paik, Larry Austin who published an avant-garde music periodical called *Source*. She remembers the work of these US-based music-makers as 'vibrant and exploratory' in ways she had experienced in London in the 1960s, but which, she says, 'seemed to be settling' since the turn of the 1970s. She singles out Cornelius Cardew – charismatic composer and co-founder of the improvising Scratch Orchestra – as a major factor in what she felt was becoming an English new-music monoculture. 'His position, the positions he took on, became more and more central to the London scene,' she notes. 'And it wasn't a perspective I was interested in. The American scene looked more and more open. Full of all sorts of low- and high-level opportunities. Especially low-level opportunities. Those tended to be the most exciting.' Her Ingatestone chapter came to a close in 1973. Was it painful to uproot from her *Piano Garden*? 'Well,' she ponders, closing her eyes a moment, 'I have the tendency to move on and not look back.'

. . .

It was Pauline Oliveros who introduced Lockwood to the woman with whom she would spend the next forty-six years of her life. Ruth Anderson: a fellow composer, a maker of electronic music and a virtuosically sensitive listener. Ruth Anderson: playful, practical, capable and tenacious.

Anderson was born in 1928 and grew up in a forestry family in Montana. She studied at Princeton and in Paris with Darius Milhaud and Nadia Boulanger. In her twenties she worked as a flautist, including in the role of principal flute of the Boston Pops Orchestra. In 1968, Anderson became one of the first three female electronic music studio directors in the USA when she headed up the new studio at Hunter College in New York City. In 1973, she wrote a blithely satirical collage work called *SUM (State of the Union Message)*, which lasts for exactly the duration of Nixon's State of the Union Message. The piece flits from the president's voice through fragments of outrageously patronising television adverts, making a dark, zany farce of it all. Anderson admitted her intention was to say 'as little and, by extension, as much as the president'.

The summer of 1973, Anderson took a sabbatical and asked Oliveros to cover her teaching at Hunter College. Oliveros was unavailable, but she recommended a certain Ms. Lockwood, a UK-based New Zealander who was interested in deep and tender sounds. For her part, Lockwood was wary. She had never done any hands-on work with the sort of voltage-controlled equipment she would need to navigate in Anderson's teaching studio. (Again, that tendency to doubt her own technical capability.) Anderson reassured her. Her teaching ethos was all about *play*, she said. Students treated the place like their own homes. They brought in slippers, a sofa, a lamp. 'I give lots of facts,' Anderson wrote to Lockwood when she was still in Essex, encouraging her to make the move,

> And I am very demanding – that they know, that they have self-respect, that they only DO – and sometimes I see it's not yet the time to DO and they will . . . and leave them alone, or help when I see they need it . . . and from students who have been with me before, begin to understand this is not a course, but some equipment and a safe place to be. As soon as the students so-called begin to know each other, to hear a great variety of music, or also experience acoustics, experience each other through sound, like the skin-resistance oscillators, they learn and do, or dream.

Here is an exercise that Anderson wrote for her students in 1973. It's called *Sound Portrait: Hearing a Person*.

In a darkened room, find a comfortable, totally relaxed position.

Listen to a piece of music.

Think of someone you love.
Do not think of the music.

When you find your thought of the person is gone, bring it
  back gently.
Let other thoughts come, and then let them go.

As the music progresses, let the thought image of the person
  be central.
Be unaware of the music.

Let anything which happens happen, except keep easily bringing
  back, letting, the person image occupy you.

You will find explanations of the person – the music will explain
  the person.

The music ideas, counterpoint, extensions, contrasts, repetitions,
  variants,
Rhythms, textures, qualities of sound, all music elements are
  of the person,

sometimes very literally, sometimes suggesting, sometimes exact,
  sometimes
understood, sometimes leading to understanding, sometimes
  verging on language,
always primarily nonverbal, always a known sense, a coming
  of a known sense.

You will find after, an understanding of the person you did not have,
and a personal relationship to the music.

The music, too, will be known.

Lockwood was heartened by Anderson's methods. Moreover, she was keen for any excuse to get herself to the United States, and so she accepted the teaching post. On the day they met, Anderson wore a blue shirt, white shorts and a pair of trainers with a hole in the toe. Within three days, romance had seized the two of them like an ambush. 'It was inescapably clear within a couple of weeks,' Lockwood smiles. 'Very clear. Very fast. A mutual recognition of some sort. We were both mavericks by nature. Both came from societies which in gender terms were really conservative. Both propelled ourselves into radical milieus. Oh,' she sighs, 'and Ruth was totally enchanting. How could I not fall in love with her on the spot?'

During that first summer, with Lockwood teaching in New York and Anderson on sabbatical in Hancock, New Hampshire, the two of them talked on the phone constantly. Unbeknownst to Lockwood, Anderson taped the calls and made a sonic love letter out of the recordings. She called the piece *Conversations* – a collage of the two women's voices, their sweet nothings, their in-betweens and laughter. She interwove snatches of old popular songs like 'Yes Sir, That's My Baby' and 'Oh, You Beautiful Doll'. 'Yes, conversations', Anderson wrote to Lockwood, 'replayed at another time are like photographs, a framed, kept, high-tuned awareness for flow of rhythm from a person, that person's composition & a composition of that person, how people cope with that one medium we must all share, of speech.'

Lockwood was thirty-four when she met Anderson, who was forty-five. They would live together for nearly five decades. A friend told them about a house going cheap in the woods north of New York City near a hamlet called Crompond. The house had a yard and enough space for two composers to make music without disturbing each other. They bought the place and loved it, but they both still yearned for the mountains. Ruth's brothers had inherited the Anderson family cabins out West, so she and Lockwood decided to build their own. In 1975 they purchased a plot of land near Flathead Lake in Montana and spent every holiday for the next fourteen years working as part-time construction labourers. They felled trees and designed a floor plan. They built frames and siding, exteriors and tongue-and-groove interiors. They finished the house in time for Christmas of 1989.

Back in New York State, they composed alongside each other but never together, respecting an unspoken rule of creative independence. Lockwood tells me how much she hates to talk about her pieces until they're pretty much finished. 'You can', she warns, 'talk out a piece until it dissolves under you and the enticements have disappeared!' That leave-me-alone rule applied to Anderson as much as it did to anyone. Feedback in the Anderson–Lockwood household was delivered with fiercely guarded delicacy, one woman making a gentle suggestion only after the requisite compliments had been dispatched. Sometimes it went horribly wrong. When Anderson ventured that the repeated B-flat harmonics in Lockwood's piano work *Red Mesa* perhaps 'went on a bit', Lockwood sulked for days. 'Only when I got over the affront that there was something I needed to do to the piece . . . of course I realised she was entirely right.'

They didn't compose together, but they did teach together. In fact, they fundamentally rewrote the syllabus of their 'Introduction to Music' class at Hunter College, so that students would spend the first part of the course learning about psycho-acoustics and the second part studying the musical cultures of their various ethnic backgrounds. Hunter being a college in inner-city New York, they were not short of different ethnic backgrounds to explore. Students were required to keep an 'ear journal' in order to focus their listening on the environments around them. 'New Yorkers' ears are so darned *defended*,' Lockwood shakes her head. 'So we asked them to open up.'

They also introduced a new class, which they called 'Women in Music'. 'Ruth, being a practical person, said that one of the problems for young women coming out of a music degree was what on earth to do with it. How to form a career given substantial barriers and the extent of male dominance that existed in almost every part of the industry. So we thought: let's bring in women and prove it's possible. I remember when [jazz singer] Betty Carter came in. She sat down on the chair with her legs splayed and said, "OK, whadda ya want from me?" Now, that was what the students needed!'

In 1975, Lockwood teamed up with the installation artist Alison Knowles to create a landmark publication called *Womens Work* – a collection of playful text-based instructional scores that they stapled together into a lo-fi magazine. Three years later they made a follow-up edition in the shape of a fold-out poster. Works by twenty-five women were included in that first edition. Lockwood herself contributed step-by-step instructions on how to enact her *Piano Transplants*. Pauline Oliveros detailed tactics on how to cause subversion on a college campus. Mary Lucier denoted triangles and circles in various landscapes. Bici Forbes, who went on to become the genre-defying artist Nye Ffarrabas, poked irreverent fun at the language of a 'women's studies' university honours programme:

** Elocution
  - On a cloudy day, scream, until rain falls.
  - On a foggy day, scream, until you have dispersed the fog.

. . .

As we talk, the West Coast of the United States is burning. Wild-fires are raging across California, Oregon and Washington, while a significant portion (roughly 20 per cent) of the United States popu-lation still denies the essential science of climate change. What can artists do? What message might cut through the denial? For the first time in our many conversations, Lockwood seems weary at the question. 'Don't know,' she shakes her head, staring at the table. 'I don't have a concrete answer to that. Ruth always used to say she believed in respite. That respite was what we could offer. We could give people a sense of ease. Help them to take a deep breath and come back into their bodies. Respite. I think I like that as much as anything. I think that is really my answer.'

The house that Lockwood and Anderson bought together in Crompond, NY, is about five miles from the banks of the Hudson river. In the 1980s, that mighty waterway swept in a new phase of Lockwood's work after she applied for a job at the Hudson River Museum and the astute personnel director, clearly having got the measure of her, responded: 'You're an artist, not an administrator. Why don't you make us an art proposal?'

Her river fixation had in fact started many decades earlier, back with those childhood camping trips in the Southern Alps of New Zealand. In her music, too, Lockwood had long been testing the waters. In the mid-1960s she launched a sprawling project called *Play the Ganges backwards one more time, Sam*, in which she whim-sically set out to create a sound archive of all the world's rivers. She asked friends to lend a hand by making recordings wherever they went. Oliveros posted her sounds from Massachusetts; Carolee Schneemann sent tapes from the Himalayas. For a 1970s performance at The Kitchen in New York, Lockwood gathered foam-rubber mattresses, projected old nineteenth-century river postcards onto the wall and pumped ozone (ozone!) into the room, thus accidentally getting everyone high while they listened to the sounds of water.

Lockwood's purpose with *Play the Ganges backwards* was to probe the possible connection between river environments and mental well-being. Like Éliane Radigue and her secret Occam scores, Lockwood loves the spontaneity of water, the way it shapes the land. Like Radigue, she loves the creative parallels. She loves how river sounds are layered, the fact her audio cortex has to do a slow scan down from the most obvious high-frequency splashes to mid- and low-frequency rumbles and rhythms that churn rhapsodically underneath the surface. She loves the scanning process, the patience it takes, the acceptance that as she scans – which requires time – the river sounds are constantly changing. She loves the interaction between the various sounds, which is especially marvellous when little series of mid-range pitches come and go and she manages to follow the dance in her listening. She finds the *aperiodicity* of those pitches delicious. It's a kind of flux and unpredictability that feels so innately natural she knows she could never construct it from scratch.

Spurred on by the commission from the Hudson River Museum, Lockwood set to work mapping rivers. Her landmark album *A Sound Map of the Hudson River* charts the sounds of the waterway from the Adirondack Mountains to the Atlantic Ocean, beginning at Lake Tear of the Clouds in upstate New York and following the water south to Staten Island. Mixed in a separate audio file, we hear the voices of fishermen, river pilots, a ranger in the Adirondacks, a farmer near the city of Troy – people who worked the river. The broader politics of the Hudson, its eddies of colonialism and industry, are left unsounded. 'It's not my history,' Lockwood says. 'In New Zealand, rivers are not so storied as they are in the United States and Europe and Asia. They are wild things.'

Above all what she wanted to do with her *Sound Map of the Hudson River* is trigger a sense of care. Back then, New Yorkers hardly swam in the river because it was too polluted. 'They loved the Hudson, but for most of them it was only a visual entity. They didn't have the feeling on their bodies of how powerful that river is. I wanted to get at that. Wanted to bring the sound of the river to people who live near it, some sense of the river's energy. Its physicality.'

There were more river maps to come. Two decades after the Hudson, Lockwood travelled down the Danube making recordings with hydrophones she borrowed from the composer Maggi Payne. She following the river's currents from its source in the Black Forest. In Austria she found strong whirlpools near Grein – an extremely narrow part of the river cleft. She wended through Slovakia and Hungary as the Danube snaked south. In the town of Vukovar, Croatia, where Serb forces committed mass killings, she found a tributary – the Vuka Rijeka – which raged through the centre of town. She recorded that ferocious sound up close and kept its boiling energy high in the final mix. In Serbia, at Bačko Novo Selo, the river flowed slowly, lapping against a small metal boat that was nestling on the shore. She encountered 200 geese grazing in a dried-out channel, and lingered on the way their calls echoed around the distant trees. Finally she followed the water through Romania and Bulgaria to the wide delta on the Black Sea. She did not record the river in Vienna or Budapest or Belgrade: the great Danube cities pave their banks with stone and rocks, and she preferred to record in unsuspecting places where the river really *sounds*. She zoomed in on aquatic insects and riverbank rodents. She spoke to people along the way. She asked: 'What does the river mean to you? Could you live without it?' The question she asked most was: 'What is a river? I.e. what is the *being* of a river?'

A Sound Map of the Hudson River was released in 1989, the year of the *Exxon Valdez* oil spill. Lockwood claims she is no overt activist, that she makes an effort to avoid being didactic in her work. 'Whenever I've tried to be,' she says frankly, 'it hasn't worked.' (In the late 1970s, she wanted to make a work about violence inflicted on women. She went to a district in Queens, NY, that reported particularly high incidents of domestic abuse. She talked with women who were working with victims, and she talked to women who were experiencing the abuse. She made a piece called *Woman Murder*. She says: 'It was so overt, so simplistically overt, that I set it aside and didn't come back to it.') And yet – with their awe, their reverence, their sense of acute attention, Lockwood's river maps connect body with environment in a way that speaks obliquely and powerfully. Her work insists on a personal connection. Her work counts as activism whether in name or not.

. . .

In the early 2000s, Pauline Oliveros and her partner Ione headed to Canada to get married. Afterwards they called up Anderson and Lockwood and suggested they do the same. In 2005, around the thirtieth anniversary of felling their first trees at Flathead Lake in Montana, the couple took up the recommendation. They drove north across the border and married in Cranbrook, British Columbia.

Ruth Anderson died of lung cancer in November 2019 at the age of ninety-one. Now Lockwood is learning to inhabit their shared spaces alone. She shows me around the quiet house in Crompond. She takes me out the back door, across a broad porch with a couple of chairs set out for long conversation. Every evening, she and Ruth would meet here at 5 p.m., drink a beer, discuss the day and listen to the gathering twilight. The garden is full of tall trees. Regular visitors include deer, chipmunks, squirrels and groundhogs. ('Groundhogs: easier to handle than the bears in Montana!' Lockwood educates me. 'Actually, not true. The bears are easy to handle. You just stay out of their way.') There is a special thing that Lockwood wants to show me in the middle of the garden. A small wooden chair, a seat for a child, has been wedged up high between the four broad trunks of a tulip tree. It is part of Anderson's final installation piece, which she called *Furnishing the Garden*. Across the lawn, a pair of rusty bar stools are being invaded by rose bushes. The last music Anderson heard before she died was Mahler's Fourth Symphony. In the final movement, a soprano – Judith Blegen on the recording in question – sings of an idyllic life over low harps and lush, grassy strings.

'Kein' Musik ist ja nicht auf Erden / Die unsrer verglichen kann werden.' (There is no music on earth that can compare to ours.)

Lockwood says she was unable to even think about listening to music for a long while after Anderson's death, let alone to try composing again. Almost every sound felt too close, too shared. Only after nearly a year did she feel able to return to *Conversations*, that sonic love letter which Anderson wrote for her when they met in 1973. She travelled back to Hancock, where Anderson had spent that summer sabbatical, and made new field recordings in and around the village and at the lakes where they swam together. She revisited their love-dizzy voices from that very first summer, and she wove them into a new work full of deep, quiet fondness. She called it *For Ruth*.

Here is a piece that Lockwood and Anderson wrote together a couple of years after they met. It contains just three lines of text. This is the score.

Softest Sound

Search out the softest sound you can hear. Rest in it.

Find the softest sound you can produce with the materials
    in a favorite room.
Explore it, taking an ear-journey inside it.

                    Ruth Anderson and Annea Lockwood, 1975–76

                        • • •

A sense of being *bothered*. For me, that's what sits at the heart of
Lockwood's work, and why her approach feels an essential point
of arrival at the end of this book about new routes of listening.
Without hysteria or dogma, her music connects us to ourselves,
to each other, to the earth. There is a porousness in her process,
an openness to others, a relinquishing of compositional control in
favour of – well, connection. She confirms what John Muir said,
that 'when we try to pick out anything by itself, we find it hitched
to everything else in the universe'.

Lockwood claims she is no activist, but her music awakens and
alerts us. She unmakes us, she steadies us again. At the close of a
century whose excesses pushed the planet to breaking point and
polarised its populations to mutual destruction, she put it like this:

The vital importance of developing recognition of our non-
separation from the other phenomena of the world. It's been
what I've been moving to all the time, ever since I started
recording the environment. The necessity of reattachment to
the natural world, and a deep-level reattachment to ourselves.

Listening to the natural world, looking, taking it in, smelling it
. . . all of that is vitalising. All of it re-awakens recognition.

Here is the text score to a piece that Lockwood wrote in 2018.
This one is called *listening with the neighborhood*.

listening with the neighborhood

at midnight, or at dawn, indoors or outside.

Listening with an awareness that all around you are other
    life-forms simultaneously listening
        and sensing with you – plant roots, owls, centipedes,
        cicadas – mutually intertwined
within the   web of vibrations which animate and surround
our planet.

Listening to feel that 'I am one with all these phenomena.
Can I know it?' I listen to know it.
    What we are at one with, we cannot harm.

Annea Lockwood, 2018

Timeline

1900   Amy Beach premieres her Piano Concerto with the Boston Symphony Orchestra. Sibelius's *Finlandia* premieres in Helsinki. Kodak launches the Brownie, a cheap camera which democratises photography.

1901   Guglielmo Marconi transmits a transatlantic radio signal from Cornwall to Newfoundland. The Uganda Railway links Mombasa to Lake Victoria.

1902   **Julián Carrillo** presents his Symphony no. 1 as a graduation piece in Leipzig. The United States declares victory at the end of the Philippine–American War.

1904   Nadia Boulanger begins teaching music theory lessons in her apartment in Paris.

1905   Mass unrest erupts against Tsar Nicholas II in the First Russian Revolution.

1906   The Muslim League forms in Dhaka.

1907   Annie Besant becomes president of the international Theosophical Society in Madras. Alfred Stieglitz makes his photograph *The Steerage*, documenting segregated classes on a transatlantic crossing. Joseph Marx coins the term 'atonality'.

1908   Béla Bartók goes on his first field-trip recording folk tunes. The Austro-Hungarian Empire annexes Bosnia and Herzegovina, sparking the Bosnian crisis. Canadian actor Florence Lawrence, the 'Biograph Girl', becomes the first movie star.

1910   Revolution breaks out in Mexico. Boutros Ghali is assassinated in Egypt. *Frankenstein* becomes the first widely recognised horror film.

1912   Schoenberg's *Pierrot lunaire* premieres in Berlin after forty rehearsals. The Chinese Empire falls.

1913   Stravinsky's *Le Sacre du printemps* premieres in Paris. Mahatma Gandhi is arrested for protesting against the treatment of Indians in South Africa. Buenos Aires opens South America's first subway rail network.

1916   The Easter Rising marks the beginning of armed conflict in the Irish revolution.

1917   Bolsheviks seize power in Russia. Erik Satie's surrealist ballet *Parade* premieres in Paris with a scenario by Jean Cocteau and sets/costumes by Pablo Picasso.

1918   Women over the age of thirty win the right to vote in the UK, though it takes another decade for equal suffrage to be achieved.

1922   T. S. Eliot publishes *The Waste Land* in London. James Joyce publishes *Ulysses* in Paris. **Ruth Crawford** writes her first piece, *Little Waltz*, in Chicago. Ezra Pound declares a new era.

1923   Bessie Smith signs to Columbia Records. Mustafa Kemal Atatürk becomes first president of the Republic of Turkey. In Mexico, **Julián Carrillo** publishes his *Teoría del Sonido 13* (Theory of the Thirteenth Sound).

1924   Pablo Neruda publishes *Veinte poemas de amor y una canción desesperada* (Twenty Love Poems and a Song of Despair).

1925   Alban Berg's opera *Wozzeck* premieres in Berlin. Sergei Eisenstein's film *Battleship Potemkin* radicalises film editing in the Soviet Union and around the world.

1926   Leopold Stokowski conducts the premiere of Edgard Varèse's *Amériques* in New York. Gertrude Ederle becomes the first woman to swim from France to England.

1928   Joseph Stalin launches his first Five-Year Plan. Alexander Fleming discovers penicillin. *Die Dreigroschenoper* (The Threepenny Opera) by Kurt Weill and Bertolt Brecht opens in Berlin.

1929   Stock markets crash on Wall Street, triggering the Great Depression.

1931   **Ruth Crawford** writes her *String Quartet 1931* while living in Berlin as the first female recipient of a Guggenheim composer fellowship.

1933   Florence Price's First Symphony is the first work by an African-American woman to be played by any major orchestra.

1934   Umm Kulthum sings for the inaugural broadcast of Egypt's state station, Radio Cairo.

1936   Stalin walks out of Shostakovich's *Lady Macbeth of the Mtsensk District* and two days later the Soviet state newspaper *Pravda* slams the opera as 'Muddle Instead of Music'.

1936   Haile Selassie flees Addis Ababa after Benito Mussolini's troops invade Ethiopia.

1937   Silvestre Revueltas travels to Europe to fight for the republican side in the Spanish Civil War. **Walter Smetak** moves to Brazil. **José Maceda** moves to Paris.

1938   Significant oil reserves are discovered in Saudi Arabia.

1940   **Else Marie Pade** joins the Danish resistance. Conlon Nancarrow moves to Mexico. Also in Mexico: Frida Kahlo paints *Self-Portrait with Thorn Necklace and Hummingbird*, Trotsky is assassinated and Silvestre Revueltas dies of alcohol-induced pneumonia.

1944   In Cairo, Halim El-Dabh creates *The Expression of Zaar*, the first piece of *musique concrète*.

1945   In Buenos Aires, Jorge Luis Borges publishes his short story collection *El Aleph* (The Aleph).

1946   The Philippines gains independence from the USA. In Addis Ababa, **Emahoy Tsegué-Mariam Guèbru's** visa application is rejected and she turns to God.

1947   India and the newly created Pakistan gain independence from the UK.

1948   A young Peggy Seeger goes missing in a department store in Washington DC and is rescued by Elizabeth Cotten. Israel is created, and the Palestinian Nakba begins.

1949   Indonesia wins sovereignty as Dutch forces withdraw.

1950   Le Corbusier is commissioned to design Chandigarh as a new capital city for India's Punjab and Haryana states.

1951   Akira Kurosawa's film *Rashomon* wins the Grand Prix (the Golden Lion of St Mark) at the Venice Film Festival and an Oscar, introducing Japanese cinema to the West.

1952   **Else Marie Pade** and **Éliane Radigue** encounter the *musique concrète* works of Pierre Schaeffer via radio programmes in Denmark and France. The pianist David Tudor premieres John Cage's *4'33"* in Woodstock, NY.

1956   Peggy Seeger performs in London and meets Ewan MacColl; the following year he writes *The First Time Ever I Saw Your Face* for her.

1957   Tōru Takemitsu writes his Requiem. John Lennon and Paul McCartney meet at a church garden fete in Liverpool. Laika, a Soviet dog, becomes the first animal to be launched into space.

1958   The United Arab Republic is born with the merger of Egypt and Syria, heralded as the dawn of pan-Arabism (it lasts three years). The Campaign for Nuclear Disarmament (CND) holds its first meeting with philosopher Bertrand Russell as president. Honda releases the Super Cub motorcycle, bringing mobility to millions. At the World Fair in Brussels, **Julián Carrillo** displays his metamorphoser pianos and Belgium stages a human zoo. In Nigeria, Chinua Achebe publishes *Things Fall Apart*.

1959   Ornette Coleman releases *The Shape of Jazz to Come*.

1960   Delia Derbyshire joins the BBC, transferring to the Radiophonic Workshop two years later. George Maciunas founds the Fluxus movement.

1961   Ligeti's *Atmosphères* premieres at the Donaueschingen Festival in Germany.

1962   A nuclear standoff between Krushchev and Kennedy escalates into the Cuban Missile Crisis. Judson Dance Theater stages its first performances in New York City.

1963   Anna Akhmatova's *Requiem* is published in Munich. **Emahoy** records her debut album, *Emahoy Tsegué-Mariam Guèbru spielt eigene Kompositionen*, in Bonn. The Association for Humanistic Psychology – a significant split from Freudianism and Behaviourism – holds its first meeting in Philadelphia.

1964   Stan Getz and Astrud Gilberto release 'The Girl from Ipanema' by Antônio Carlos Jobim.

1965   Malcolm X is assassinated. The Association for the Advancement of Creative Musicians is founded on the South Side of Chicago. The Second Vatican Council (Vatican II) comes to a close in Rome.

1966   China's Cultural Revolution begins. Mikhail Bulgakov's *The Master and Margarita* is published (in a censored, serialized form) in the Soviet Union.

1967   Hélio Oiticica coins the term *Tropicália* at an exhibition in Rio de Janeiro. The AACM opens its school with Roscoe Mitchell as the first dean. The Republic of Biafra attempts independence, triggering civil war in Nigeria. In Colombia, Gabriel García Márquez publishes *One Hundred Years of Solitude*. In South Africa, the world's first heart transplant is performed at the Groote Schuur hospital in Cape Town.

1968   The Troubles begin in Northern Ireland. **Annea** (then Anna) **Lockwood** stages glass concerts at Middle Earth in London.

1969   Mulatu Astatke returns to Addis Ababa with vibraphone, electric keyboards and wah-wah pedals in his suitcases. The Stonewall riots in New York City instigate the gay rights movement. Muammar Gaddafi establishes the Libyan Arab Republic.

1970   **Else Marie Pade** creates *Face It*, sampling the voice of Hitler. **Éliane Radigue** moves to New York and begins working with synthesisers. Janis Joplin dies of a heroin overdose aged twenty-seven.

1971   Idi Amin takes power in Uganda.

1973   **Annea Lockwood** meets Ruth Anderson, having been introduced by Pauline Oliveros.

1974   **José Maceda** stages his vast work *Ugnayan* using thirtyseven radio stations across the entire city of Manila. In Addis Ababa, a Marxist-Leninist faction of the Ethiopian Army overthrows the empire and establishes rule by military junta.

1975   Microsoft is founded in Albuquerque, New Mexico.

1976   In Soweto, police open fire on students protesting against Apartheid and white minority rule. In Lagos, Fela Kuti releases *Zombie* and the Nigerian government responds by destroying his commune. In New York City, Steve Reich premieres *Music for 18 Musicians*.

1977   Manhattan Plaza opens in New York City, with 70 per cent of apartments reserved for artists. Pierre Boulez's electronic music laboratory IRCAM opens under the pavement outside the Pompidou Centre in Paris. Nan Shepherd publishes *The Living Mountain*. *Star Wars* becomes the highest-grossing film of all time.

1978   Pina Bausch creates *Café Müller* for her dance company Tanztheater Wuppertal.

1979   The Iranian monarchy is overthrown by popular revolution. The first Sony Walkman goes on sale in Japan.

1980   Yuji Takahashi writes *Kwangju, May 1980* as a memorial to victims of South Korea's dictator Chun Doo-hwan.

1981   bell hooks publishes *Ain't I A Woman*. Bob Marley dies in Miami and is given a state funeral in Jamaica. Aids is clinically observed for the first time.

1982   The CD is launched as a music platform.

1983   Birth of the internet. The Québécois composer Claude Vivier is murdered in Paris by a man he picks up in a bar.

1984   George Lewis unveils *Rainbow Family* for 'interactive virtual orchestra'. Audre Lorde publishes *Sister Outsider: Essays and Speeches*.

1986   In the Philippines, the Marcos regime is ousted in the non-violent People Power Revolution. Ferdinand and Imelda Marcos flee to Hawaii.

1986 No. 4 reactor explodes at Chernobyl Nuclear Power Plant.

1988 **Galina Ustvolskaya** composes her sixth and final piano sonata.

1989 The Berlin Wall falls. Nicolae Ceauşescu is executed in Romania. Chinese troops open fire on student protesters in Tiananmen Square. An oil supertanker gushes 37,000 tonnes of crude oil off the coast of Alaska in the *Exxon Valdez* oil spill. Pauline Oliveros coins the term 'Deep Listening' to describe a practice of radical attentiveness. **Annea Lockwood** releases *A Sound Map of the Hudson River*.

1990 End of Augusto Pinochet's dictatorship in Chile.

1991 Boris Yeltsin becomes the first president of Russia.

1992 The Rio de Janeiro Earth Summit acknowledges the scale of global ecological crisis.

1993 Karlheinz Stockhausen finishes his *Helikopter-Streichquartett* (Helicopter String Quartet), the third scene of his opera *Mittwoch aus Licht*. Each member of the quartet is required to take flight in a separate helicopter.

1994 Nelson Mandela is elected president of South Africa. Jeff Bezos founds Amazon in Seattle.

1995 Thomas Vinterberg's film *Festen* introduces the Dogme 95 'vows of chastity' to film culture, and spearheads the use of small digital cameras. Windows 95 is released.

1996 Tupac Shakur is murdered in Las Vegas. The Taliban takes control of Afghanistan for the first time.

1999 Hugo Chávez becomes president of Venezuela. Vladimir Putin becomes president of Russia. Tania León writes *Horizons* for orchestra, described as a sonic creolisation.

2000 **Éliane Radigue** writes her last electronic piece, *L'Île Re-sonante*.

Thanks

To those around the world who shared expertise and insights, who guided my investigations, rerouted my dead-ends and entrusted me with invaluable contacts and research materials: thank you.

Thank you to Alejandro Madrid and Carmina Escobar, to Pascale Criton, Roberto Kolb Neuhaus, Juan Sebastián Lach Lau, Pablo Chemor and Alexander Bruck. Thank you to Judith Tick and Barbara Smetak, to Chico Dub at Novas Frequências, Luis Alvarado at Buh Records, Marco Scarassatti, Paulo Costa Lima and &. Migracielo (Edson Migracielo). Thank you to Aki Onda, Chris Brown, LaVerne C. de la Peña and Dayang Yraola, and to the University of the Philippines Center for Ethnomusicology. Thank you to Konstantin Bagrenin, Frank Denyer, Rebecca Saunders and Andrei Bakhmin, to Ilan Volkov, Maya Dunietz, Alasdair Campbell, Peter Meanwell and Hanna M. Kebbede, and to Patrick and Mark Gilkes. Thank you to Henrik Marstal, Andrea Bak and Eva Havshøj Ohrt at Edition S. Thank you to Jacob Kirkegaard: I hope we can make it to Bakken together someday. Thank you to Leonard Jones, Taylor Ho Bynum, John Hollenbeck and Petr Kotik, to John Chantler and to Rhodri Davies.

Thank you, Peggy.

Thank you, Emahoy.

Thank you, Éliane.

Thank you, Annea.

To George Lewis: deepest thanks for the warmth of your encouragement, the generosity of your time, and for your own work, which has shifted my thinking and opened my ears.

Thank you to my editor, Alexa von Hirschberg, for seizing the threads and weaving these pages into shape so expertly. Thanks to Dan Papps, Mo Hafeez, Joanna Harwood, Hannah Knowles, Amanda Russell and all at Faber for the energy, deft nudging and general classiness in bringing this book into the world. Thanks to Kate Hopkins for applying the most astute eye in the business.

Thank you to Patrick Walsh for showing early love for the project, and to John Ash for running with it so stylishly.

Thank you to those who cajoled, reassured, read drafts and gave perspective along the way: to Jonathan Cross, Philip Clark, Charlotte Higgins, Lucy Scholes, Stephen Johnson, Nate Wooley, Tom Service and Francis Bickmore.

To my brilliant producers at Radio 3 who supported, advised and accommodated my time away: thank you.

Thank you to Michael Rossi and Natacha De Bivar Palhares Rossi for the Portuguese translations. Thank you to Mark Cousins for the film history, to David Grinly for the photographs, and to Adam Molleson and Sam Woods for broadening the timeline.

Thank you to John and Maggie Matthews for writing space in the Cairngorms. Thank you to Sara Mohr-Pietsch and to Monica and Jackie Rushforth for writing space in the city.

Thank you to my parents, John and Chris, for widening the horizons.

And – always – thank you to Aidan.

Further Reading: The Essentials

Alonso-Minutti, Ana R., Eduardo Herrera and Alejandro L. Madrid (eds), *Experimentalisms in Practice: Music Perspectives from Latin America* (New York: Oxford University Press, 2018)

Cizmic, Maria, *Performing Pain: Music and Trauma in Eastern Europe* (New York: Oxford University Press, 2012)

Denyer, Frank, *In the Margins of Composition* (Oxfordshire: Vision Edition, 2019)

Eckhardt, Julia, and Éliane Radigue, *Intermediary Spaces / Espaces intermédiaires* (Brussels: Umland editions, 2019)

Gerlach, Julia (ed.), *Smetak's Inventions: Die vermischten Welten des Erfinders, Klangkünstlers und Musikers Walter Smetak (1913–84) / The Interfused Realms of Inventor, Sound Artist, and Musician Walter Smetak (1913–84)* (Hofheim: Wolke Verlagsges. Mbh, 2019)

Gottschalk, Jennie, *Experimental Music since 1970* (New York: Bloomsbury Publishing, 2016)

Hakobian, Levon, *Music of the Soviet Era: 1917–1991*, 2nd edn (Abingdon and New York: Routledge, 2018)

Johnson, Stephen, *How Shostakovich Changed my Mind* (Kendal: Notting Hill Editions, 2018)

Lewis, George E., *A Power Stronger than Itself* (Chicago and London: University of Chicago Press, 2008)

Madrid, Alejandro L., *In Search of Julián Carrillo and 'Sonido 13'* (New York: Oxford University Press, 2015)

Marstal, Henrik, *Else Marie Pade* (Copenhagen: Multivers, 2019)

Mautner, Itay (ed.), *Emahoy Tsegué-Mariam Guèbru: Music for Piano* (Jerusalem: Jerusalem Season of Culture, 2013)

Rutherford-Johnson, Tim, *Music After the Fall: Modern Composition and Culture since 1989* (Oakland: University of California Press, 2017)

Santos, Ramón Pagayon, *Tunugan: Four Essays on Filipino Music* (Quezon City: University of the Philippines Press, 2005)

Scarassatti, Marco, *Walter Smetak: O Alquimista dos sons* (São Paulo: Editora Perspectiva, 2009)

Seeger, Peggy, *First Time Ever* (London: Faber & Faber, 2017)

Smetak, Walter, *O enxerto do Takaká & outros textos*, edited by &. Migracielo (São Paulo and Ondina: EDUFBA and Outrem Editorial, 2019)

Tick, Judith, *Ruth Crawford Seeger: a Composer's Search for American Music* (New York: Oxford University Press, 1997)

Various artists, *Womens Work* (New York: Primary Information (reissue), 2019)

Various authors, *Spectres: Composer l'écoute / Composing listening* (Rennes: Shelter Press, 2019)

Sources

Unless otherwise stated, all direct quotes attributed to George E. Lewis, Alejandro L. Madrid, Carmina Escobar, Juan Sebastián Lach Lau, Pascale Criton, Peggy Seeger, Paulo Costa Lima, Barbara Smetak, LaVerne C. de la Peña, Dayang Yraola, Chris Brown, Rebecca Saunders, Frank Denyer, Andrei Bakhmin, Emahoy Tsegué-Mariam Guèbru, Henrik Marstal, Andrea Bak, Leonard Jones, Taylor Ho Bynum, John Hollenbeck, Éliane Radigue, Rhodri Davies and Annea Lockwood are from interviews with the author.

Epigraphs

our habitual vision of things is not necessarily right: Nan Shepherd, in *The Living Mountain* (Edinburgh: Canongate, 2011 reissue), p. 101.

for some time, historians of experimentalism in music have stood at a crossroads: George E. Lewis, in *A Power Stronger than Itself* (Chicago and London: University of Chicago Press, 2008), p. xiii.

Introduction

the guarded privilege of an ever-smaller section of British society: Graham Vick, in 'Enter the fat lady', the *Guardian*, 20 October 2003.

based mostly upon the absence of mention of them: Charles Seeger, quoted in Judith Tick, *Ruth Crawford Seeger: A Composer's Search for American Music* (New York: Oxford University Press, 1997), p. 116.

we know that there are different types of Black life: Muhal Richard Abrams, quoted by George E. Lewis in 'Lifting the Cone of Silence From Black Composers' in the *New York Times*, 3 July 2020.

now is the time to explore other logics and music potentials: José Maceda in conversation with Michael Tenzer, quoted in 'José Maceda and the Paradoxes of Modern Composition in Southeast Asia' in *Ethnomusicology* Vol. 47, No. 1 (Urbana-Champaign: University of Illinois Press, Winter 2003), p. 116.

when we try to pick out anything by itself, we find it hitched: John Muir, in *My First Summer in the Sierra* (Edinburgh: Canongate, 1997 reissue), p. 91.

Julián Carrillo

Assuming – and this is no small assumption – that symphony composers: Julián Carrillo, quoted in Alejandro L. Madrid, *In Search of Julián Carrillo and 'Sonido 13'* (New York: Oxford University Press, 2015), p. 40.

THERE IS NO symphonist who has tried to write an opera and has not succeeded: Julián Carrillo quoted in Madrid, ibid., p. 41.

embrace both camps: Madrid, ibid., p. 42.

WE ARE ON THE VERGE OF WITNESSING THE MOST TRANSCENDENTAL EVENT: Madrid, *In Search of Julián Carrillo and 'Sonido 13'*, p. 110.

IMPOTENT TO CONTINUE THE POLEMIC WITHIN THE CONFINES OF STRICT SCIENTIFIC RIGOUR: Madrid, ibid., p. 151.

'Byzantine' attitude of the 'dilettanti who by questioning what they do not understand get at least to see their names in print!': Madrid, ibid., p. 151.

'PROVE' his theories 'with facts and decent reasons for the benefit of his reputation and the dignity of Mexican musicians': Madrid, ibid., p. 146.

I send you some facts about myself that you can arrange as you please: Silvestre Revueltas, quoted by Roberto Kolb Neuhaus in 'Silvestre Revueltas's *Colorines* vis-à-vis US Musical Modernisms: A Dialogue of the Deaf?' in *Latin American Music Review / Revista de Música Latinoamericana*, Vol. 36, No. 2 (Austin: University of Texas Press, Fall/Winter 2015), p. 209.

foreign music whose morbid character depresses the spirit: Partido Nacional Revolucionario, quoted in Ilene V. O'Malley, *The Myth of the Revolution: Hero Cults and the Institutionalization of the Mexican State, 1920–1940* (Westport, CT: Greenwood Press, 1986), p. 119.

fruit of true Mexican tradition: Carlos Chávez quoted in Madrid, *In Search of Julián Carrillo and 'Sonido 13'*, p. 35.

I am through with Europe, Carlos: Aaron Copland, quoted in Leonora Saavedra, *Carlos Chávez and His World* (Princeton: Princeton University Press, 2015), p. 102.

highly spiced, like Mexican food: Aaron Copland, quoted in Leonora Saavedra, ibid., p. 104.

a bold collage that deconstructs folklorist nationalism: Roberto Kolb Neuhaus, 'Silvestre Revueltas's *Colorines* vis-à-vis US Musical Modernisms: A Dialogue of the Deaf?', p. 210.

his fullest music in his sonorous silence: Pablo Neruda's 'Oratorio in a Minor Key on the Death of Silvestre Revueltas', quoted by Robert Parker in 'Revueltas in San Antonio and Mobile', *Latin American Music Review / Revista de Música Latinoamericana*, Vol. 23, No. 1 (Austin: University of Texas Press, Spring/Summer 2002), p. 127.

Ruth Crawford

Makes caves under the piano: Peggy Seeger, in *First Time Ever* (London: Faber & Faber, 2017), p. 9.

I folded my wings and breathed good friendly dust: Ruth Crawford, quoted in Joseph N. Straus, *The Music of Ruth Crawford Seeger* (Cambridge: Cambridge University Press, 2003), p. 300.

sling dissonances as mean as any of them: Edward Moore, writing in the *Chicago Daily Tribune* (1928), quoted in Judith Tick, *Ruth Crawford Seeger: a Composer's Search for American Music* (New York: Oxford University Press, 1997), p. 4.

real lady musician, with nice manners: Clara Crawford, quoted in Judith Tick, p. 24.

I see her plainly now: Peggy Seeger, in *First Time Ever*, p. 11.

All I had been trying to do: Sergey Prokofiev, quoted by Daniel Jaffe in *Sergey Prokofiev* (London: Phaidon, 1998), p. 98.

I feel myself broadening: Ruth Crawford writing to her mother, quoted in Judith Tick, p. 34.

cut such capers when the wind found its cup: Ruth Crawford writing in her diary, quoted in Judith Tick, ibid., p. 58.

What do you think of the name!!!: Ruth Crawford, quoted in Judith Tick, ibid., p. 40.

'For you are the sun': lines from Ruth Crawford's poem 'Creator' (1925), quoted in Judith Tick, ibid., p. 47.

I am beginning to think life is what I want: Ruth Crawford writing in her diary, quoted in Judith Tick, ibid., p. 99.

Tall, aristocratic, ultra-refined, a bit cold: Ruth Crawford, quoted in Bill C. Malone, *Music from the True Vine: Mike Seeger's Life and Musical Journey* (Chapel Hill: University of North Carolina Press), p. 16.

Five feet of ice and ten feet of books: observation by Ruth Crawford of Charles Seeger, quoted in Matilda Gaume, *Ruth Crawford Seeger: Memoirs, Memories, Music* (Metuchen, NJ: Scarecrow Press, 1986), p. 68.

gentlemen are not musicians: Charles Seeger's father, quoted in Judith Tick, *Ruth Crawford Seeger: a Composer's Search for American Music*, p. 130.

your integrity compelled my admiration: Charles Seeger writing to Ruth Crawford, quoted in Judith Tick, ibid., p. 122.

Approach a note by a slide from below, and sustain the note: Ruth Crawford, quoted in the preface to *Three Chants*, unpublished score.

Germans simply can't stand the hurt: Ruth Crawford writing to Charles Seeger, quoted in Judith Tick, *Ruth Crawford Seeger: a Composer's Search for American Music*, p. 160.

more Schoenberg worshipper than I would have thought: Ruth Crawford on Alban Berg, quoted in Matilda Gaume, *Ruth Crawford Seeger: Memoirs, Memories, Music*, p. 83.

dear quiet shy little person: Ruth Crawford on Béla Bartók, quoted in Matilda Gaume, ibid., p. 82.

career vs love and children battle: Ruth Crawford writing to Charles Seeger, quoted in Judith Tick, *Ruth Crawford Seeger: a Composer's Search for American Music*, p. 173.

What's going to happen to me?: Ruth Crawford, quoted in Judith Tick, ibid., p. 133.

there is no obstacle to the loving: Charles Seeger writing to Ruth Crawford, quoted in Judith Tick, ibid., p. 169.

you're on the right track and we're on the wrong track: Charles Seeger to Aunt Molly Jackson, quoted in Ann M. Pescatello, *Charles Seeger: a Life in American Music* (Pittsburgh and London: University of Pittsburgh Press, 1992), p. 135.

You'd be in trouble if you tried to argue with her: Charles Seeger, quoted in Judith Tick, *Ruth Crawford Seeger: a Composer's Search for American Music*, p. 86.

he worked her too hard and she cooked too much: Virgil Thomson, quoted in Judith Tick, ibid., p. 86.

all during the housecleaning: Ruth Crawford, quoted in Judith Tick, ibid., p. 293.

As a budding eco-feminist: Peggy Seeger, in her introduction to *The Essential Ewan MacColl Songbook* (Windsor, NJ: Loomis House Press, 2009), reproduced as 'Songmaker' on the website Working Class Movement Library: Ewan MacColl.

We were a close family: Peggy Seeger, in *First Time Ever*, p. 27.

I came in after school one day and found Libba playing it left-handed: Peggy Seeger, in ibid., p. 44.

closet oneself in one's comfortable room: Charles Seeger, quoted in Elizabeth Tucker and Ellen McHale (eds), *New York State Folklife Reader: Diverse Voices* (Jackson: University Press of Mississippi, 2013), p. 205.

sung as though they might continue off into space: Ruth Crawford, quoted in Judith Tick, *Ruth Crawford Seeger: a Composer's Search for American Music*, p. 331.

all of you make such a good team that I'd say America's wakingup: Woody Guthrie, quoted in Judith Tick (ed.) with Paul Beaudoin (assistant ed.), *Music in the USA: A Documentary Companion* (New York: Oxford University Press, 2008), p. 522.

I believe when I write more music: Ruth Crawford, writing to Edgard Varèse, quoted by Roberta Lamb in 'Composing and Teaching as Dissonant Counterpoint', in Ray Allen and Ellie M. Hisama (eds), *Ruth Crawford Seeger's Worlds: Innovation and Tradition in Twentieth-Century American Music* (Rochester: University of Rochester Press, 2007), p. 170.

Ugliness is also a very beautiful thing: Ruth Crawford, quoted in Judith Tick, *Ruth Crawford Seeger: a Composer's Search for American Music*, p. 326.

I believe I'm going to work again. More! If I live to be 99: Ruth Crawford, quoted in Jean
R. Freedman, *Peggy Seeger: a Life of Music, Love, and Politics* (Urbana-Champaign:
University of Illinois Press, 2017), p. 62.

propped up in bed trying to write a poem about America: Carl Sandburg, quoted in Joseph
Haas and Gene Lovitz, *Carl Sandburg: A Pictorial Biography* (New York: Putnam,
1967), p. 168.

Walter Smetak

*a new genre of music: a poor music, a music of the beggars (Eu vou criar um novo gênero de
música)*: Walter Smetak, in *O enxerto do Takaká & outros textos*, edited by &. Migracielo (Salvador: EDUFBA and Outrem Editorial, 2019), p. 282.

the land of possible impossibilities: Walter Smetak, in 'O Alquimista dos Sons', interview
with Renato de Moraes in *Veja* magazine, 5 March 1975, p. 3.

'O céu se chove, um barco furado?': Walter Smetak, in *O enxerto do Takaká & outros
textos*, p. 87.

a society given to contacts, exchanges, interpenetrations: Antonio Risério, *Avant-Garde na
Bahia* (São Paulo: Instituto Lina Bo e P.M. Bardi, 1995), p. 72.

It was summer. People were wearing many colours: Walter Smetak, quoted in Julia Gerlach
(ed.), *Smetak's Inventions: Die vermischten Welten des Erfinders, Klangkünstlers und
Musikers Walter Smetak (1913–84) / The Interfused Realms of Inventor, Sound Artist, and
Musician Walter Smetak (1913–84)* (Hofheim: Wolke Verlagsges. Mbh, 2019), p. 55.

*a very Brazilian Brazilian, with my feet in the water up to my knees (E eu como brasileiro
brasileiríssimo, com os pés n'água até os joelhos)*: Walter Smetak, in *O enxerto do Takaká
& outros textos*, p. 134.

'desordem e a liberalidade dos trópicos': , in 'O Alquimista dos Sons', interview with Renato
de Moraes in *Veja* magazine, p. 3.

'A verdade é uma só: são muitas' ('The truth is only one: there are many'): Antônio Brasileiro,
quoted by Paulo Costa Lima in 'Cultural Perspectives in Music Composition: the
case of the composition movement in Bahia-Brazil', *Orfeu*, Vol. 5, No. 1 (Flori-
anópolis: Universidade Federal de Santa Catarina, 2020), p. 13.

Music represents the reflection of social reality: Agenda of *Música Viva*, quoted by Paulo
Costa Lima in 'Koellreutter, Widmer, Smetak e a floração do movimento de com-
posição na Bahia', in Antonio Risério and Gringo Cardia (eds), *Cidade da Música da
Bahia*, Vol. 1 (Salvador: Prefeitura Municipal de Salvador, 2020), p. 286.

If we divide the word in half: Walter Smetak, writing in *Simbologia dos instrumentos*,
quoted in Julia Gerlach (ed.), *Smetak's Inventions: Die vermischten Welten des Erfinders, Klangkünstlers und Musikers Walter Smetak (1913–84) / The Interfused Realms of
Inventor, Sound Artist, and Musician Walter Smetak (1913–84)*, p. 33.

floating on a block of ice, drifting from the North Pole: Walter Smetak, in *Simbologia dos instrumentos*, quoted in Julia Gerlach (ed.), ibid., p. 61.

Love must be a soft thing (O amor deve ser uma coisa suave): Walter Smetak, in *O enxerto do Takaká & outros textos*, p. 78.

critical, grumpy, sometimes elusive (Como amigo foi crítico, rabugento, às vezes esquivo, outras glorioso, humilde, radiante, severo e irreverente): Ernst Widmer in 1984, quoted by Paulo Costa Lima in 'Koellreutter, Widmer, Smetak e a floração do movimento de composição na Bahia', *Cidade da Música da Bahia*, Vol. 1, p. 299.

IN PRINCIPLE WE ARE AGAINST (Em princípio, estamos contra todo e qualquer princípio declarado): Grupo de Compositores da Bahia, quoted by Paulo Costa Lima in ibid., p. 290.

fertilisers, nutrients and compost: Tom Zé, quoted by Andy Beta in 'The Story of Tropicália in 20 Albums', *Pitchfork*, 19 June 2017.

I have nothing to do with this purity: Gilberto Gil, quoted by Maya Jaggi in 'Blood on the ground', the *Guardian*, 13 May 2006.

'Smetak, Smetak, e Musak e Smetak': Caetano Veloso, 'Épico', on the album *Araçá Azul* (Philips, 1973).

'Smetak tak tak tak (tak tak tak tak tak)': Gilberto Gil's 'Língua do Pê', on the album *O sol de Oslo* (Blue Jackel, 1998).

microtonise yourself, never to be exalted again with the Pythagorean harmonies: Walter Smetak's 'Microtonização', quoted by Marco Scarassatti in *Walter Smetak: o Alquimista dos Sons* (São Paulo: Editora Perspectiva, 2009), p. 117.

We can squeeze almost nothing more out of our old musical system: Walter Smetak, quoted in Julia Gerlach (ed.), *Smetak's Inventions: Die vermischten Welten des Erfinders, Klangkünstlers und Musikers Walter Smetak (1913–84) / The Interfused Realms of Inventor, Sound Artist, and Musician Walter Smetak (1913–84)*, p. 75.

a free form of composition: Walter Smetak, in *O enxerto do Takaká & outros textos*, p. 228.

Aqueles que sabem cantar, cantem (Those who know how to sing, sing): Walter Smetak, ibid., p. 228.

I have to go back home. I have to work: Walter Smetak, writing to Helga Retzer, Head of Music at the DAAD Artists-in-Berlin Programme, on 5 December 1982. Quoted in Julia Gerlach (ed.), *Smetak's Inventions: Die vermischten Welten des Erfinders, Klangkünstlers und Musikers Walter Smetak (1913–84) / The Interfused Realms of Inventor, Sound Artist, and Musician Walter Smetak (1913–84)*, p. 84.

He liked to shock (Smetak gostava de chocar, catapultando o ouvinte da inércia para novas reflexões): Ernst Widmer in 1984, quoted by Paulo Costa Lima in 'Koellreutter, Widmer, Smetak e a floração do movimento de composição na Bahia', *Cidade da Música da Bahia*, Vol. 1, p. 299.

a predominance of rewiring (a predominância do religar): Marco Scarassatti in *Walter Smetak: o Alquimista dos Sons*, p. 82.

to build every idea you have in your head: Walter Smetak writing to Helga Retzer, Head of Music at the DAAD Artists-in-Berlin Programme, on 5 December 1982. Quoted in Julia Gerlach (ed.), *Smetak's Inventions: Die vermischten Welten des Erfinders, Klangkünstlers und Musikers Walter Smetak (1913–84) / The Interfused Realms of Inventor, Sound Artist, and Musician Walter Smetak (1913–84)*, p. 83.

It's all over; the rest is siiiiiiilence (Está tudo acabado; O resto é silênciooooooo): quoted by Marco Scarassatti in *Walter Smetak: o Alquimista dos Sons*, p. 83.

José Maceda

maze of sounds, where musical function becomes a recreation: José Maceda, quoted by Ramón Pagayon Santos in *Tunugan: Four Essays on Filipino Music* (Quezon City: University of the Philippines Press, 2005), p. 147.

As coming from anywhere. Not Nigeria or Madagascar: José Maceda in conversation with Chris Brown, 1992. Recording shared with the author.

There were more and more pianists: José Maceda, ibid.

what has all this got to do with coconuts and rice?: José Maceda, quoted in Michael Tenzer, 'José Maceda and the Paradoxes of Modern Composition in Southeast Asia' in *Ethnomusicology*, Vol. 47, No. 1 (Urbana-Champaign: University of Illinois Press, Winter 2003), p. 94.

Portability meant a 10-kilo Uber: Dayang Magdalena Nirvana T. Yraola, 'José Maceda Exhibit Series: a Curator's Reflection' in *Humanities Diliman: A Philippine Journal of Humanities* (Diliman: University of the Philippines Diliman, 2020), p. 102.

an intense situation … almost inaudible twangs and heavily cluttered noises: José Maceda, quoted in Ramón Pagayon Santos, *Tunugan: Four Essays on Filipino Music*, p. 135.

Where new musical horizons are being sought: José Maceda, *Gongs & Bamboo: a Panorama of Philippine Music Instruments* (Quezon City, University of the Philippines Press, 1998), p. 59.

so stiff that I wanted to jump out of the plane: José Maceda in conversation with Chris Brown, 1992.

Good vs. evil, being vs. nothingness, presence vs. absence: Jacques Derrida, quoted by José Maceda, 'A Concept of Time in a Music of Southeast Asia' in *Ethnomusicology*, Vol. 30, No. 1 (Urbana-Champaign: University of Illinois Press, Winter 1986), p. 46.

The recordings are my dictionary: José Maceda in conversation with Chris Brown, 1992.

They used me. They changed the word: José Maceda, ibid.

As a creative ideology for unity and community: quoted in Ramón Pagayon Santos, 'Ugnayan: Society and Power as Music Composition', *RECTO Lecture Series* (January, 2007), p. 7.

the idea that only large groups of people: José Maceda in 1974, quoted in Arsenio Nicolas, 'From *Atmospheres* to *Ugnayan*: the Music of José Maceda' (PhD research paper for College of Music, Mahasarakham University, Thailand, 2015), p. 6.

emphasis on the identity and the history: Cedrik Fermont and Dimitri della Faille, *Not Your World Music: Noise in South East Asia* (Berlin and Ottawa: Syrphe & Hushush, 2016), p. 100.

rituals in villages where people converged: Arsenio Nicolas, in 'From *Ugnayan* to *Udlot-Udlot*: the Music of José Maceda'. Paper given at the first International Conference on Ethnics in Asia: Life, Power and Ethnics (Naresuan University, Pitsanulok, Thailand, 20–21 August 2015), p. 3.

'Look at me!': José Maceda in a filmed performance of *Udlot-Udlot* at Yerba Buena Gardens in San Francisco, 2000.

They went into my closets looking for skeletons: Imelda Marcos to reporters in 2001, quoted in 'Homage to Imelda's Shoes', BBC News online, 16 February 2001.

practically invading the exclusive domain: Ramón Pagayon Santos, *Tunugan: Four Essays on Filipino Music*, p. 152.

Time without beginning without end: Yuji Takahashi on José Maceda, sleeve notes to *José Maceda: Music for Five Pianos* (ALM Records, AlCD-54, 2000).

actually that of a drifter: Dayang Yraola's curator's note for the exhibition 'Listen to my music' at the University of the Philippines Jorge B. Vargas Museum and Filipiniana Research Center, 2013.

now is the time to explore other logics and music potentials: José Maceda in conversation with Michael Tenzer, quoted in 'José Maceda and the Paradoxes of Modern Composition in Southeast Asia', p. 116.

Galina Ustvolskaya

Fingers smart as they strike against the keys' hard edges: Maria Cizmic, *Performing Pain: Music and Trauma in Eastern Europe* (New York: Oxford University Press, 2012), p. 89.

will achieve world fame: Dmitri Shostakovich, quoted in Semyón Bokman, *Variations on the Theme Galina Ustvolskaya: The Last Composer of the Passing Era* (Bloomington, Indiana: Xlibris, 2019), p. 21.

spirituality is what remains of a person if you disregard the rest: Galina Ustvolskaya, in *Scream Into Space / Schreeuw in het heelal*, a documentary film directed by Josée Voormans (VPRO Holland, 2005).

He sees no way out. He falls with every step. He keeps falling and asks God for help: Galina Ustvolskaya, in *Scream Into Space / Schreeuw in het heelal.*

no single word in English renders all the shades of 'toska': Vladimir Nabokov, in the annotations of his 1964 translation of *Eugene Onegin* (Princeton: Princeton University Press, 1991 reissue), p. 141.

ability to submerge into darkness: Nikolai Berdyaev, quoted by Elena Nalimova in *Demystifying Galina Ustvolskaya: Critical Examination and Performance Interpretation* (PhD thesis for Goldsmiths College, University of London, 2012), p. 122.

we often played four-hand duets: Galina Ustvolskaya, quoted in Elena Nalimova, ibid., p. 57.

linguistic phantasmagoria: A. S. Byatt, 'A poll tax of souls', the *Guardian*, 30 October 2004.

Shostakovich's musical conscience: 'Galina Ustvolskaya: Shostakovich's "musical conscience"' in the *Independent*, 27 December 2006.

optimistic and healthy people irritated her: Elena Nalimova in *Demystifying Galina Ustvolskaya: Critical Examination and Performance Interpretation*, p. 94.

'Don't look at me! Don't look!': Valentin Silvestrov, quoted by Elena Nalimova in *Demystifying Galina Ustvolskaya: Critical Examination and Performance Interpretation*, p. 12.

The winds of politics swirl around Galina, but she stays solid and true to herself: Maria Cizmic, quoting a student of Ustvolskaya, told to Andrew Morris in 'The Inner Mountain: Memories of Galina Ustvolskaya', *VAN Magazine*, 2018.

Emahoy Tsegué-Mariam Guèbru

Everyone knows how a mother's love sacrifices itself: Emahoy Tsegué-Mariam Guèbru, preface to 'Mother's Love' in *Emahoy Tsegué-Mariam Guèbru: Music for Piano*, edited by Itay Mautner (Jerusalem: Jerusalem Season of Culture, 2013), p. 20.

Else Marie Pade

sponges splashing and dripping in the washstand: Else Marie Pade, 'The Compositional Possibilities are Endless', republished by *The Wire*, June 2017, originally published in the Danish edition of *Lettre Internationale*, no. 4, June 2004.

I learned very quickly that some of the sounds came: Else Marie Pade, ibid.

These and many other fairy-tale characters became my friends: Else Marie Pade, ibid.

I thought they were saying something, these shiny marbles – or rather, that they were singing. But what?: Else Marie Pade, ibid.

It gave rise to a righteous indignation: Else Marie Pade, ibid.

'The day that went away, the night that's black': Else Marie Pade, lyrics of 'Du og jeg og stjernerne' (You, me and the stars).

A sound collage of shouting and screaming: Else Marie Pade, 'The Compositional Possibilities are Endless'.

I'm in the future, writing music: Else Marie Pade, quoted by Andrea Bak in conversation with the author.

How does art unite with the kitchen? (Hvordan forenes kunsten med køkkenet?): quoted by Henrik Marstal in *Else Marie Pade* (Copenhagen: Multivers, 2019), p. 112.

variegated, joyous and distinctive sound world: Else Marie Pade, 'The Compositional Possibilities are Endless'.

Sound is the vocabulary of nature: Pierre Schaeffer, in *Treatise on Musical Objects: An Essay Across Disciplines*, translated by Christine North and John Dack (Oakland: University of California Press, 2017), p. 527.

The big OB wagon came driving, full of people: Else Marie Pade, quoted by Henrik Marstal in *Else Marie Pade*, p. 119.

dwarfs and the giants, the dancing flowers and the quivering leaves: Else Marie Pade, in 'When Time Took on Tonal Colouring', translated by Maja and Bill Arthy, quoted in the sleeve notes to the album *Et Glasperlespil* (Dacapo Records, 2002).

Production of lightning is attempted: Else Marie Pade, quoted by Henrik Marstal and Ingeborg Okkels in the sleeve notes to the album *Face It* (Dacapo Records, 2002).

NOW the mermaid sang as mermaids should: Else Marie Pade, 'The Compositional Possibilities are Endless'.

Moderated sweep generator with web modulator: listed in the sleeve notes to *Else Marie Pade: Electronic Music* (Dacapo Records, 2001).

making an epic forever out of a single passing ordinary day: Ali Smith on James Joyce in *Artful* (London: Hamish Hamilton, 2012), p. 37.

blow wide open the musical world and let in sound: Edgard Varèse, quoted in Vivian Perlis and Libby Van Cleve, 'Edgard Varèse: (1888–1965)', in *Composers' Voices from Ives to Ellington: An Oral History of American Music* (New Haven and London: Yale University Press, 2008), p. 95.

a deluge of phone calls: Else Marie Pade, 'The Compositional Possibilities are Endless'.

'nauseating' [...] *'physically uncomfortable'*: Knudåge Riisager, quoted by Henrik Marstal in *Else Marie Pade*, p. 86.

'To lovely Else Marie Pade': Stockhausen's Christmas card, 1995, quoted by Henrik Marstal, ibid., p. 95.

When my sonic experiments began to cohere and become compositions: Else Marie Pade, 'The Compositional Possibilities are Endless'.

hardening of the arteries: Edgard Varèse, quoted in Wilfrid Mellers, *Caliban Reborn: Renewal in Twentieth-Century Music* (New York: Harper & Row, 1967), p. 121.

she is the grandmother of all of us electronic musicians: Thomas Knak, in *Politiken*, 19 October 2002, quoted in 'Else Marie Pade', online article on the website *Ja Ja Ja: a Nordic Music Affair*, 4 November 2014.

Muhal Richard Abrams

He was a basket of curiosity: Leonard Jones, in conversation with the author.

No licks. I don't want anyone playing no licks: Muhal Richard Abrams, quoted by Leonard Jones in conversation with the author.

It was like I had found a teacher: Joseph Jarman, quoted in George E. Lewis, *A Power Stronger than Itself* (Chicago and London: University of Chicago Press, 2008), p. 68.

Muhal was the inspiration: Jack DeJohnette talking to Nate Chinen, quoted in '50 Years On, Association for Advancement of Creative Musicians Influences Jazz', the *New York Times*, 6 March 2015.

While segregation created the blues: Mike Rowe, *Chicago Blues: the City and the Music* (New York: Hachette, 1981), p. 26.

the greatest entertainment section in the world: George E. Lewis, *A Power Stronger than Itself*, p. 218.

Forrestville was a standard public school: Muhal Richard Abrams, quoted in George E. Lewis, ibid., p. 7.

We are dealing with something that is intuitive and *scientific*: Muhal Richard Abrams, quoted in George E. Lewis, ibid., p. 122.

'crude' [. . .] *'a failed contrapuntalist'*: Joseph Schillinger, quoted in Marc Edward Hannaford, 'One Line, Many Views: Perspectives on Music Theory, Composition, and Improvisation through the Work of Muhal Richard Abrams' (PhD paper, Columbia University, 2019), p. 168.

everywhere he went over the next four years: George E. Lewis, *A Power Stronger than Itself*, p. 58.

A positive approach to the theory of musical composition: Henry Cowell's introduction to Joseph Schillinger, *The Schillinger System of Musical Composition*, 2 vols (New York: Carl Fischer, 1946), Vol. 1, p. ix.

unstable polyphony of voices: George E. Lewis, *A Power Stronger than Itself*, p. 498.

Abrams, [Jodie] Christian, [Philip] Cohran and [Steve] McCall sent postcards: George E. Lewis, ibid., p. 97.

the conventional wisdom that casts improvisation in general: George E. Lewis, ibid., p. 96.

That's a high vibration to live up to: Muhal Richard Abrams, quoted in George E. Lewis, ibid., p. 110.

Yes [. . .] It does in the sense that we intend: Muhal Richard Abrams, quoted in Bill Quinn, 'The AACM: A Promise', *DownBeat Music '68* (1968), p. 46.

To cultivate young musicians and to create music: AACM charter, quoted in George E. Lewis, *A Power Stronger than Itself*, p. 116.

No one's excluded [. . .] You may not be Duke Ellington: Muhal Richard Abrams, quoted in George E. Lewis, ibid., p. 106.

It is our hope that intelligent definition of the past: Jeff Donaldson, quoted by Lisa Gail Collins and Margo Natalie Crawford (eds) in *New Thoughts on the Black Arts Movement* (New Brunswick, NJ: Rutgers University Press, 2006), p. 291.

Muhal Richard Abrams, the name commands respect: sleeve notes to the album *Levels and Degrees of Light* (Delmark, 1968).

What is here is what we are and what we hope to be: sleeve notes to *Levels and Degrees of Light*.

technology-laden sonic uncanny valley: Marc Edward Hannaford, 'One Line, Many Views: Perspectives on Music Theory, Composition, and Improvisation through the Work of Muhal Richard Abrams', p. 165.

Masters went to great lengths to discipline plantation soundscapes by insisting: Mark M. Smith, *Listening to Nineteenth-Century America* (Chapel Hill: University of North Carolina Press, 2001), p. 68.

Mr. Abrams did relatively little experimentation with electronic music: Matt Schudel, in 'Muhal Richard Abrams, pianist who expanded the limits of jazz, dies at 87', *Washington Post*, 2 November 2017.

tradition in African-American music is wide as all outdoors: Julius Hemphill, quoted by Suzanne McElfresh in 'Julius Hemphill', *Bomb Magazine*, 1 January 1994.

Basically, we're musicians. It's music: Muhal Richard Abrams, quoted by Jim Macnie in 'Muhal Richard Abrams: Yesterday & Tomorrow' on the music blog *Lament for a Straight Line*, 1 December 2010.

let's make it our poor. It should be the actor's bedroom: Alexander H. Cohen, quoted in *Miracle on 42nd Street*, a documentary film about Manhattan Plaza directed by Alice Elliott (2017).

very vivid New York education working from 11 o'clock: Samuel L. Jackson, quoted in *Miracle on 42nd Street*.

a crest on the wave of immigrant musicians recently arrived from St Louis: Gary Giddins in *The Village Voice*, May 1977.

knew about it before the New York cats did: George E. Lewis, *A Power Stronger than Itself*, p. 336.

The great composers did a lot of improvising: Muhal Richard Abrams, talking on 15 January 2016 to Frank J. Oteri, published online in 'Muhal Richard Abrams: Think All, Focus One', *NewMusicBox*, 1 April 2016.

Éliane Radigue

'Mon rêve familier' / 'My familiar dream': Paul Verlaine, in the collection *Poems under Saturn / Poèmes saturniens*, translated by Karl Kirchwey (Princeton: Princeton University Press, 2011), p. 26.

A sunny place for shady people: W. Somerset Maugham, quoted in John Baxter, *French Riviera and its Artists: Art, Literature, Love and Life on the Côte d'Azur* (New York: Museyon, 2015), p. 212.

The sonic landscapes of the Nice region were inexhaustible: Éliane Radigue, in 'Le temps n'a pas d'importance' ('Time is of no importance') in *Spectres: Composer l'écoute / Composing listening* (Rennes: Shelter Press, 2019), p. 50.

The director patently assessed my anatomy much more than my potential talent: Éliane Radigue, quoted by Julia Eckhardt in *Intermediary Spaces / Espaces intermédiaires* (umland editions, 2019), p. 68.

We never see a plant move: Éliane Radigue, in 'Le temps n'a pas d'importance' ('Time is of no importance'), in *Spectres: Composer l'écoute / Composing listening*, p. 49.

Annea Lockwood

we were burning American flags, political effigies, the status quo: Annea Lockwood in 'How To Prepare a Piano', *Sound Scripts: Proceedings of the Inaugural Totally Huge New Music Festival Conference 2005*, vol. 1 (2006), p. 20.

'Piano Transplants': text score. Permission to reprint given by Annea Lockwood.

I'm really hung up on serenity-inducing sounds: Annea Lockwood in conversation with Pauline Oliveros on the 'Ode to Gravity' programme on KPFA FM, 20 December 1972.

as little, and by extension, as much as the president: Ruth Anderson, quoted by Annea Lockwood in 'Hearing A Person – Remembering Ruth Anderson (1928–2019)', *NewMusicBox*, 19 December 2019.

I give lots of facts, and I am very demanding: private letter from Ruth Anderson to Annea Lockwood, reprinted with permission from Annea Lockwood.

'Sound Portrait: Hearing a Person': text score. Permission to reprint given by Annea Lockwood.

*'**Elocution - On a cloudy day, scream, until rain falls'*: Bici Forbes, in *Womens Work*, Issue 1 (1975) (reissued by Primary Information, 2019).

'Kein' Musik ist ja nicht auf Erden / Die unsrer verglichen kann werden': 'Das himmlische Leben' (Heavenly Life) from Gustav Mahler, Symphony no. 4 (Universal Edition, 1911).

'Softest Sound': text score. Permission to reprint given by Annea Lockwood.

When we try to pick out anything by itself: John Muir, in *My First Summer in the Sierra*, p. 91.

'listening with the neighborhood': text score. Permission to reprint given by Annea Lockwood.

Image Credits

Inventor of metamorphic piano Julián Carrillo at home. Joseph Scherschel
The LIFE Picture Collection/Shutterstock.

Silvestre Revueltas. Credit and source unknown.

Ruth Crawford Seeger. © Peggy Seeger

Peggy Seeger. The Estate of David Gahr / Getty Images.

Walter Smetak, Tak Tak. Collection of the Smetak Family.

Jose Maceda – 19 November 1996. © Co Broerse.

Jose Maceda in Paris, 1938, Jose Maceda Collection. UP Center for
Ethnomusicology, University of the Philippines Diliman, Quezon City.

First page of Jose Maceda's score for *Uganayam*: Music for 20 Radio
Stations – Jose Maceda, *Ugnayan*. Music score, 1974. UP Center for
Ethnomusicology, University of the Philippines Diliman, Quezon City.

Galina Ustvolskaya, 1956. Courtesy of St Petersburg Philharmonia.
Printed with permission.

Galina Ustvolskaya, 1940s. © ustvolskaya.org

Autographed cover of *Emahoy Tsegué-Mariam Guèbru Plays Own Earlier
Compositions*. Courtesy of the author.

Else Marie Pade. © Lisbeth Damgaard

Circles of Sevenths (1959) Else Marie Pade. © Edition·S, Copenhagen,
Denmark. Printed with permission.

Jazz musician and composer Muhal Richard Abrams stands holding a
saxophone in front of the musicians of the AACM's experimental
band (Association for the Advancement of Creative Musicians) as he
conducts their performance, Chicago, Illinois, *c*.1965. Photo by Robert
Abbott Sengstacke / Getty Images.

Eliane Radigue from the cover of *Vice–Versa, Etc.* (LP). Jacques BRISSOT
courtesy Fondation A.R.M.A.N.

Annea Lockwood – *Burning Piano*, 1968, the Chelsea Embankment.
© Geoff Adams

Annea Lockwood and Franco Evangelisti at Darmstadt in 1961. Courtesy
of Annea Lockwood.

Index

Subjects of chapters are indicated in **bold** type, and images in *italics*.